TAX & DEVELOPMENT
SOLVING KENYA'S FISCAL CRISIS THROUGH HUMAN RIGHTS:

A Case Study of Kenya's Constituency Development Fund

TAX & DEVELOPMENT
SOLVING KENYA'S FISCAL CRISIS THROUGH HUMAN RIGHTS:

A Case Study of Kenya's Constituency Development Fund

Attiya Waris

lawAfrica

Published by:

LawAfrica Publishing (K) Ltd.
Top Plaza, 3rd Floor
Kindaruma Road, (Off Ngong Road)
P.O. Box 4260-00100 GPO
Nairobi, Kenya
Wireless: +254 20 249 5067
Cell: +254 708 898 189
Fax: +254 20 249 5067

LawAfrica Publishing (U) Ltd
Office Suite, No. 2
Plot 10A Jinja Road (Opposite NEMA House)
P.O. Box 6198
Kampala, Uganda
Phone: +256 41 255808
Fax: +256 41 347743

LawAfrica Publishing (T) Ltd
Co-Architecture Building, 7th Floor
India/Makunganya Street
P.O. Box 38564
Dar-es-Salaam, Tanzania
Phone: +255 22 2120804/5
Fax: +255 22 2120811

Email: sales@lawafrica.com

Website: www.lawafrica.com

© Attiya Waris 2013; LawAfrica

ISBN 9966-031-00-6

lawAfrica

TABLE OF CONTENTS

DEDICATION

I dedicate this book to Allah and To my dear and wonderful parents, who have been there for me every single inch of the way.

ACKNOWLEDGEMENTS

In the course of my writing I was assisted in so many ways by many people who made this process richer. Especially my supervisor Prof Sol Picciotto, who is the most incredible guide and mentor anyone could have during an academic journey of discovery.

I am particularly grateful to the support and guidance I received over the seven years it has taken to produce this work from the numerous other friends, colleagues and resource persons who have assisted me through this process up to and including turning this into a publishable manuscript.

I am also grateful to my family: My Mother and Father, Feroze, Adil, Tazmina, Nawaal, Nabiha and Nusaybah.

This has truly been a journey of Mind, Body and Soul.

ABBREVIATIONS

ACHPR .... African Charter on Human and People's Rights

BOP .... Balance of Payments

BRP .... Budget Rationalization Program

CDC .... Constituency Development Committee

CDF .... Constituency Development Fund, Kenya

CDFC .... CDF Committee, Kenya

CEDAW .... Convention on the Elimination of All Forms of
.... Discrimination against Women

COP .... Participatory Budgeting (PB) Council, Brazil

CRC .... Convention on the Rights of the Child

CSOs .... Civil Society Organisations

CAG .... Controller and Auditor General

DC .... District Commissioner

DDO .... District Development Officer

DO .... District Officer

DPC .... CDF District Project Committee, Kenya

DRD .... Declaration on the Right to Development

DS .... Development Seminars

EA .... East Africa

EAA .... East African Association

EAC .... East African Community

EACA .... East African Court of Appeal

EACSO .... East African Common Services Organisation

GDP .... Gross Domestic Product

FPE .... Free Primary Education

Habitat .... United Nations Habitat Programme

HRC .... Human Rights Council

HRCom.. Human Rights Committee

IBP ....International Budgetary Project

ICCPR .... International Covenant on Civil and Political Rights

ICESCR International Covenant on Economic, Social and Cultural Rights

ICERD International Convention on the Elimination of All Forms of Racial Discrimination

IDASA...Institute of Democracy in Africa

IMF.. International Monetary Fund

KANU .... Kenya African National Union

KBS.. Kenya Bureau of Standards

KESSP..................... Kenya Education Sector Support Programme

KRP... Key Resource Persons

KRA .... Kenya Revenue Authority

KIPRA................. Kenya Institute of Policy Research and Analysis

Kshs...Kenya Shillings

KTWA .... Kavirondo Taxpayer's Welfare Association

LADP................................. Local Area Development Programme

LASDAP..................Local Authority Service Delivery Action Plan

LATF .... Local Area Transfer Fund, Kenya

LegCo ....Legislative Council

MDG ....Millennium Development Goals

MoF... Minister of Finance

MP .... Member of Parliament

MTEF ....Medium Term Expenditure Framework

NCC.. Nairobi City Council

NDP .... National Development Plan

NGOs ....Non-Governmental Organisations

NMC................. CDF National Management Committee, Kenya

NTA .... National Taxpayers Association

OECD Organisation of Economic Cooperation and Development

PAYE .... Pay As You Earn

PA .... Porto Alegre, Brazil

PB .... Participatory Budgeting

PC .... CDF Project Committee, Kenya

PDP .... Participatory Development Plans

PFE .... Policy Framework for Education

PIP .... Public Investment Program

PMC .... CDF Project Management Committee, Kenya

PRFB .... Programme Review and Forward Budget

PRSP .... Poverty Reduction Strategy Paper

REPLF .... Rural Electrification Programme Levy Fund

RMLF .... Road Maintenance Levy Fund

RTD .... Right to Development

SAP .... Structural Adjustment Programme

SEBF .... Secondary School Education Bursary Fund

UDHR .... Universal Declaration of Human Rights

UK .... United Kingdom

UN .... United Nations

UNDP .... United Nations Development Programme

UNGA .... United Nations General Assembly

UNICEF United Nations International Children's Education Fund

US .... United States of America

USD .... United States of America Dollars

VAT .... Value Added Tax

WB .... World Bank

WP .... Worker's Party

WSF .... Belem World Social Forum, 2009

FOREWORD

For most people, taxation is a dry and boring technical topic. Yet taxes are an essential foundation for a civilised society. Attiya Waris in this book takes on the ambitious task of showing how the tax system both reflects and shapes society, as well as exploring ways in which tax reform could contribute to both economic development and social justice. Basing her analysis on the perspective of fiscal sociology pioneered by Joseph Schumpeter, she extends the work done by Euro-centric scholars by focusing on the fiscal state in post-colonial societies, more specifically Kenya.

It is not surprising that in post-colonial states such as Kenya there are deep-rooted fiscal problems, amounting to a crisis. During the colonial period, taxation inevitably took the form of, and was seen as, part of the system of imperial rule. But in the post-colonial period little has been done to establish a stronger basis of legitimacy. Indeed, both mismanagement and corruption in public expenditure have further added to the crisis of taxation. While large transnational corporations, and the wealthy and powerful, are able to take advantage of sophisticated forms of international tax avoidance, small business and ordinary people feel that they are left to shoulder the bulk of the burden. As in many developing countries, the relatively low level of tax revenues exacerbates the dependence on foreign aid.

Some progress has been made in improving tax administration, with administrative and technical reforms. However, the problems are so deep-rooted that more radical approaches are needed. One such is the movement for participatory budgeting, which was pioneered in Porto Alegre in Brazil. Dr Waris traces the emergence of this system, as well as its international spread in many countries. Kenya also has been experimenting with an approach on these lines, with the Constituency Development Fund. Regrettably, however, as the book shows, the approach adopted in Kenya has lost most of the democratic impetus which powered the Porto Alegre model, and seems to have resulted in reinforcement of political clientelism.

Nevertheless, Dr Waris, in my view rightly, argues that establishing a legitimate basis for the tax system requires forms which re-connect accountability in public expenditure with forms of levying taxes which are accepted as fair. To this end, she explores the contribution that could be made from the perspective of international human rights principles. Certainly, governments' human rights obligations are now understood to extend to social and economic rights, including the right to development. Too often, however, these obligations are said to be subject to availability of resources. The merit of bringing a human rights perspective into the issue of taxation and state expenditure is that it could provide a basis for forms of government accountability and responsibility, which could help to re-legitimise taxation. At the same time, as the participatory budgeting initiatives have shown, success depends also on the solidity and vibrancy of forms of democratic participation.

Attiya Waris succeeds admirably in this book in discussing with verve and passion, as well as clarity and insight, issues which are of central importance to the future of Kenyans as well as citizens of all countries. The book makes an important contribution to global scholarship as well as public policies. It deserves to find a large readership, which I hope will help to contribute to the worldwide debates about the crucial issues of tax justice and the future of collective social institutions and the state.

Sol Picciotto

Emeritus Professor, Lancaster University (UK) .

Scientific Director, Oñati International Institute for he Sociology of Law (Gipuzkoa, Spain)
6th March 2011

PREFACE

This book is broken into three separate parts or sections not including the introduction and conclusion. The introduction and methodology are set out initially. Part one consists of chapters one, two and three; Part 2 consists of chapters four and five and finally part three consists of chapters six and seven. Chapter 8 makes recommendations and concludes.

The first section enquires into the legitimacy of the existence of the post-colonial fiscal state, sets out the theory of the fiscal state in the context of post-colonial developing states with specific reference to Kenya and attempts to place modern day Kenya using fiscal sociology and the typology of the fiscal state. The history, background and development of the colonial and post-colonial fiscal state is analysed to bring out the typological gaps and to begin to construct the vacuum in the post-colonial developing state as regards the state's fiscal responsibility towards its citizens by setting out the diverse attempts being made in the Kenyan context.

The second section explores human rights principles and the right to development through the lens of resource constraints and the problems posed in their realisation, together with the possibilities for their realisation that are currently being developed. Within the human rights realm, there are several arguments that are used to maintain and encourage this separation. They include the issues of domestic sovereignty; budgetary policy; the illusion that civil and political rights are more important than economic and social rights; and finally, the lack of interest, until recently, of human rights specialists in taxation as a source of finance. This section will also go a step forward and propose the utilisation of human rights benchmarks with which to re-distribute tax revenue

Section 3 is the application section and sets out the interplay between the state and citizens that currently exists in the world today. This section will set out the definition, background, history and reasoning behind the introduction of PB. It will then apply this concept through the lens of fiscal sociology with the aim of discovering whether there is the realisation of human rights through the PB process. The legitimising of the post-colonial fiscal states' right to tax is thus analysed by focussing on the state-society relationship as it is expressed through the CDF.

CHAPTER 1

INTRODUCTION

There is hardly any other aspect of history ... so decisive for the fate of the masses as that of public finances. Here one hears the pulse beat of nations at its clearest. Here one stands at the source of all social misery[1]

One fundamental purpose for acknowledging basic rights is to prevent or eliminate the degree of vulnerability that leaves people at the mercy of others.[2]

The spirit of a people, its cultural level, its social structure, the deeds its policy may prepare ... is written in fiscal history. He who knows how to listen to its message here discerns the thunder of world history more clearly than anywhere else.[3]

The honouring of basic rights is an active alliance with those who would otherwise be helpless against natural and social forces too strong for them.[4]

Legitimacy arises out of the confidence of the ruled and this book will discuss society and taxation by arguing that the fiscal legitimacy should arise out of the confidence in the fiscal behaviour of the state and its handling of the fiscal resources placed in its trust.[5] Citizens in developing countries, both individually and as a society, perceive taxation as firstly, a necessary burden or obligation to the state and secondly, as a remission that has no commensurate benefits or guarantees.[6] The concept of 'necessary burden' has resulted in revenue collection disparities in developing countries as the relatively large size of the economy is not reflected in the proportionately small amount of tax revenue collected. There are numerous reasons for this including but not limited to the societal perception of tax as

---

1   Goldscheid (1962) 2

2   Chapman (1996) 37

3   Schumpeter (1991) 101

4   Shue (1996) 33

5   Weber (1972) 267

6   See Bratton, Mattes and Gyimah-Boadi (2005) 142 for examples of citizens perceptions of evasion and avoidance of tax.

a burden leading to both avoidance and evasion of tax. The effects of both domestic and global policies, which allow inputs of diverse actors as well as poor governance practices, fuel this perception.[7] The perception of governance practices extends societal perceptions towards the lack of accountability, transparency and responsibility of the state in its collection and use of fiscal resources in the eyes of citizens, taxpayers and society or the tax bargain. In the latter element, there is a distinctly slow and minimal improvement of human well-being in developing countries. Although developed countries were granted the right or power to levy tax, the 'no commensurate benefits or guarantees' was softened and the 'burden' alleviated by developing social welfare provisions that led to the improvement of the lives of citizens. This fiscal re-distribution policy has not been undertaken, adopted or achieved in most developing countries. This book thus seeks to explore not only how to improve tax collection but also tax distribution with reference to developing countries and Kenya specifically. Thus, the aphorisms set out above together are the links that this book will seek to draw together.

Taxation must be recognised in terms of not only the law and society movement but also the racial, ethnic, historical, economic, political, ideological, and belief systems in which it exists.[8] In addition, States go through stages of historical development and it has been argued by some scholars that a social welfare state is a fundamental characteristic of the penultimate level of development: the fiscal state.[9] The social welfare state and the guarantees it provides to society include the provision of goods and services that improve the well-being of individuals and groups within society. It has been extensively applied in developed countries worldwide but has not yet taken root effectively in developing countries. All these elements are engaged with to different extents within this book.

---

7   The Kenyan government since 1997 has not released audited accounts and a recent government statement stated that all audited accounts would be released by July 2005 but this has not been done to date. See Kenya National Audit Office (2009). The last published report is the 2006-7 report The Report of the Controller and Auditor General Together with the Appropriation Accounts Other Public Accounts and the Accounts of the Funds of 2006-2007 (2006-7)

8   Mumford (2008) 219

9   Schumpeter

Over the past 50 years, there has been the development of another model of the well-being of peoples: human rights. Human rights are defined as the basic moral guarantees that people in all countries and cultures have simply because they are people.[10] If human rights principles, which set out 'benefits and guarantees' of individuals and society is an element of well-being, it can thus be extended to international human rights principles and explore whether these are a possible tool in solving the crisis of the developing fiscal state.

The focus of this book is on human rights law, which has been chosen to test whether in fact it can be an alternative or additional guide to tax law and policy for the fiscal state to use in legitimising not only its continued existence but also its collection and distribution of tax resources in the eyes of society. This in turn will enable analysis as to whether societal perception of taxation can change with the intention of removing or minimising the perception of 'burden' by providing 'benefits and guarantees' to society.

1.1.   RE-LEGITIMATING THE FISCAL STATE THROUGH REALISING HUMAN RIGHTS

This research arose and developed through an initial two-pronged question. Firstly, how, when and under what circumstances does the fiscal state receive and maintain the legitimacy to collect and distribute tax? Secondly, how can international human rights treaties–to which many states worldwide are party–be realised within the domestic realm? The connection between these two questions is thus the overall objective of this book, which is to explore whether re-legitimation of the fiscal state can be achieved through the realisation of human rights law. The re-legitimation of the fiscal state's right to collect tax and the realisation of human rights are thus, the twin pillars upon which this thesis rests. At an initial glance, one might perceive an immediate disjuncture between the two. Firstly, the joining of the discourses of two seemingly unconnected areas of law: taxation and human rights. Secondly, an enquiry into achieving two separate and disparate legal concepts: re-legitimation and realisation.

---

10   Nickel (1987) 561-562

The commonality between the above two questions rests on the relationship between the state and society: the social contract. The state on the one hand, is a creation of society tasked with responsibilities towards its citizens. The right to collect tax; amount of tax revenue collected; the source from which it is collected; the manner of collection as well as the use and distribution of the collected revenue is traditionally a constitutional right or power of the national government of any particular state. Tax policy and national resource collection and distribution have always been placed within the discretion of government/political party in power in a state.[11] Thus, the priority use of these funds is decided upon by the 'rulers' often with no requirement that reference be made to the people/ citizens who contributed to the funds now at the state's disposal. Over time and through history these funds and hence tax policy has been analysed and spending priorities have remained largely in the discretion of rulers.[12] Society on the other hand, contributes its members to the state to allow its creation and functioning for certain fixed purposes. These functions need to be fulfilled, and include basic issues such as security, recognising that it requires resources in one form or another. These add onto the demands placed on the state's resources at its first and most basic state developmental level of existence. However, with the growing complexity of the state and its undertaking to provide more goods and services, there is a commensurate growing requirement for resources. This leads to the recognition that there is a limited resource base and thus the needs or requirements must be prioritised.

In the modern developing state, the use of limited resources and its prioritisation has been left traditionally to the state. Societal and state priorities do not always reflect each other. The questions that arise in the conflicting priorities of the state and society are how to bring these choices closer together, whether there is a necessity that they be a compromise and how this compromise should function. This book will reflect on the use of the limited resources available to the developing state, not only to legitimise the state and allow its continued collection of resources but also to argue for and propose

---

11   See generally Brennan and Buchanan (1980)

12   See generally Levi (1988)

how re-prioritisation could continually improve the well-being of society and increase collections in the long-term. However, the discussion here will follow a more anecdotal approach strengthened with statistical data currently available.[13]

As opposed to perceiving citizens as mere subjects of the state and its activities, the book will posit that participation of society in the re-distribution of tax revenue can form part of a society-state compromise. As a result, starting questions include: How was taxation first introduced in developing countries? How would tax revenue be linked to tax expenditure? Was there a link? If there is a link, had it been broken in developing countries and why? Could human rights be a tool for linking revenue to expenditure? Can law contribute to linking tax revenue to tax expenditure using human rights? Suggested conclusions, I imagined were that the inherited history of the application of tax, force and threats is what keeps tax collection going but that no one in Kenya would link the payment and collection of tax to expenditure or to human rights.

Accountability, responsibility and transparency of an efficient and effective fiscal system are critical where the state is responsible to those who have entrusted it with their limited resources for their betterment. The interplay between limited resources that are

---

13   A search of various sources to pinpoint fiscal data on Kenya showed that information that exists is limited and hard to find. Kenya National Archive data from the commencement of British colonisation to independence is sporadic as a colonial office fire is said to have destroyed many of the records, resulting in the use of mainly secondary data and some primary data in the form of a few reports in this thesis. There are also limited fiscal and other records available for the years 1963-1970 but no reason could be ascertained for this state of affairs in Kenya. Data is available for 1970-2007 but is interrupted. In addition, it is limited by the absence of a published Hansard and law reports since 1980. Publication re-commenced in 2005 and currently there is a project to publish the past missing volumes of these publications. However, at the time this research was conducted in 2007 access to both was still impossible. However, in 2009 certain Hansard publications and Law reports have been periodically released and withdrawn on the official government website. In addition, the most recent Welfare Monitoring Survey is for 1997; The last time a population census was taken was in 1999; The last Integrated Labour Force Survey (ILFS) available is of 1998/1999 while the most recent poverty line statistics available at the Kenya Bureau of Statistics are for 2005 and the most recent Kenya Integrated Household Budget Survey (KIHBS) is for 2005/2006. Statistical analysis was also further limited due to the absence of data locally and this translates into inaccurate analysis undertaken both locally and internationally for example by the international reports such as the WB and IMF 2009 reports on Kenya which officially utilise all these as well as specifically 2004 data.

distributed at the discretion of fiscal states based on their spending priorities has resulted in development, poverty alleviation and the improvement of the lifestyles of the people in some states. While recognising the complexity of state-society relations, that are different for different groups of people, the relationship that seems to have developed between citizens and the developed state through state mechanisms and institutions has not been as successful in improving the lives of citizens in the post-colonial developing state. The improvement of these spending priorities in the context of the current fiscal crisis with greater resource constraints and specifically for the post-colonial developing state is thus where this thesis is situated. The unsettled concept of state fiscal responsibility towards its citizens is the underlying issue that pushed the direction this book has taken of an exploration of the link between tax revenue levying and collection, to tax expenditure use and distribution, on behalf of citizens.

Is it time for a developing state model of the social welfare state?[14] However, the current fiscal crisis, which is not, only a crisis of the fiscal but also of the welfare state with its high expenditure obligations has led to an aversion to the adoption of this idea. Hence, a problem addressed by this book is to find an alternative to the social welfare state concept, and the possible solution explored is to reinterpret and attempt to translate it into a 'human rights state' with socio-economic rights to replace social welfare provisions and the maintenance of state structures and administration as part of civil and political rights.

Why should human rights be the tool of choice? Collection and distribution deliberately does not have any 'benefits and guarantees.' Human rights principles evolve and develop and are given importance by individual states at the international level. Human rights can be said to have a normative force that many people worldwide acknowledge. In addition, states also acknowledge its importance through the signing of treaties and covenants. In other words, one could argue that human rights are *prima facie* important to the state. Thus, interest in human rights internationally gives all states and

---

14   Cobham (2006)

citizens in the world an international platform of a basic minimum benchmark of qualifying and partially quantifying well-being and needs of all peoples and societies. Consequently, one possible reading of the significance of human rights theory centralises the notion of realisation in order to turn the ideal into real, concrete and crystallised. Human rights principles, similarly, are international and also domestically constitutional obligations undertaken by states. However, these rights are ideals and aspirational and their realisation remains within the discretion of the state. The nature of the case study that uses the term 'development' allows the book to narrow focus by placing all of these rights under the wide umbrella of development and the right to development. As a result, the book will query whether taxation and the re-distributive policy of tax should be re-assessed in light of human rights, from the point of view of state policy and legislation as a state approach to the fulfilment of human rights obligations in the post-colonial fiscal state.

At a larger level this book will draw in the discussion around several wider areas. These include sociology, philosophy, law, economics and history. The aim will be to set out the diverse discourses taking place in these different fields in the context of both legitimation of tax and the realisation of human rights. Within these wider areas, emerging themes in no particular order include state-building, social contract, colonialism, the welfare state, tax, participation, citizenship, human rights, development and poverty alleviation. These themes form the commonalities that run through the entire document and are part of the threads that will be drawn out and applied to Kenya.

The rationale of this book flows out of the common themes set out above. The failure of the fiscal state to provide for the needs of the people and the inability of the people to voice their concerns despite the use of representative democracy in many parts of the world today provides grave concern for the continuing and needless death of many millions of people from poverty and the lack of development in their regions all over the world. If the argument of limited resources is to be analyzed then the need to make the best possible use for these resources is critical and must be addressed from a different approach. The needs have been clearly and concisely set out in human rights discourse and the use of resources clearly set out in tax discourse yet neither look to each other to find the link in order to use the resources for the people, and this is a lacuna that this book will attempt to address.

This is but a first step in a discourse on human rights and taxation that remains separate and there is room for its justification, analysis and building in the future. Budgetary analysis as well as tax policy in thematic forms has already begun in many countries through the work of non-governmental organizations and this should be continued. In addition, the creation of poverty alleviation and development indicators and benchmarks could also be re-assessed using concrete fiscal terms and analyzed within the parameters of each individual state.

1.2.   LINKING TAXATION AND HUMAN RIGHTS IN DEVELOPING STATES THROUGH THE LENS OF FISCAL SOCIOLOGY

The concept of realisation of human rights through taxation proposed by this book has not been explored in either human rights discourse or fiscal/taxation discourse. An exploration in human rights discourse is only now beginning to take root,[15] through among other practical methods, the retrospective budgetary analysis by civil society organisations including the IBP and IDASA. However, budgetary analysis in developing countries is difficult to monitor and requires complex data gathering from both the current period and tracing of trends over time. It also requires content specific data relating to a state's level of development and available resources. Thus, it is difficult to evaluate state compliance with their obligations through measurement against these criteria,[16] especially over a limited period of research, with limited data available.

Tax law analysis traditionally ignores reference to society and societal requirements and simply analyses the collection and distribution of tax at a technical level, in order to fulfil government functions with importance placed on recurrent expenditure. The

---

15   See generally Roper and Barria (2009)

16   Steiner, Alston and Goodman (2007) 305-306

issue of tax policy alternatives as explored within traditional tax analysis leaves the concept of the unchecked discretionary power of government unchallenged and limits societal participation to the electoral vote.

Although human rights originated and evolved through the state and thus, like tax policy have a state centric basis, they have been accepted by the international community and specific states as being the basic minimum requirements for the general well-being of citizens.

The issue of resource scarcities within domestic capabilities includes among other sources of government revenue–taxation. This link of resource scarcities to the well-being of citizens and society allowed the possibility of connecting into the growing field of socio-legal theory and fiscal sociology, the argument for the bridging of taxation in the state-society relationship to human rights. It is with this in mind that fiscal sociology was chosen as the guide for the discussion in this book.

1.3. DEFINING FISCAL SOCIOLOGY FOR THE DEVELOPING STATE

Schumpeter's fiscal sociology is best defined by Backhaus as the analysis of taxation and public finances undertaken by studying the 'lives of individuals, groups and societies'. It includes in it the unintended impact of taxation as well as regulation and has implications for almost every activity of government that somehow affects the private sector.[17] Goldscheid defined fiscal sociology as the historical nature of the state at a point in time and its functional interdependence between finances and social development.[18] The space created by fiscal sociology to allow multidisciplinary discourse on fiscal relations between society and the developing state while allowing for diversity in state forms is thus where this thesis will situate itself. It will use the political, economic, legal, cultural, institutional and historical factors of a society to link in the state. It will also add the discourse of human rights as a measure of the

---

17   Backhaus (2002) 73

18   Goldscheid as quoted by Musgrave (1992) 99

complex social interactions through their participation of society and citizens in the institutional processes of the fiscal state.

However, it does analyse the transient state as Schumpeter develops it and attempts to make changes to his paradigm in order to allow the developing state in its reality – a reality that he would appreciate – to manifest itself in his theory in order to better understand it from the socio-legal perspective. In addition, despite an extensive discussion on tax revenue, Schumpeter failed to expand on the issue of tax expenditure; instead, public expenditure was seen as a circumstance to which tax must adjust.[19] The connection of taxation to citizens evolving rights and thus the realisation of these rights progressively through history gets ignored in Schumpeter's theory of the fiscal state and the denial of progressive realisation or improved well-being is the core of the problem this thesis attempts to grapple with in the context of the post-colonial fiscal state.

Human rights principles are the principles and policy consideration benchmarks being explored in this book as a measure of the effectiveness, efficiency and accountability, responsibility of the state to society. Thus, human rights are added into the discourse in order to attempt to create concrete provisions that are progressively enforceable and realisable. This thesis will argue for the widest possible interpretation of human rights claims, principles, policies, laws and values. The use of this extremely wide scope is firstly to pragmatically attempt to point out the potential breadth of human rights considerations that can be linked into taxation through fiscal sociology. Secondly, to normatively assert that human rights are appealing by virtue of the standards that they set and there is a need to test their practical realisation.

---

19   *Ibid.* 103

The need to see whether a state can be self-sustainable[20] while providing for the society therein leads to the discussion and use of fiscal sociology not only at the overall theoretical level, but also at the more detailed level of discourse in developing countries as is broken down into the macro and the micro levels of fiscal sociology.

1.3.1. THE MACRO LEVEL OF FISCAL SOCIOLOGY

Goldscheid's stand can thus be summarised by his statement that public finance decides the fates of the masses that this is where one would hear the pulse beat of the nation clearest.[21] Schumpeter in responding to Goldscheid stated that:

> The spirit of a people, its cultural level, its social structure, and the deeds and policy may prepare is written in its fiscal history and that public finances are one of the best starting points for an investigation of society.[22]

Schumpeter argued that a good fiscal administration could delay or even avoid a fiscal crisis. Goldscheid broadly stated after the war that the state could no longer sustain itself and thus it must seek either revenue or services from the people. He argued that the development of fiscal institutions was as a result of the forces of class struggle. The feudal state was wealthy because it was controlled by the ruling classes; the state became impoverished when feudalism broke down. Thus if a state is to be rendered useful, the lost wealth must be reinstituted so that it can meet its welfare function.[23] This led to the development of individual taxation and the 'tax state'.[24]

This book thus commences with a methodological map of the levels and different models of the fiscal state using fiscal sociology as created by Schumpeter and expounded by the Ormrod-Bonney model as the tool for understanding the stage of fiscal development a state has attained. This concept of the typology of the fiscal state

---

20   Group of Experts on the UN Programme on Public Administration and Finance (1997) paragraph 12

21   Musgrave (1992) 99

22   Schumpeter (1954) 19, Schumpeter (1991) 4

23   Goldscheid (1962) 202-13

24   *Ibid.*

will be discussed in this thesis in the context of its application on the 'post colonial fiscal state' in order to understand whether one can in fact apply the concept of the fiscal sociology and the typology of the fiscal state. Schumpeter's theory, however, has certain limitations in its application to developing states, including shrinking borders, self-sustainability policies, labour mobility, globalisation, the shadow economy, all of which push Schumpeter's vision of freedom from economic restraint.[25] He made no allowance for a society where the state of distribution would be a legitimate concern of democracy.[26]

The mapping of the stages of the fiscal state is the critical contended tool for approaching the crisis of the fiscal state for several reasons. Firstly, it is based on the historical development of states. Secondly, it places states into categories based on a multiple number of factors including resource availability and level of development. Thirdly, it is a holistic interpretation of the state and taxation as well as citizens and their rights.

Schumpeter and Goldscheid were offering fiscal sociology as a macro-**historical** paradigm that captured, embodied and lay bare the dominant drivers of **societal, economic** and **political** change[27] to which this book will add the already developing area of tax **law** and legal change.[28] Modern scholars have used Schumpeter and Goldscheid's theory and extended it in diverse fields. Fiscal history has been expounded by McClure and Van Veen who argue that the collection of taxation necessitates the emergence of the fundamental elements of **societies, government** and **markets**. Daunton has stated that the history of taxation comprises a combination of four elements, the **institutions** of tax assessments and collection, the **different forms** of income and **economic activity**, and the **political** processes of tax revision and the purposes of public action.[29] Webber and Wildavsky argue in their **historical** analysis of tax expenditure that the **political** regime determines the type of

---

25   Musgrave (1992) 104

26   *Ibid.* 105

27   Marques (2004) 2

28   See Mumford (2008)

29   Daunton (2001) 22

budget system adopted.[30] Most recently, Mumford posited that the legitimization of tax could be seen through the **culture** of taxation prevalent in a society, the method of collection, the ease as well as the societal response to the use of state's resources and the forms that their redistribution takes.[31] Thus, fiscal sociology has been expanded in the past 10 years to include influences from both the socio-legal school and constitutional law influences on public finances. Current analysis includes tax revolts in Japan on one hand and support for the welfare state in Finland on the other,[32] to which this thesis will add on and explore—human rights law.

The substantiation of the possibility of adding on both the post-colonial state and human rights as a benchmark is thus explored. It is made possible by several arguments. Firstly, that the typology of states inherently recognises the uniqueness of each state. Secondly, it also recognises the evolving meanings and allows for the contextualised analysis of terminology that benchmark the progression of states such as 'state', 'well-being', 'administration', 'tax' and 'welfare'. Thirdly, scholars argue that Schumpeter wrote in an era when economists still cared about the 'real world'. Fourthly, Schumpeter also argued for the interconnection between the development of a state and the tax regime as long as the state could be distinguished from private interests. It will be argued that these developments as well as the inherent flexibility in the theory of fiscal sociology allows for not only the extension of fiscal sociology to apply to developing states but to also use human rights as a possible benchmarking alternative to the social welfare state.

Participation is the tool used in the application of this theory to analyse whether in fact there can be a link made between human rights and taxation at a macro level. Schumpeter stated that economic analysis deals with the questions of how people behave at any given time, the economic effects of their behaviour. Economic sociology he added deals with the question of how the people came to behave as they do. He then defined human behaviour as including actions, motives, propensities, social institutions, relevant to economic

---

30   See generally Webber and Wildavasky (1986)

31   Mumford (2001) 2

32   As quoted by Mumford (2008) 219

behaviour.[33] This reference to human behaviour is what allows the discussion to then flow into the area of participation and PB as an analysis of how budgeting decisions are made by society and thus allows one to consider if the behaviour of society can be tied into human rights.

In conclusion, in order to analyse the link in developing countries, like Kenya, between the issues of tax revenue and tax expenditure this thesis shall be using fiscal sociology. The inquiry requires a foray into how this connection or link can be made on the basis of history, societal needs and future regionalism in developing countries especially Kenya, in the context of fiscal sociology. The use of fiscal sociology shall be the methodology in not only developing policy proposals but also analysing present policies in the case of the linkage and or connection being made between revenue and tax expenditure and how the link can be used to finance and or strengthen the financing of human rights, development and the alleviation of poverty by increasing redistribution in order to reduce inequalities.

This study will thus generally analyse the jurisprudence on the right of government to levy and disburse taxation through the fiscal state. It shall specifically look to demonstrate the applicability or lack thereof of human rights principles, adopting a critical analysis and comparative approach in the study, with the essential research data being gathered mainly from both primary and secondary literature as well as interviewing of tax and human rights specialists and implementers of legislation in Kenya and Brazil.

1.3.2. The Micro level Context

Schumpeter stated that fiscal demands are the sign of life of the modern state.[34] In addition, he argued that this theory could be applied to localised questions of **economy** and **governance** within an international framework while maintaining focus on localised questions.[35] At the micro level, since 2000, the analysis has been

---

33   Schumpeter (1954) 19

34   Schumpeter (1991) 110

35   See generally Schumpeter (1950)

predominantly limited to the field of economics. More recent efforts include discourse into taxpayer motivations, strategic decisions, rational calculation and meso determinants such as interactive or threshold effects. Some authors like Backhaus limit themselves to the economist perspective while others like McLure[36] combine economics and sociology.

The challenging part of this project is to not only attempt to bring together two seemingly unconnected fields of taxation and human rights at a theoretical level but to also attempt a practical application by analysing existing state systems using this approach. The specific focus chosen for the purposes of this book was the Constituency Development Fund in Kenya. The fund has several critical elements that are pertinent to this study. Firstly, there was the legal provision that specified direct allocation of tax revenue to tax expenditure, creating the link that this thesis proposes. Secondly, the revenue allocation was specified for development purposes leading to the development of the fiscal state. Thirdly, the allocation of tax revenue is to the smallest grass-root electoral area (constituency) which allows the highlighting of a microcosm of the state-society relationship. Fourthly, it specifies the use of local citizenry in the constituency to decide on their needs or requirements based on their priorities for the year, which had to be undertaken by people in the area, and allows for an analysis based on well-being and social welfare as posited by Schumpeter.

The CDF uses the term development but does not define it. This allowed not only for the use of the economic interpretation of development tying in Schumpeter's arguments on tax development and state development but also allows space for inclusion of the right to development as well. These two terms together are the stands that begin to build up the link between taxation and human rights. The 'right to development' as it has developed through international law inherently requires a link to resources and this adds another strand to the tax-human right link. Finally, the acceptability of the use of the right to development as a human right in the past 30 years is contextualised based on three grounds. Firstly, that this is the most

---

36   See generally Marques (2004)

modern and recent interpretation of a human right. Secondly, it was proposed by developing states, the subjects of this thesis. Finally, independently through different mechanisms, states are already making attempts to apply it, albeit indirectly.

Participation is a key issue in the PB discourse. Downs credited Schumpeter with formulating the premise that politicians do not seek elections to offer programmes but vice versa.[37] However, Musgrave argues that Schumpeter himself argued for a stronger leadership, with the state acting as a rational instrument and not a villain, a theory that is not well fitted in developing country discourse.[38] Thus, here too the issue of society will be extended further than foreseen by Schumpeter to include elements of direct democracy.

Although the specific focus of this study is Kenya and the variation over time of the choices that rulers made in the collection and distribution of tax, the aim of the thesis is to enquire into the tax policy choices and the results of their application. Although there is concern with reforms of tax systems, and some statistical data is provided, there is no attempt undertaken here to calculate the amount collected, lost or stolen. The main purpose is thus, to locate whether the participatory process of citizens through the articulation of their needs in state budgeting processes can result in not only re-legitimating taxation but also realising of human rights, while recognising the limitations of the system and this research.

---

37   Downs (1956) 29

38   Musgrave (1992) 112

PART 1

LEGITIMISING THE POST COLONIAL STATE

CHAPTER 2

LEGITIMISING THE POST-COLONIAL FISCAL STATE THROUGH FISCAL SOCIOLOGY

There is hardly any other aspect of history ... so decisive for the fate of the masses as that of public finances. Here one hears the pulse beat of nations at its clearest here one stands at the source of all social misery.[39]

The spirit of a people, its cultural level, its social structure, the deeds its policy may prepare ... is written in fiscal history. He who knows how to listen to its message here discerns the thunder of world history more clearly than anywhere else.[40]

The modern state cannot exist where all centres of life rest in the community. It only emerges with a setting where bonds of community have disintegrated and the individual-the lesser lord and the voting citizen-moved to the centre of gravity. Only there does the state become necessary either by a common need or the community even broken retains functions which the newly created individuals are unwilling or unable to take over.[41]

The state, society and taxation are inextricably intertwined. Their interconnectivity is expressed in the tax bargain between the state and society that grants the state the fiscal legitimacy to collect and distribute tax. Fiscal legitimacy is based on the confidence that a society has in the governance of the fiscal state. The tax bargain as it has been negotiated between the state and society is constantly changing and is reflected in the laws and policies that govern the levy and distribution of taxation. As long as the evolving tax bargain is perceived by society as being fair and equal, the fiscal legitimacy of the state is maintained and a fiscal crisis is averted.

Fiscal legitimacy and fiscal crisis are weights on either side of a balance. The pivot of the balance is society's confidence in the fiscal state. This confidence can be assessed through a variety of ways and can be perceived through diverse characteristics in the evolving

---

39   Goldscheid (1962) 2

40   Schumpeter (1991) 101

41   Musgrave (1992) 92 quoting Schumpeter (1991) 110

relationship between the state and society. Traditional areas of state activity included defence, foreign affairs, the administration of law and order and the protection of private property. However, there is a growing concern for economic and social welfare not only of the state as a whole but of individual citizens as well. Fiscal legitimacy can be described as an accountable, responsible and transparent fiscal system that is effective and efficient and just and fair. Movement away from this description is movement away from fiscal legitimacy and towards fiscal crisis.

Measuring the perception of citizens and the confidence they have in a fiscal state is a technical process. In addition, perceptions and confidence change with constantly changing fiscal laws and policy. The tax bargain involves the tax levied on the state and the expenditures undertaken by the state that society perceives as being justifiable and for their benefit. State expenditure is divided into recurrent and development expenditure. Recurrent expenditures are preconditions to the existence of the state including political and social roles of governance consisting of defence (both internal and external), foreign affairs, and administration of justice. Development expenditure on infrastructure, health and education and social security may be considered as investments to stimulate economic growth but will be considered necessary for a political regime to maintain societal loyalty and increase fiscal legitimacy.[42] This thesis while recognising the importance of gauging these perceptions makes a first foray into the area. As a result, this first step and the measurement of citizen's perceptions and confidence levels will be addressed for the perspective of the fiscal laws and policies of the state: tax revenue and developmental expenditure.

Traditional analysis of taxation is not multi-disciplinary and limits analysis to the state's role in the collection and distribution of tax. Although this approach to taxation is important in addressing the traditional areas of state activity, it has not succeeded in improving upon the concerns of economic and social welfare that affect fiscal legitimacy of post-colonial states. With this in mind, the overall purpose of this thesis is to engage with the state-society relationship

---

42   Heller (1974) 255

as it concerns the tax bargain in the distribution of taxation in order to increase fiscal legitimacy and reduce the propensity of fiscal crises in post-colonial states. Approaching tax law from a state-societal perspective makes the thesis a multidisciplinary study and allows the ensuing discussion to situate itself in the theoretical framework of the socio-legal school.

The central problem facing post-colonial fiscal states is how to increase its legitimacy and develop. The underlying intention of this thesis is that the location and application of a method of increasing legitimacy will result in an improvement in the well-being of its constituent society through an effective and efficient fiscal system that is accountable, responsible and transparent.

The evolving tax bargain between the state and society, and the confidence that society has in the state can be best assessed through history. The analysis of the background to the commencement of taxation, its growing complexity in collection and distribution, and the reactions of society to this process are some of the key elements in understanding the level of fiscal legitimacy of a state. This requires that the thesis draw on historical, economic, political, cultural, sociological and legal perspectives. Fiscal sociology approaches the analysis of taxation and public finances by studying the lives of individuals, groups and societies through history. This includes the unintended impact of taxation as well as regulation and has implications for almost every activity of the state that somehow affects the private sector and society[43] as expressed by the anagrams set out above.

Studies based on fiscal sociology have been undertaken mainly by historians,[44] sociologists,[45] economists[46] and political scientists[47] with growing discourse in the socio-legal school by tax law scholars.[48] Their collective works have resulted in the creation and

---

43   Backhaus (2002) 73

44   See generally Ormrod, Bonney and Bonney (1999), Daunton (2001) and Tilly (1992)

45   See generally Schumpeter (1991) and Goldscheid (1962)

46   See generally Campbell (1993) and Backhaus (2002)

47   See generally Moore (2004)

48   See generally Mumford (2008)

development of a historical analysis of the development of the fiscal state setting out types and models of fiscal states with categories and sub-categories to delineate transition from one type of state to another.[49] However, these analyses are based on the historical evolution of European states with only a cursory analysis of the post-colonial fiscal state. The overall approach of this thesis is thus further narrowed down in this chapter to the application of fiscal sociology to an analysis of the post-colonial fiscal state and a methodological critique of the existing typologies and types of fiscal states in order to address the issue of the increase of its fiscal legitimacy.

This chapter will argue that the post-colonial fiscal state is a specific type of a fiscal state that needs to have separate and distinct consideration. It is further argued here that this has not been fully considered theoretically in the context of the fiscal legitimacy of the state and that a more complete analysis of the post-colonial fiscal state has important implications for both law and policy, especially in perceiving the problems peculiar to the post-colonial fiscal state. The main intent is to attempt to address the fiscal crisis of the post-colonial state focussing on Kenya and to suggest the possible prevention or alleviation of the fiscal crisis through a human rights perspective to participatory budgeting.

The analysis will firstly, analyse and discuss the source of the legitimacy of the existence of post-colonial fiscal states; where this legitimacy stems from, the challenges it faces and, what allows the fiscal state to continue to exist. Secondly, it will analyse the importance of using fiscal sociology to analyse the post-colonial fiscal state and finally, it will use fiscal sociology to analyse the typology of the fiscal state by drawing out characteristics within the different types of fiscal states in order to establish the challenges to the placement and transition of the post-colonial fiscal state within the existing typology.

---

49   See generally Schumpeter (1991), Ormrod, Bonney and Bonney (1999), Daunton (2001) and Tilly (1992)

2.1.   Conceptualising Fiscal Legitimacy for the Post-Colonial State

Legitimacy is a complex and multidisciplinary issue.[50] It has been explored mainly in political science with some limited forays by legal scholars. Weber argues that legitimacy arises out of the confidence of the ruled.[51] As long as the ruled-citizens continue to have confidence in and obey the state, it remains legitimate. Citizens, however, will only continue to obey as long as they believe in the fairness of the policies and laws being implemented. As a result, fiscal legitimacy is a reflection of the confidence society has in the state's performance in collecting and spending its tax revenue as expressed in accepted laws and policies. Fiscal legitimacy is but one small facet of legitimacy, which this thesis will seek to explore.

Fiscal legitimacy is critical to the existence of the post-colonial fiscal state as it is the source of its support, it assists in state building and it promotes sovereignty and independence by reducing reliance on foreign aid. This fiscal state has two roles to play in the maintenance and improvement of fiscal legitimacy: political and legal. Although government as a political actor assumes the responsibility of deciding what ends are to be pursued and what resources it is prepared to commit in dealing with problems, as a legal actor the state must then proceed to establish the mechanisms to further these ends.[52] This discussion, while recognising the importance of political legitimacy, will limit itself to improvement of legitimacy from a legal perspective. It will proceed on this premise without seeking to replace politics with law. The enhancement of fiscal legitimacy will thus be discussed from the point of view of how to harness the law and policy-making process to create an optimum condition for increasing well-being and state development.

Good governance paves the way to fiscal legitimacy by building people's faith in the state and ensuring their acceptance of its laws and policies. Good governance has today become the centre of

---

50   See generally McAuslan and McEldowney (1985) for a discussion on legitimacy from a legal perspective, and Connolly (1984) for a discussion on political and social legitimacy.

51   Weber (1972) 267

52   Nonet and Seznick (2000) 112

attention for many post-colonial fiscal states in the drive to improve efficiency and effectiveness through transparency, accountability and responsibility practices of the fiscal state in order to be both just and fair. States can enhance fiscal legitimacy, by firstly, involving independent third parties in the auditing and evaluation of public policies to strengthen transparency and accountability. Secondly, promoting better, fairer and more public spending; thirdly, broadening the tax base and making tax systems fairer and more balanced. Finally, reinforcing the capacity, authority and accountability of sub-national government bodies. Fiscal legitimacy is not only an issue of capacity, in addition to strengthening administrative capabilities, societal participation and open and informed debate can result in more transparency. Independent actors with the capacity and the financial independence to carry out a critical evaluation of policies and proposed reforms can also add to the good governance and fiscal legitimacy.

In post-colonial fiscal states in Africa citizens of all classes have sought to avoid paying taxes and state fees,[53] decreasing the state's extractive capacity. This has been compounded by the effects of both domestic and global policies, which allow fiscal and policy inputs of diverse actors, as well as poor governance practices including corruption, clientelism and patronage fuel this perception.[54] There is a distinctly slow and minimal improvement of human well-being in developing countries. Comprehensive fiscal re-distribution has not been undertaken, adopted or achieved in most developing countries. As a result, civic indiscipline in some states has arisen reducing fiscal legitimacy and increasing the fiscal crisis. If these states are to develop in addition to reduction of reliance on foreign aid, the trust and loyalty of citizens and society must be recovered. Laws and policies that reflect societal thought must be put into place and pursued in order to convince citizens of the state's ability and right to continue

---

53   See Bratton, Mattes and Gyimah-Boadi (2005) 142 for examples of citizens' perceptions of evasion and avoidance of tax.

54   The Kenyan government since 1997 has not released audited accounts and a government statement stated that all audited accounts would be released by July 2005 but this has not been done to date. See Kenya National Audit Office (2009). The last published report is the 2006-7 report, The Report of the Controller and Auditor General Together with the Appropriation Accounts Other Public Accounts and the Accounts of the Funds of 2006-2007 (2006-7)

to collect revenues for the public good. The state will not succeed until citizens believe they are participating fully in public life and that their tax payments will not be lost to government corruption. This thesis thus seeks to explore not only how to improve tax collection but also tax distribution in post-colonial fiscal states in Africa and Kenya specifically through the strengthening of the state-society relationship in order to alleviate poverty and achieve development.

2.2.   CONCEPTUALISING FISCAL SOCIOLOGY FOR THE POST-COLONIAL FISCAL STATE

The method of analysis, measurement and improvement of the fiscal legitimacy of the post-colonial fiscal state is a difficult challenge that has been partially explored but largely ignored. As a result, the manner in which to undertake such a challenge generally remains unsettled.[55] Goldscheid defined fiscal sociology as the historical nature of the state at a point in time and its functional interdependence between finances and social development.[56] Schumpeter concurred with this argument by stating that the best starting point from which to study the state is fiscal sociology when he stated that

> The budget is the skeleton of the state stripped of all misleading ideologies.[57]

Schumpeter included in fiscal sociology the political, economic, legal, institutional and historical factors of a society as they were linked to the fiscal state.[58] Mumford from a legal perspective recently added to these elements by arguing that taxation be recognised in terms of not only the law and society movement but also the cultural, racial, ethnic, historical, economic, political, ideological, and belief systems in which it exists.[59]

Schumpeter and Goldscheid were offering fiscal sociology as a macro-**historical** paradigm that captured, embodied and lay bare

---

55   See generally Collignon (2007) and Everest-Phillips and Sandall (2008) for recent attempts to meet the challenge of measuring fiscal legitimacy.

56   Goldscheid as quoted by Musgrave (1992) 99

57   Schumpeter (1991) 100

58   *Ibid.* 100-101

59   Mumford (2008) 219

the dominant drivers of **societal, economic** and **political** change[60] and this thesis will attempt to add to the already developing area of tax **law** and legal change.[61] Modern scholars have used Schumpeter and Goldscheid's theory and extended it in diverse fields. Fiscal history has been expounded by McClure and Van Veen who argue that the collection of taxation necessitates the emergence of the fundamental elements of **societies, government** and **markets**. Daunton has stated that the history of taxation comprises a combination of four elements, the **institutions** of tax assessments and collection, the different forms of income and economic activity, and the **political** processes of tax revision and the purposes of public action.[62] Webber and Wildavasky argue in their **historical** analysis of tax expenditure that the **political** regime determines the type of budget system adopted.[63]

Mumford posited that the legitimization of tax could be seen through the **culture** of taxation prevalent in a society, the method of collection, the ease as well as the societal response to the use of state's resources and the forms that their redistribution takes.[64] Moore argues most recently that Schumpeter's fiscal sociology is extremely pertinent in the analysis of **developing states**.[65] Thus, fiscal sociology has been expanded to include influences from both the socio-legal school and constitutional law influences on public finances[66] as well as post-colonial states. This thesis will approach the analysis of tax law by following the conceptualisation of fiscal sociology in the tradition created by Goldscheid and Schumpeter and distilled by Mumford and Moore.

However, there is a difference between Schumpeter's fiscal sociology which was developed at a macro level and the manner in which it is applied and interpreted today and thus by extension the

---

60   Marques (2004) 2

61   See generally Mumford (2008)

62   Daunton (2001) 22

63   See generally Webber and Wildavasky (1986)

64   Current analysis includes tax revolts in Japan on one hand and support for the welfare state in Finland on the other. See Mumford (2001) 2

65   See generally Moore and Rackner (2004)

66   As quoted by Mumford (2008) 219

manner in which this thesis will apply it. This thesis does not follow Schumpeter to his end discourse of full socialism. However, it does analyse the transitioning of the fiscal state as Schumpeter developed it and attempts to add to his paradigm in order to allow the post-colonial fiscal state in its reality – a reality that he would appreciate – to manifest itself in his theory in order to better understand it from the socio-legal perspective.

Schumpeter argued that the social welfare was only achievable after the state transitioned from the domain state to the tax state. The social welfare state and the guarantees it provides to society includes the provision of goods and services that improve the well-being of individuals and groups within society. This characteristic is found in developed states especially Europe but has not yet taken root effectively in post-colonial states. The subsequent analysis will be undertaken with the aim of assessing how the fiscal states have developed historically and thus how the post-colonial fiscal state's development reflects similarities and differences historically. This analysis will be geared towards attempting to discern how fiscal legitimacy can be increased by achieving the improvement of well-being of society and social welfare.

2.3.   THE DEVELOPMENT OF THE FISCAL STATE

The concept of the fiscal state[67] has its origin in an article by Joseph Schumpeter that was first written in the late days of World War I on the basis of the wartime financial experiences of the Austro-Hungarian Empire. In it, Schumpeter argues that war justifies the collection of taxes from the populace, and further, that the viability of any state can be measured by its ability to draw taxes from the citizenry.[68] He further argues that without the financial need, the immediate cause for the creation of the fiscal state would have been absent.[69] Thus, the infringement of the individual liberties imposed by the ruler in order to further his interests is argued by Backhaus as

---

67   The addition of the avenue of borrowing to fund government activities arose with time, in addition to the existence of taxation levied to form the fiscal state.

68   Schumpeter (1991) 111

69   *Ibid.* 108

being the crisis of the fiscal state where needs arising outweigh the resources at the disposal of the state.[70]

Ormrod and Bonney support Schumpeter in arguing that fiscal history shows that change arises with the need for modernity and this pushes states forward into modernity and fiscal crisis.[71] The fiscal state is defined as the state that uses both taxation and other forms of revenue formation in order to not only maintain itself but by also obtaining additional income in order to develop. This theory has led to the development of the types of states that classifies the forms of revenue acquisition used.

It should be noted at the offset of this analysis that fiscal systems and models are at best sub-optimal and a compromise between limited resources and unlimited requirements. In addition, no state's development mirrors another. However, while recognising the incompleteness of any solution, the attempt being undertaken in this section and thesis is to utilise fiscal sociology and the work of scholars as they have analysed the development of European fiscal states, to attempt to draw a parallel between their diverse developmental processes. This analysis will in turn be tested in the following chapters by analysing the historical development of the Kenyan post-colonial fiscal state.

2.3.1. STAGES OF DEVELOPMENT OF THE FISCAL STATE

The stages of development of the fiscal state can be broken into different stages or types based on the existence, the extent of reliance and the complexity of application of taxation. There have been 4 types of states set out, analysed and subcategorised. These are all set out in the table below.

---

70   Backhaus (2002) 58

71   Ormrod, Bonney and Bonney (1999) 3 and Schumpeter (1991) 108

Figure 1: Types of Fiscal States

Characteristics	Primitive State	Domain State	Tax State	Fiscal State
Synonyms		Demesne state Rentier state[73]	Finance state	Welfare state[72] Resource state
Scholars who have tried to build models using these states	Ormrod-Bonney	Schumpeter Kruger Ormrod-Bonney	Ormrod-Bonney Kruger	Schumpeter Ormrod-Bonney
Developed the sub-types		Primitive[74] Less primitive Entrepreneurial Colonial	Capital–coercive[75] Capital-intensive Coercive-intensive	

In the analysis of the fiscal development and transitioning of the Austrian state, Schumpeter first developed and utilised fiscal sociology to categorise its development into two types: the domain[76] and tax[77] states. He argued that the main difference between these two states was that domain states were not supported by tax but by estates predominantly while the tax state relied more on tax.[78] Tilly analysed the imperial history of European states based on alternative histories of state formation. He posits that continuously varying combinations of capital, coercion, war and the position of the state within the international system,[79] divided imperial tax states

---

72   Moore (2004) 299

73   See generally Musgrave (1992)

74   Ormrod, Bonney and Bonney (1999) 14

75   Tilly (1992) 18-32

76   Tilly describes this by stating that in the middle ages rulers relied on their own estates or domains for resources and on the provision of goods and services by dependants. Resources might have also been obtained by plunder or colonization, by coercion or trade. *Ibid.* 18

77   During the wars, there was a search for additional revenues outside those already levied and thus began the levy of tax by the state. Bonney (1995) 14

78   Schumpeter (1991) 102-110

79   Tilly (1992) 14

in Europe into 3 types: coercion-intensive,[80] capital-intensive[81] and capitalised-coercion.[82]

Ormrod and Bonney have subsequently added two new types of states: the tribute state[83] that relied mainly on plunder and the fiscal state[84] that not only relied on taxes but also used them to improve societal well-being. Daunton[85] set out the pre-cursors of the modern fiscal state as the domain state and the tax state adopting Ormrod and Bonney's definitions while making no reference to primitive states.[86]

In considering colonial states, Bonney added on a sub-category to the domain state of the primitive, less primitive, entrepreneurial and colonial states but did not address the placement of the post-colonial state.[87] However, Moore added the term rentier state to refer to the post-colonial state that relies mainly on rent from resources and other strategic interests as well as foreign aid calling it a pre-tax state without addressing where in the models it fitted.[88]

Although these classifications and definitions of states are conceptually admirable and very effective in setting out how best to deal with a state at the policy level, the sentiments of Ormrod

---

80   State formation led to the creation of tax farmers who forcibly sold animals and imprisoned leaders as hostages when communities defaulted in tax payments. Customs and excise did not yield high returns in these relatively non-commercial economies. This then led to creation of head taxes and land taxes administered through property owners and village heads. *Ibid.* 18-28, 30

81   States were commercial economies and tax was levied mostly on commerce. *Ibid.* 18-28, 30

82   A mixture of the coercion-intensive and capital-intensive systems, which included use of property owners and merchants creating a duality of tax structures on land and trade. *Ibid.* 30-32

83   They defined the tribute state as a state that relies on plunder and extortion where a surplus is produced by the colonised from domain or otherwise. Ormrod, Bonney and Bonney (1999) 4-8

84   This state also combines a high level of tax revenue with large-scale borrowing. *Ibid.* 13-14

85   Daunton (2001) 4-5

86   *Ibid.* 4-7, relied on the Ormrod-Bonney model in his analysis of the types of states and adopts the evolution of states from one form to the other by using the model as his reference point.

87   Ormrod, Bonney and Bonney (1999) 14

88   Moore (2004) 299

and Bonney and Tilly must be re-echoed here: an ideal model for the purposes of the rest of the world remains incomplete. The disadvantages of using an ideal type analysis is that it fails to take into consideration states that did not move from the domain to the tax state.

The ensuing analysis will proceed on the basis that although all states may not recapitulate the European experience, the European analysis of the fiscal states' development can be used in several ways: firstly, to pinpoint durable characteristics and secondly, to identify the principles of variation. Basing the analysis on this two-pronged approach of the model will allow other states to be better placed to identify firstly, their distinctive characteristics, secondly, their historically imposed constraints and finally, the relationships among the characteristics of particular types of states.[89] However even an incomplete model is better than no model at all and hence this chapter will proceed following on Tilly's train of thought.

2.3.2. THE MODELS OF THE FISCAL STATE

Schumpeter argued that a good fiscal administration could delay or even avoid a fiscal crisis.[90] He stated in his analysis of the collapse of the Austrian tax state, that its failure was not merely to do with the budgetary crisis but also was a superficial sign of the link between fiscal affairs, the social structure and the understanding of its historical structure.[91] In delineating the development of states into two he broadly set out the characteristics that transitioned the domain state into the tax state.[92] Kersten Kruger subsequently in 1987 proposed a model of transition of a state from a domain to a tax state based on Schumpeter's analysis.[93]

---

89   Tilly (1992) 16

90   Schumpeter (1991)116-119

91   Musgrave (1992) 90

92   Schumpeter (1991) 102-116

93   This table can be found in Ormrod, Bonney and Bonney (1999) 4-8. This table is almost identical in content with the Ormrod-Bonney model on the following page except for the addition of the columns describing the tribute and fiscal states and the removal of the two rows on loans and taxes and the addition of rows discussing expenditure, credit structure, and the causes of instability.

In 1999, Ormrod and Bonney analysed the Schumpeter-Kruger's model and added to it to create their typology of the stages of development of the fiscal state. They posited that there was a necessity to add upon the Schumpeter-Kruger model for two reasons. Firstly, it was too limited to a particular era and part of Europe. Secondly, it failed to address the issue of the interaction between expenditure, revenue and credit and the causes of instability and change in a fiscal system; instead, they argued that Schumpeter had posited that public expenditure was a circumstance to which tax must adjust which has been supported by Musgrave.[94] They then set out the following table.

---

94   Musgrave (1992) 103

Figure 2: The Ormrod-Bonney Model[95]

Characteristic	Tribute State	Domain State	Tax State	Fiscal State
Financial Theory	Beginning of a general theory.	Relatively undeveloped theory.	'Mercantilism' and 'cameralist'	Highly developed theories.
Form of Government	'Predatory', peripatetic rulers (dynastic) or tribes.	Personal, few limits in decision making.	Highly developed institutions and legal procedures.	Precise credit and tax legislation and 'fiscal constitution'.
Central Administration	Kinsmen, marital allies and clients of the ruler.	Small staff in more primitive forms.	Well staffed; specialised departments, defined authority.	Sophisticated organisation of departments, planning; administration
Local administration	High levels of local autonomy but with the sanction of royal intervention and/or punishment		Regularly controlled by central government.	Highly developed control by the centre.
Office holders	Royal kinsmen and families of rank. Sometimes Church officials.		Professionally trained personnel.	
			Many of these may still be holders of venal offices.	Appointments more or less on merit and presumed competence.
State Responsibilities	Maintenance of law and order.			
			Plus active influence on, and regulation of, all aspects of life.	
				Process of regulation may include elements of 'social engineering'.
Method of financing	Mix of payments in money and in kind.		Mainly Monetization.	High levels of monetization.

95 Derived from the Ormrod-Bonney Model see Ormrod, Bonney and Bonney (1999) 4-8

Characteristic	Tribute State	Domain State	Tax State	Fiscal State
Public finance	Plunder and extortion. Surplus produced by those colonized.	Surplus produced by domain or other regalian rights. Exploitation.	Increasing importance of taxation.	Precise planning of taxation with reference to the economy and public opinion.
Expenditure	Heavily related to scale of military effort.			Not heavily related to scale of military effort.
	Reliance on booty and conquests to meet expenditure.		Increasing size of armies, technological developments, and simultaneous military and naval armament	
		In more advanced systems, scaling down of household costs and all military costs (except for emergencies) in relation to predicted income.	Escalating military costs which spiral out of control in periods of sustained warfare. Costs of debt servicing acute in periods of wartime. Other costs may be curtailed.	Lead to the development of 'fiscal-military' states, some of which gain superpower status. 'Modern' sophisticated states may incur considerable levels of expenditure on health, social security and other 'welfare' costs for the population.

Characteristic	Tribute State	Domain State	Tax State	Fiscal State
Revenues	Taxes an infrequent aid, limited to specific purposes. Exactions and extortions play an important role. Systematic debasement of the coinage in wartime.	'Renewal' of coinage in peacetime.	Regular direct and indirect taxes, no longer limited to specific purposes. Exactions and extortion play little or no role. Debasement of the coinage, even in wartime, becomes unusual. Attempts to unify the tax structure, avoiding regressive taxes and relating the burden of taxation much more closely to the sources of wealth.	Direct and indirect taxes of a highly sophisticated kind, with income taxes, property taxes and other duties levied with a view to maximizing fiscal efficiency and assisting economic development. Unified tax structure with greater or emphasis on 'progression'. Levels of economic growth and inflation play an increasing part in taxpayers' expectations.
Credit Structure	Some short-term loans, but lack of a settled structure for public credit. Weak private finance corporations.	Short-term bridging loans against interest in kind or mortgaging of domain land. Some reliance on external, urban credit markets.	Sophisticated credit structures, with variable but often low rates of interest. Long-term loans guaranteed by the state or representative institution. Interest paid in money and potentially taxable. Credit structures may lack integration: potential tension between domestic and international markets for credit. State banks in certain countries.	Closer integration of domestic and international markets for credit. Capacity of the state to borrow sums on a scale unthinkable in earlier eras without any expectation of significant debt reduction. State banks play a role in regulation and market guidance, but large private banks and a multiplicity of financial institutions act collectively as a 'financial market'.

Characteristic	Tribute State	Domain State	Tax State	Fiscal State
Role in economy	Circulation of accumulated precious metals and foodstuffs.	Independent, active and profitable producer.	Taxation as means of participation in profits made by subjects..	
Economic Policy	Colonization and slavery may assume importance; securing of food supply fundamental to the system.	Market intervention to keep prices down; securing of food supply fundamental to the system.	Market supervision; subsidies for potentially profitable enterprises in trade and industry. 'Mercantilist' intervention in trading policies between states. Acquisition of overseas empires for trade and raw materials.	At times of internal crisis in wartime, highly interventionist role in the economy. In peacetime, more laissez-faire approach to trade and industry, although regulation remains the norms. Crucial role in influencing interest rates and the money supply. Possible manipulation of inflation in the interests of government borrowing. Collapse of control and 'hyperinflation' in others.
Public Enterprises	None except perhaps the army itself.	Agricultural and mining enterprises in conjunction with domain.	Monopolies with guaranteed supply and fixed prices an early example. Supervision of grain supply and other commodities during shortage. Royal or 'state' sponsored, trading companies.	Growth of the state sector as the state assumes greater responsibilities. Rise in costs of certain parts of the state sector (e.g. health and social security costs) help ensure self-sustained growth in the size of the state sector..

Characteristic	Tribute State	Domain State	Tax State	Fiscal State
Political Participation	Restricted to a small number of families.	Little and infrequent activity of the estates of the realm.	Initially on the increase; authorization and administration of taxes, in some countries later limited or removed by 'absolute' rulers.	Highly variable, but tendency towards participation because of the reliance on and sophistication of, credit structures.
Social Consequences	Negligible; stabilization of agricultural economy except in wartime. Exemptions and concessions for privileged groups.		Compulsion to increase productivity. Social disciplining; redistribution of purchasing power.	Exemptions and concessions for privileged groups largely removed in the interests of fiscal efficiency; unless groups benefit from special tax or social security advantages. Relatively small tax changes can assume electoral significance in democracies.
Statistics	Rare; surveys only to assist estimation of output except in more advanced systems. Difficulty in establishing any sort of balance sheet in 'primitive' systems.		Frequent productivity surveys; tax registers of house, landowners, tradesmen and artisans. Sophisticated accounting.	Much greater statistical sophistication of the state. Tendency towards frequent production of, and reliance on, statistics. Monthly figures and a periodic decennial census of population.

Characteristic	Tribute State	Domain State	Tax State	Fiscal State
Causes of Instability / precipitants of change in the system	Civil war, foreign invasion, collapse of control over outlying regions—all potentially leading to the overthrow of the state, and with it, the prevailing fiscal system.	Active military conflict with larger armies in an era of technological change and increasing military costs might overwhelm all but the most sophisticated domain states. The absence of reliable loan and tax income becomes crucial in a long conflict.	High debt servicing costs or debt-revenue ratios leading to quasi-bankruptcy. Inability to renege on public debt owing to its contractual nature. Political impasse between the crown and powerful sectional groups over the nature of a revised 'fiscal constitution'. Potential overthrow of the state.	Ideologically-inspired attempts to 'roll back' the state have yet to prove successful in the long term. Inherent tendency of health and social security payments to rise with increased life expectancy. Technological costs of warfare prohibitive for 'sustained' conflict other than with nuclear or biological weapons.

Since the development of this table, there has been no challenge to it. As a result, it can be concluded that the durable characteristics that vary with the level of fiscality of the state include: the financial theory, the form of government, the central administration, the local administration, the office holders, state responsibility, the method of financing, public finance, expenditure, revenues, credit structure, the role of the economy, economic policy, public enterprises, political participation, social consequences, statistics and finally the causes of instability. The principles of variation include the uniqueness of individual states and that they are a combination of a diverse set of characteristics that may not lend themselves to being categorised clearly and precisely. However, the presentation of these variations are not as clear cut when applied to individual states.

An immediate critique that arises in the context of the post-colonial state that is clearly evinced in the table is that this table is drawn from the point of view of an imperial state and not a colony or previously colonised state. In addition, neither Schumpeter nor Ormrod and Bonney refer to the limitation of the possibility of wars, conquests and colonisation in the twenty-first century as their analysis are not only historically based but were undertaken in the twentieth century while analysing the past.

2.4.   CHALLENGES TO CATEGORISING THE POST-COLONIAL FISCAL STATE

The Schumpeter-Kruger model and the additions by Ormrod and Bonney as set out above developed the above table as a synthesis for mainly heuristic purposes.[96] The following analysis will be based on the approach that the model has clarified both the durable and variable characteristics in the development of fiscal states. The mapping of the stages of the fiscal state becomes a critical contended tool for approaching the fiscal legitimacy of the post-colonial fiscal state.

---

96   *Ibid.* 2, 12,14

2.4.1. The Creation of the Post-Colonial Fiscal State

Schumpeter as discussed earlier in the chapter stated that without a financial need, the immediate cause for the creation of the fiscal state would have been absent.[97] The literature on the development of the fiscal state and its theories are extensive and covers many types of states but do not address the deliberately created states, which do not naturally develop or evolve based on a fiscal need but instead were created through the process of plunder, colonisation and whose introduction to tax was a result of the fiscal requirements of another state and society. The basis of financial need on which the fiscal state develops as argued by Schumpeter is not apparent to the colonised society that is being plundered and colonised.

All the characteristics that describe the fiscal state – the forms of financial theory, form of government, administration, and who the office holders were, the state responsibilities, revenue, expenditure, credit structures, economic policy, level of participation, social consequences, statistics and causes of instability that were implemented were decided upon by the imperial state with little or no reference to the created colony. In addition the continuing process of colonisation in Africa by the British was undertaken by first setting up trade and this gradual growth of control of a society that did not result in a comprehension of the fiscal legitimacy of the system being put into place and that to avert fiscal crisis this fiscal system could be used to improve society. As a result its immediate implementation was solely for the benefit of the imperial state.

2.4.2. The Colonial Fiscal State

Schumpeter in his discussion on the existence of people recognises the possibility of their existence not forming part of a state. He stated that they belong to the world as working–animals. He divided the world based upon an assumption of continued imperialism where there will inevitably always be 'states' of workers not in the form of states by and within themselves but mainly a resource and labour economy for another dominant state, in this situation the imperial

---

97   Schumpeter (1991) 108

state.[98] These territories he does not however place or recognise within his typology.

Bonney in a one paragraph discussion of colonial fiscal states outlines their stages of development and locates them within the Ormrod-Bonney model by placing them within the typology of the domain state. He however argues that they go through a development slightly different from the normal progression of the European fiscal state without joining them onto the larger scheme of the fiscal state. Using colonialism as a key difference he develops an alternative model that divides into primitive,[99] less primitive,[100] entrepreneurial[101] and colonial[102] types of domain states.

Both Tilly and Daunton discuss the development of colonies and their addition to the imperial states revenues. Tilly states that from the end of the 18th century, Great Britain, Spain, Portugal, the United Provinces and France all had large overseas empires and a worldwide trade system. Thus by the beginning of the 20th century, one quarter of the world's lands surface was redistributed as colonies among six states. However, the colonial states did not emerge, evolve or develop uniformly or follow the development pattern of other already existing states. Capital-intensive states like, the Dutch Republic and Venice pursued trading monopolies without military conquest or colonisation. Coercion-intensive states like, the Norse and Spanish concentrated on settlement, enslavement and importation of labour and tribute. Capital-coercive states like Britain and France combined capitalism and coercion.[103] Daunton quotes Tilly and states that there was a low amount of revenue collected within the imperial state during the colonial era where

---

98   *Ibid.* 108

99   The ruler is obliged to consume the produce of his state *in situ* without any market or sales or central collection point for transfer of goods and services into cash. Ormrod, Bonney and Bonney (1999) 14

100   This state has a central administration system allowing for collection, storing and consumption of goods. *Ibid.*

101   This state allows for the collection of taxes in kind and as a result, was safe from price fluctuations or shortages. *Ibid.*

102   A primitive fiscal system that is a tax state in its own right but which continues to remit income to a dominant state. *Ibid.*

103   Tilly (1992) 18-32

revenue would be obtained from the colonies by exploitation or plunder, as well as by coercion or the use of capital in trade.[104]

In the process of colonisation, the introduction of a capitalist economy was cemented by the levy of taxation on the African continent. The imperial British state undertook this through the introduction of a chartered company, namely the British East African, West African or South African Companies which were mandated for a fee to run the colonised territories as a company and gain profit from it but at the same time remit a fee to the British Crown. The Chartered Company not only engaged in trade but also introduced taxation in the colonies to add to their income rationalising that this would also lead to the development of the colonised state into a Western form economy. It can therefore be argued that if the colony was relying mainly on tax revenue as its main source of income, it was in fact already a tax state. The imperial state falls into the category of a tax state. After the British tax state ascertained that the colonisation was indeed fiscally productive, it would take over from the Chartered Company and run the colonised state thus taking over the structures introduced and continuing to benefit from taxation but in a more direct manner.[105] Most colonial regimes in Africa imposed both Hut and Poll Taxes. Vickery adds that the application of taxation in particular the hut tax had a twofold purpose; firstly, to provide remuneration for the administrative authorities that were under pressure to become self-sustainable and secondly, to compel participation of the colonised in the economy.[106]

However, as colonisation developed, taxation was also used as a means of applying colonial policies. It was argued that the colonies must supplement rather than compete with the imperial economy. The two major aims of colonial taxation was to firstly, try to ensure that the colonies at least covered the costs involved in their administration, and secondly, to shape their economic development in line with the policies of the Empire, which mainly meant developing primary production to complement British industrialisation. This decision to develop self-sufficiency of the

---

104   Daunton (2001) 2

105   Vickery (1986) at 41–43

106   *Ibid.* 71

colony in line with the fiscal policy in the British tax state gave the colony before independence the characteristic of a tax state, with the predominant fiscal reliance of the state on taxation. Portuguese imperial policy conversely treated their colonies merely as sources of revenue and booty placing them into the domain state. Whichever form of state one perceives the colonial state to be placed in there was no engagement between the state and the society to create a fiscal social contract.

2.4.3.   THE POST-COLONIAL FISCAL STATE

Moore while referring to both Schumpeter and Ormrod and Bonney refers to the post-colonial fiscal state as a rentier state.[107] He argues that since it does not rely predominantly on tax revenue it cannot be termed a tax state. He does not attempt to use or critique the OB model or analyse the post-colonial state from a historical perspective, and as a result, he sidesteps the categories entirely. However he alludes to the rentier state as existing at a stage before the transition to a tax state. In addition, similar to Bonney's argument on the colonial state he argues for a separate developmental path for the post-colonial fiscal state in Africa using fiscal sociology.[108]

Moore's analysis does categorise one type of post-colonial state. However, his description is limited to the post-colonial states that are rich in resources, and/or receive large amounts of development aid or debt-relief which he terms as rents. By putting forward another model rather than a type, that also does not cover all post-colonial states and although it has merit, it is an additional critique to the ideal type and as a result falls into the same trap. His analysis does however point to the issue that not only subjects pay taxes. However he does strengthen the argument of the importance of reliance on subjects and the undermining influence that tax can have on society.

Kenya, the focus of this thesis is a state that does not predominantly rely on rents to support it and has been striving for the increased

---

107   States that have a high dependence on natural resource rent (including mineral and resource revenue) and strategic rent (development aid) as opposed to the domain, tax and fiscal states are seen as states dependant on their own earned income. See generally Moore (2001) and Moore (2004)

108   Moore (2004) 299

levy of taxes. Although the levy of tax is not the sole characteristic that pushes a state from one level of the typology to another, it is the most important characteristic and the concern of this thesis. As a result despite Moore arguing for a separate typology to be developed for post-colonial states since Kenya does predominantly rely on tax revenue, the OB model becomes a real possibility in guiding the ensuing analysis.

There are, however, areas of concern for post-colonial states that are not addressed in the categories. They include no discussion on the issue of shrinking borders, self-sustainability policies, labour mobility, globalisation, the shadow economy, all of which push Schumpeter's vision of freedom from economic restraint.[109] In discussing democracy, he made no allowance for a society that has not achieved the level of the fiscal state and yet had a legitimate concern for the manner in which the state distributed revenue.[110] Although the conditions necessary for the operation of democracy were considered by him including civil liberties, tolerance of others' opinions, national character and habit of a certain kind,[111] Schumpeter limited citizen's participation to voting for leaders and discussion and did not consider universal suffrage as necessary.[112]

Another difficulty in placing the post-colonial developing state is that all the characteristics in effect in the colonial state upon independence were put in place by the imperial state with some changes. Thus, despite the struggle of independence in many colonies that resulted in the legitimacy of the state, the ensuing failure to make changes to the state-societal relationship has resulted in the continued absence of a fiscal social contract and the achievement of fiscal legitimacy of the post-colonial state. Even if one chooses to overlook the issue of the absence of a fiscal social contract the continuation of the implementation of taxation that has been perceived in the colonial society as a method of oppression results in a continued response to taxation as oppressive and forced with no benefits.

---

109   Musgrave (1992) 104

110   *Ibid.* 105

111   Schumpeter (1954) 295-96

112   *Ibid.* 244-45

In addition from the perspective of the ex-imperial state, the resources and the economy continue to benefit from the economies of their ex-colonies. The OB model, fails to reflect the effect of these colonies as satellite economies on the development of the Imperial States and the tax revenue that they generated for them. In placing the modern developed state, the OB model also fails to reflect the continued effect that past colonies have on their ex-colonial masters through the existing structures of trade and tax law..

Generally in post-colonial states today, the financial theories and financing methods in place reflect those found globally and tend to be those set out in the fiscal state. The form of government, central and local administration as well as office holders can be a mixture of all the categories with issues of patronage and clientelism existing hand-in-hand with more complex and well developed institutions and precise legislation. State responsibilities, the credit structure and the role in the economy possibly fall into that of the tax state. The public finance, economic policy and public enterprises are that of the tax state and the fiscal state. Political participation, revenues, statistics and the causes of instability varies between all four states. Social consequences can be a combination of the primitive and the domain states. Expenditure is not always related to military effort and thus this characteristic does assist in the placement of the post-colonial fiscal state and its development. Certain elements within the characteristics that were seen to be inherent to the development of the fiscal states in Europe such as colonialism, the use of war to develop finance and settle borders are no longer applicable. As a result the resource options of post-colonial states follow a seemingly different route from the proposed OB model.

Schumpeter argued that the most important achievement of the fiscal state is the increased welfare of the state. Thus, no matter what type of state one is considering, the arguments posited and analysed in this thesis based on the assumption that post-colonial states are aiming to achieving the characteristics of the fiscal state geared towards fiscal self-sufficiency and state-building resulting in increased fiscal legitimacy. More specifically as this thesis will argue, they are attempting to develop the core concept within the fiscal state: improved welfare and societal well-being. The ensuing analysis and critiques in the subsequent chapter will undertake a detailed analysis of the historical development of the Kenyan fiscal state with the final goal of improving well-being.

2.4.4.   TRANSITIONING FROM ONE STATE TYPE TO ANOTHER

Although the classification of states as analysed above is a very helpful guide, the Ormrod and Bonney[113] model apart from its widened application to Europe cannot be adopted wholly as the guide for the post colonial state. Apart from the gaps in the model in the context of historical development of the post-colonial state, it critically does not address how the post-colonial state will transition towards a fiscal state.

The next question to be asked is what will move the post-colonial fiscal state from either the domain state or the tax state onwards to the fiscal state? The movement of a state from one type to another is seen to develop because of a financial crisis of need. The infringement of the individual liberties of society members imposed by the ruler in order to further his interests is argued by Backhaus as being a crisis of the fiscal state, where rising needs outweigh the resources at the disposal of the state.[114] Crises and societal upheavals move states from one type to another, but not necessarily in a linear manner. Ormrod and Bonney add that fiscal history shows that change arises with the need for modernity and this pushes states forward into modernity.[115] They argue that the transition of domain to tax state and to the fiscal state took place because first, crises that occur within fiscal systems do not change the nature of the system. Secondly, revolutions move a fiscal state on, and finally, that self-sustained growth is the model for development within the fiscal state.[116]

The entire discourse surrounding the development of the fiscal state is centred around fiscal crises that push the state from one level

---

113   Ormrod, Bonney and Bonney (1999) 4–8
114   Backhaus (2002) 58
115   See generally Ormrod, Bonney and Bonney (1999)
116   Bonney (1999) 13

to the next that can be averted or prevented through increasing fiscal legitimacy. However, the categorisation of the post-colonial fiscal at the theoretical level can be possibly either a domain or a tax state. How, when or where the transition takes place is thus critical in the context of the post-colonial state if well-being is to be improved and poverty reduced.

In addition the transition is not as clear-cut as in the European states. Ormrod and Bonney, although expanding their model to include many European states, make clear-cut distinctions between the categories and posit that a certain characteristic perceived as belonging to one category does not continue past a certain point to another category. For example, in the category of the office holders, while in the primitive stage the kinship ties are utilised in the allocation of positions, whereas this no longer exists in either the tax or fiscal state. If using these categories as distinct, the existing analysis by both Bonney and Moore will place both the colonial and the post-colonial fiscal state and its development into the category of the domain state as kinship ties, patronage and clientelism remain strongly in place in most post-colonial African fiscal states whether or not they predominantly rely on tax revenue.

The challenge is to not only place the post-colonial fiscal state but to attempt to find a parallel or similar route to charting its development and allowing it to achieve the level of the fiscal state. Achievement of the level of the fiscal state would involve and include all the durable characteristics set out in the table. However, the key characteristic in the fiscal state is the existence of social engineering and a social welfare state, with all the efficiency and effectiveness that the administration of such a state would require.

2.5. MEETING THE CHALLENGE TO FISCAL LEGITIMACY THROUGH WELL-BEING

Social welfare rested on the idea, that social provision of goods and services be treated as a right by all citizens, rather than an act of charity, a gift from some to others,[117] an idea that Schumpeter has adopted as being a constituent element of the ultimate level of the

---

117   See generally Kelley (2000)

state: the fiscal state. The modern welfare state can be approached in many different ways, as an instrument of social control or betterment. As a part of a state or a stage in the development of capitalism; as a minimum safety net for those in need, social insurance for the middle classes or everything a government needs to do to improve the well-being of the people.[118] Social welfare objectives include among others, direct spending for income security, housing, health care, education, employment and training, and social services. People see social welfare states as a guarantee for a minimum standard of living, protecting citizens from loss of income beyond their control, especially retirement, sickness, disability or unemployment. Thus, this includes public assistance and social insurance, serving both the poor and the middle class.[119] However, Scandinavian authors add a third dimension to the welfare state, which is ensuring that all citizens receive the standards available of a certain level of services without discrimination.[120] Wilensky has also stated that the 'essence of the welfare state is government-protected minimum standards of income, nutrition, health, housing and education assured to every citizen'[121]

The beginning of the twentieth century resulted in creation of the Poor Law in Britain with an old age pension, unemployment, sickness benefits, and in the 1942 Beveridge Report mapped out the development of social security.[122] In addition, other scholars have also argued that the welfare state goes through four stages namely, experimentation, consolidation, expansion and reformulation, which set out and reflect economics, politics and social policy by virtue of events and reactions.[123] However, the same was not extended to the colonies, instead these provisions were only accorded on the basis of white racial superiority that resulted in provision only for the white settler population and a certain limited provision for certain categories of civil servants. In addition the onerous fiscal burden

---

118   See generally Howard (1993), Carrier and Kendall (1986); Esping-Andersen (1990)

119   See generally Pampel and Williamson (1989); Marmor, Mashaw and Harvey (1990)

120   See generally Briggs (1961)

121   Wilensky (1975) 1

122   Kay and King (1990) 105

123   Flora and Heidenheimer (1981) 386

of the welfare state in the developed world calls into question its utility in developing states, and the need to seek a more practical and suitable alternative. As early as the 1950s a British sociologist, Richard Titmuss, called attention to the connection between tax policy and social policy.[124] He brought out the issue that concerned him: the possibility that more money would be spent on maintaining the system than in actually catering for the needs of the people.[125] This argument is reflected in many post-colonial states not only continued to curtailed and limited social services, but utilised fiscal resources instead in, for example, the creation and maintenance of a bloated civil service.

Offe also linked taxation, budgets and spending with capitalism and the welfare state with his argument that 'capitalism cannot coexist *with* neither can it coexist *without* the welfare state' (emphasis in original).[126] Flora and Heidenheimer also state that the welfare state is a product of capitalism.[127] However, there is no model welfare state; welfare states are shaped by national conceptions of welfare and social purpose and as a result are contextual at best. Apart from Plant there is no reference to the compulsory financing of human rights from the approach of social welfare theorists, nor is there the consideration that social welfare might be part of human rights or vice versa.[128] In fact, it has been argued that the equating of the welfare state with direct spending programmes has led to the neglect of social policy including tax expenditures.[129]

Peter Flora and Arnold Heidenheimer state that there are three basic means by which the welfare state pursues its goals: the indirect payment of cash benefits, the direct provisions of services in kind and the indirect extension of benefits through deductions and credits. However, they also add on a fourth means, economic policy and protective legislation. It is this fourth means, that most concerns this thesis as this is the link through which human rights

---

124   Titmuss (1958) 34–35

125   *Ibid.* 26

126   Offe and Keane (1984)

127   Flora and Heidenheimer (1981) 31

128   Plant (1986) 22–48

129   Howard (1993) 403

guaranteed constitutionally can be brought in and enforced through budgetary allocation thus at the most basic level linking tax revenue to expenditure for the welfare of the state and finally development and poverty alleviation.[130] In addition, despite this the authors themselves also have omitted reference to tax expenditure while discussing the development of the modern welfare state. In addition, discussion is centred on tax policy and budgetary reform and not social policy. The welfare state thus occupies what is a gap between social policy and tax policy literature in developing countries.

2.6.   CONCLUSION

The foregoing discussion sought to explore and extend the typology of the fiscal state to the post-colonial developmental African state. However, the Eurocentric origin of the typology makes it difficult to place developing countries today or to chart their historical development through the typology. The typology of the fiscal state in relation to some post-colonial fiscal states follows a different route from that set out in the OB model. The development of the state is pushed forward by forces that are different from those charted out and perceived through the development of European states.

During the colonial period a European-style fiscal state did not and could not emerge. Instead it seemed to almost conform to a mixture of the categories of the tribute, domain and tax states. Taxation has a broadly political value, that confirms the legitimacy of the state through its collections and the willingness of taxpayers to provide the resources that can not only maintain the state but also increase the well-being of the people. However, the various successes and failures of the post-colonial fiscal state have added on further obstacles to the legitimation of the post-colonial fiscal state, as will be discussed within the Kenyan context.

---

130   Flora and Heidenheimer (1981) 26

CHAPTER 3

THE FISCAL STATE IN COLONIAL KENYA

Fiscal sociology recognises that each state in the world has its own unique history. Schumpeter posited that in order to understand the 'thunder' of fiscal history of a state one must analyse its history.[131] The introduction of modern taxation in Kenya arose during colonisation. The objective of this chapter is to explore how the introduction and development of taxation affected Kenya as a post-colonial fiscal state. It begins with a brief discussion of the previous fiscal history of Kenya, before undertaking an analysis of the effect of British colonial fiscal policy on the Kenyan colonial fiscal state. It will attempt an exposition and analysis of the linkages made between tax income and expenditure and welfare, and will argue that there was little or no link made between tax revenue and tax expenditure in order to legitimate the colonial fiscal state in the state-society relationship.

Kenya is the specific focus of this thesis, the discussion in this chapter is limited to the colonial powers that affected East Africa and Kenya. Kenya was sporadically and partially colonised[132] from the 7th century firstly by the Arabs, then the Portuguese and finally the British[133] before gaining independence in 1963. This era of occupation and invasion cannot be clearly separated as there was a constant battle between these occupiers for control.[134] The enquiry of this chapter will be limited to the tax and welfare policies and practices of the pre-colonial societies in Kenya, then the Arabs, the Portuguese and the British. The ensuing discussion will be divided into these distinct categories, however, recognising that historically

---

131   Schumpeter (1991) 101

132   Colonialism refers to the form of intergroup domination in which settlers of significant numbers migrate permanently to the colony from the colonizing power, while imperialism refers to intergroup domination where few if any permanent settlers from the imperial homeland migrate to the colony. However, for the purposes of this thesis, I shall use these terms interchangeably to mean intergroup domination and whether or not there are, large numbers of settlers in the colony shall not limit my use of literature or exclude text. It is defined by Horvath (1972) 50.

133   Gray (1957) 3

134   Roberts (1986) 660-665

this era of occupation and invasion cannot be clearly divided and there was a constant battle between these occupying states for control over East Africa and Kenya.[135] This chapter does not however seek to analyse and discuss all the colonial fiscal encounters throughout the history of Kenya. It will instead refer to the implementation of colonial laws and policies and the societal reactions that enhance understanding of colonialism and the effect it has had in the creation of the colonial fiscal state. The analysis will approach the history of the creation and development of the colonial fiscal state from the limited focus of the creation and development of its fiscal legitimacy, and the connections that have been made between tax revenue and tax expenditure for the improvement of the welfare of colonial society.[136]

3.1.   SYSTEMS OF FISCAL EXTRACTION AND DISTRIBUTION BEFORE BRITISH COLONISATION OF KENYA

3.1.1.   PRE-COLONIAL KENYA

The limited information on the entire pre-colonial period in Kenya identifies two types of governance.[137] One type of governance posited by Ochieng' is that in this era the society were made up of a system of lodges, sectional relations and codes of justice which contributed to the corporate polity of their social groups and communities.[138] The second more complex type of governance, which is similar to Goldscheid's concept of the primitive fiscal state and its princely ruler, is characterised as an ethnic community that had a system where a payment in kind was made to a chief or ruler for the purposes of protection. This tax or tithe was payable in terms

---

135   See generally Huxley (1939) for a broad discussion on the occupation of the East African coast and Kenya from the 7th to the 19th century when the British began their colonisation of Kenya.

136   For convenience, I have adopted the encompassing term 'colony' to denote all different types of British dependencies, adopting the official nominal distinctions between 'dominions', 'crown colonies', 'colonies', 'mandated territories' and 'protectorates' only when deemed relevant.

137   Roberts (1986) 662 Bennett (1978) 4 states that there is almost no knowledge from either written sources or archaeological findings between the 5th and 10th centuries. A detailed study can be found in MacLean (2005).

138   Ochieng' (1985) 44

of the produce from the land or animals and security was provided through a system of warrior classes.[139]

At that stage many of these nations in Kenya were small and required little or no administration. Life was at subsistence level and mainly communal and thus they could be described as pre-primitive and primitive states in terms of the Ormrod-Bonney model. The areas of Kenya that subsequently resisted occupation or were unaffected by either the real or actual control of subsequent colonial administrations, maintained some elements of these ways of life.

3.1.2. THE SULTANATE OF OMAN

The Sultanate of Oman occupied the coast and the islands off the East African coast from the 7th century.[140] The policy of the Sultanate was to obtain slaves for use in agriculture in different parts of Arabia.[141] There was no intention to extend occupation over a larger area than necessary and the Sultanate was content with limiting its occupation to the islands where the city-states developed which were used mainly as ports from which to purchase goods from the African interior as well as stops on the trade routes around Africa and onwards to Arabia and Asia, and this policy was maintained throughout the occupation.[142]

The administration of taxation was done at the local level. Each area occupied was geographically controllable, consisting of islands or headlands. Each of these had local hereditary rulers called Sultans. Initially the sultans were members of the family of the sultan of Oman who were settled on the islands with others for the purpose of protecting and allowing trade with the interior tribes of Africa and the harbour access to the trade route. However, the policy of intermingling led to the eventual emergence of local rulers.[143]

---

139   Ocaya-Lakidi (1977) 137-139

140   The Arabs that colonised East Africa belonged to the Islamic jurisprudential school of the Ibadis. Although it is unclear if this had any fiscal connotations, it may have guided the general economic policy.

141   Wilkinson (1981) 279

142   Huxley (1939) 353

143   Martin (1974) 379

Each city-state had its own systems of taxation including administration and enforcement in the collection of customs duties.[144] The taxes collected were shared between the local rulers and a proportion which was sent back to the Sultanate in Arabia. The sultanate as a kingdom owned everything and all remissions went to the Sultan to be used at his discretion. However, the states were not content and there was constant conflict between them for power and resources.[145] Periodically, assistance was obtained from slaves[146] and allies that included indigenous ethnic communities that were trading partners as well the Sultan of Oman, the British and the Germans.[147]

The fiscal laws and policies applied in the collection and distribution of taxation during this period were based on Islamic law, the religious affiliation of the Sultanate. Taxation was applied on the basis of Islamic principles, which set out four taxes: *zakat, jizya, sadaqa* and *khums*.[148] As a result, the Omani fiscal policy consisted of a wide and complex tax base.

The first tax base separated the inhabitants based on their religious practices. On the East African coast, the tax base was split into Muslims, Christians and polytheists.[149] Muslims were expected

---

144   Gray (1957) 3

145   Conflicts varied between outright wars as well as attacks on farms and people as well as the kidnapping and holding of slaves for ransom. See generally Ylvisaker (1978) for some examples of the results of conflicting sultans and city-states.

146   The Sultanate of Witu freed slaves in times of war in exchange for military service. *Ibid.* 676

147   Diffie, Shafer and Winius (1977) 341

148   Zakat is a form of voluntary single capital tax levied on Muslims at a minimum rate of 2.5% on all savings and all cash assets annually accumulated. It is used specifically to finance among other things, poor relief, and emancipation of slavery, assistance to individuals serving Islam. However, it does not fall within the control of the state. *Sadaqa* is another form of voluntary tax for charitable purposes under no state control whatsoever. *Jizya* was a tax imposed on conquered non-Muslims in a Muslim nation under treaties signed between the two communities as a payment in lieu of compulsory military service, which could only be imposed on Muslims. *Khums* was a tax on assets redeemed by force and included spoils or war booty. It was considered a state asset at the disposal of the leader or war booty of the commander in chief for his personal disposal. See Kuran (1995) 159, Choudry and Rahman (1986) 63 and Ahmad (2001) 7-8

149   Polytheists in this case were the indigenous African ethnic communities or tribes that were practitioners of African traditional religion and culture.

to make voluntary and unregulated contributions of *zakat* and *sadaqa*.[150] These were, however, not expected to be remitted to the state. In addition, men who claimed to be descendants of the Prophet Muhammad through his son-in-law, Ali, were exempt from all tax and during war could claim 20% of the booty taken in the field. They were identifiable by the title Sayyid, Sharif and Sha'ikh.[151]

Polytheists were required to make annual truces with the Arabs. This policy was used by the Arabs in order to buy time to increase the immigrant Arab population to a number large enough to create an Arab/mixed race population willing to submit to Arab rule. Christians had two options. Either they submitted to a per capita tax or they provided a certain number of slaves as agreed upon. However, in the latter case, after the first year, this was automatically converted into a poll tax (*jizya*) and the Christians became protected people (*dhimmis*). This peace treaty was under the supervision of an Arab Governor and needed to be reaffirmed yearly; failing which it lapsed; allowing for looting and collection of booty considered *khums*.[152] There also existed a detailed set of laws laying down a scale of payments for trade passing between areas like East Africa and India going through Sohar in either Omani or local ships.[153]

A second tax base was also applied to trade. Islamic law upheld the right of government to levy tax if resources were insufficient with the proviso that taxes had to be raised in a just manner within bearable limits.[154] As a result, traders including the settlers[155] from the imperial state within each island city-state and foreign traders[156] were subject to a tax on goods for export. These traders were taxed by the application of a capitation tax for slaves[157], as well as customs

---

150   Kuran (1995) 159, Choudry and Rahman (1986) 63

151   Martin (1974) 371

152   Kuran (1995) 159, Choudry and Rahman (1986) 63

153   Wilkinson (1981) 279-280

154   Chapra (1976) 161

155   Settlers consisted of a mixture of Arabs, families that resulted from intermarriage and local Africans who had converted to Islam.

156   Traders from other nations included India, Europe and Mauritius.

157   A capitation tax is a head tax on each individual. It was levied on the traders and was computed by a fixed amount for each slave being exported out of the sultanate.

duty.[158] In addition certain city states that did not want certain types of traders would use tax to dissuade them from setting up shops in their cities. The Sultan of Witu, for example, charged USD 200-300 in tax for any Indian trader setting up a shop within the sultanate.[159] The currency used for exchange was predominantly gold, however; the more affluent city-states like Zanzibar had their own coinage.[160]

Thus, the city-states on the East African coast many of which are part of the modern geographical borders of Kenya could be considered to have been a combination of a worker, tribute and tax state. In addition, there was a complex system of the collection of taxes, with separate tax bases and types of taxation. Direct taxes were levied on non-Muslims while trade taxes were levied on all with some exceptions. In addition, war booty was also a source of revenue. There is no literature on whether revenue was redistributed or whether it was sufficient for the recurrent expenditure requirements of the fiscal city-state. As a result, the issue of fiscal legitimacy was built mainly on the basis of being descendants of the Omani Arabs with whom social relations were maintained.

3.1.3. THE PORTUGUESE

Between the 16th and 18th centuries the Portuguese repeatedly tried to take over the East African coastal area unsuccessfully.[161] The first recorded treaty that involved a form of taxation in this period was in 1502. The then Sultan Ibrahim of Malindi[162] was held against his wishes and forced to accept defeat. While being held hostage during negotiations on Vasco da Gama's boat, a treaty of surrender was signed with Portugal for an annual tribute of 1,500 meticals[163]

---

158   Customs duty was charged on all goods taken out of the Sultanate and the main exports included cloves, ivory and beads.

159   Ylvisaker (1978) 680. This policy proved successful as there was only 1 registered Indian trader in Witu

160   Roberts (1986) 207, 216

161   See generally Willis (2005) 1515-1518

162   A city state that was a tribute state of the Sultanate of Oman.

163   See Costa (2006) where a metical is defined as 4.83 grams of gold powder - weight of gold equivalent to the old gold coin Arabic, *Dinar* - placed inside the feathers of birds (from preferably the largest feathers of ducks), the ends were plugged with beeswax. 100 meticals were a folder, 1/8 of Metical was called a *thong*.

of gold.[164] The terms included Portuguese rights to erect forts, build garrisons and exercise control over revenue and customs duties, introduce settlers and generally exercise full rights of sovereignty.[165] In addition, the Sultan was to be allowed to receive one third of the customs revenue as his personal property.[166] Similar treaties were signed with other sultans including the Sultans of Mombasa, Zanzibar and Kilwa.[167] All of them repeatedly failed to actually pay the tribute, despite repeated demands by the Portuguese including the use of violence by destruction of private property[168] resulting in the continual failure to bring any money into the coffers of the Queen of Portugal.[169]

The aim of Portugal's fiscal policies for the administration of its colonies was to obtain an income from its colonies just as was being done at the time in the United States of America by the British Empire. This fiscal policy was already practiced by the Portuguese in Brazil in the 16th and 17th centuries. Caio argues that the Portuguese kingdom simply extended its administrative system and organisation over Brazil with little or no innovation and this policy was also practiced in Kenya, where the Portuguese took over and maintained the collection of customs revenue from the tribute city-states that had been previously collected by the Sultan of Oman. However the Sultan of Oman maintained control over certain taxes unabated such as the imposition from as early as 1722 of a capitation tax in respect of every slave exported by the French from the African dominions.[170] Only in taxation with reference to imposts, tolls, taxes, and collection methods did the Portuguese try to make adjustments to suit local conditions by taking payment of tax in kind rather than in monetary form.[171] Initially there was some revenue, however rejection of Portuguese rule and challenges continued throughout

---

164   Strandes (1961) 41

165   Gray (1957) 3

166   Strandes (1961) 3

167   Ochieng' (1985) 54–60

168   Gray (1957)108–110

169   *Ibid.* 96

170   *Ibid.* 23

171   Prado (1967) 352-53

their occupation with the effect that attempts to enforce tax policy that privileged Portuguese traders led to the eventual destruction of commerce.[172]

The connection between tax revenue and expenditure for the betterment of the local population was not a concern for Portuguese imperial policy. On the contrary, the policy pursued was not only to ensure that a minimum of expenditure be incurred in the colonisation process but also that as much profit as possible be gained from the process.[173] Caio gives the example of the Board for the Collection of Voluntary Subsidies which he states collected a special subsidy for 10 years in 1756 to defray the expenses in rebuilding Lisbon after the Great Earthquake of 1755, but which continued well after despite protests by the 'voluntary' contributors in Brazil, and was still collected during the empire period. Theoretically, the subsidy was still being used to rebuild Lisbon.[174] There were also at times extraordinary collections, for example, in 1772 there was a literary subsidy to raise money for public education; and for emergencies, for example, in 1804 for 'in view of the grievous state in which the kingdom finds itself as a result of the troubles in Europe'.[175] Brown has also stated that the Portuguese balance of payments was dependant on Brazilian remittances.[176]

In East Africa the limited expenditures incurred within the region is evidenced by the fact that Portuguese rule is described as tumultuous with no real foothold being made in the country.[177] Tax policies that they applied have not remained at all with the exception of the exemption of clergy in Portugal and Christian clergy in East Africa from all taxes including customs duty.[178] However, since the Portuguese chose to treat the East African city–states as tribute states, there was a subsequent uprising by the Arabs. The Sultan of Oman

---

172   Willis (2005) 1517

173   Roberts (1986) 231

174   Prado (1967) 374

175   *Ibid.* 378

176   Brown (1989) 179

177   The only physical memory today on Kenya's coast is the Pillar of Vasco da Gama in Malindi and Fort Jesus in Mombasa.

178   Gray (1957) 269

assisted in their liberation and regained the tribute states having lost control for 200 years.

When the British landed on the East African coast and began their process of the colonisation of Kenya, fiscally the island states and the coastline of Kenya could be best described as having been tribute states of the Portuguese and Arabs. There were elements of tax states in the complexity of taxes levied and collected, but, there was no recorded re-distribution of tax revenue. In the East African hinterland, the remainder of the ethnic communities or tribes continued to exist as they always had as a combination of pre-primitive and primitive states practicing communal self-subsistence. It is this mixture of ethnic nations, communities and city-states with a diversity of complex, simple or non-existent fiscal policies that the British encountered when they began their occupation of East Africa.

3.2. BRITISH COLONIAL FISCAL POLICY IN KENYA

British[179] colonialism or imperialism is historically divided into two stages: the 'Old Colonial system' or the 'First Empire'[180] of the British Atlantic and Asian Worlds that ran simultaneously with Portuguese occupation of the East African coast and the 'Second Empire'[181] from the late 18th century.[182] In the first phase of colonisation, Britain saw itself as mainly a trade and commerce expansionist state with policies geared towards protecting the trade routes and the sources of goods needed for the sustaining of the industrial revolution. This policy changed after the British victory in the 1763 French-Indian War,[183] when the British tried to levy tax on the American colonies

---

179   By extension, one can apply this philosophy to the imperial histories of all imperial states.

180   A. D. 1583-1783

181   A. D. 1783-1983

182   Armitage (2000) 3 and Hopkins (1999) 208 confirm that British history is taken to mean domestic history while imperial history implies the extraterritoriality. Texts and literature are as a result divided into two types, firstly, the history of political thought tends to deal with the history of the ideas of the state and ignore concepts of empire and secondly, texts that only refer to the colonised states and the colonial policies as a separate historical issue. The result is that texts on the history of taxation and its development in the imperial states ignore the effects on the empire and imperialism.

183   See generally Marston (2002). This war was between Britain, France and the native

to assist in the repayments of the war debt. However, the societal reaction was opposition, the coining of the slogan of 'no taxation without representation' and the triggering of the 1776 American war of independence.[184] If one were to apply the Schumpeterian argument of war justifying taxes and measuring state viability, then the American colonial society was not open to this and thus the colonial state failed to become viable resulting in independence. Despite the failure to collect tax from the American colonies, the French-Indian war marked a turning point for the British Imperial policy. In addition to continuing to approach colonies as a source of resources, it was required that each colony should also generate enough revenue to pay for its administrative costs.[185]

Once tax revenue was absorbed into colonial policy, the administrative costs of colonisation were accounted for in diverse ways. In discussing India's underdevelopment, Prabhakaran has set out some data on the amount of money that was extracted from India and sent to the imperial state, which show that there was repeatedly a budget deficit.[186] Subramanian also supports Prabhakaran's assertion that the budgeted and incurred gross colonial expenditure was more than the gross revenue from India in 1847. Through his analysis of these accounts and the manner of their preparation he questions the argument that tax was not a method of wealth extraction. His analysis of the breakdown of the budgetary expenditure figures reflects varied but inexplicable expenditure items. They include wars fought to expand territory, interest payable on Indian debt, interest on investment in the railways, civil and military charges incurred in England supposedly on India's behalf, expenses for maintaining India House in London and 'the wages of the Charwoman employed to clean the rooms of Whitehall.'[187] He argues that attributing these and other expenses to the colonial administration was a type of creative accounting, aimed at not reflecting a surplus in order to limit the development of India.

American population for control of the American colonies.

184   Dickinson (1970) 25–26
185   *Ibid.* 25–26
186   Prabhakaran (1990) 6
187   Subramanian (1979)10

One of the overarching principles of British colonial rule was that deficits in one colony would not be covered by revenues raised elsewhere, or by metropolitan revenues. This implied, however, that to maintain a stable system of fiscal independence, large military expenses were primarily carried by the imperial state.[188] An exception to this rule was British India, which supplied and paid for a considerable amount of the British Indian troops deployed in battles inside and outside the Indian subcontinent. However, this did not lead to a comparatively high tax burden in British India, perhaps as India was also rich in mineral resources. The amount of direct revenue raised for the metropolitan treasury or imperial military expenses using colonial taxes were not predominantly extractive.

The imperial state at the time of the Second Empire was in a state of exhaustion of resources and over population, they as a result, used the satellite economy of the colony, firstly, as a place to move populations that were unproductive or unemployed. Secondly, to introduce into a subsistence and primitive state, a type of feudalism by the introduction of British settlers as large scale land owners through latifundia that would increase production of raw materials for the imperial economy. When the occupation and colonization of Africa and Kenya began, the main aims of British imperial fiscal policy had developed to two main areas. Firstly, to develop the economy of the imperial state and any activities undertaken were firstly in order to increase domestic economic production and profits from trade. Secondly, to recover all expenditure incurred to develop the colonies for the benefit of the imperial economy by taxing the colony. These are evident from the opening anagrams to the chapter that summarize British policy in Kenya as discussed in the following sub-sections.

The levy of taxation was never posited by the authors of colonial theory, as being a reason for colonisation in Africa.[189] As a result, the collection of tax revenue and its legitimacy were never a concern of colonial fiscal policy. Perham argues that one of the principles of

---

188   See generally Davis and Huttenback (1988)

189   Knorr (1963) 59. Perham (1963) 77-78 sets out five main reasons for colonisation: the economy for trade expansion; security to protect world commerce; emigration; power and prestige; and finally, the ideal of philanthropy.

British colonial policy was that the colonies must supplement rather than compete with the imperial economy. Thus, two major aims of colonial taxation were: first, to try to ensure that the colonies at least covered the costs involved in their administration; secondly, to guide and shape the economic development of the colony in line with policies that would result in assisting in the economic development of the Empire. This generally translated into developing primary production to complement British industrialisation and assistance in satisfying the demand for raw materials in factories in the imperial state. Despite the disregard to the legitimacy of the levy of taxation by the imperial state, the effect that the lack of fiscal legitimacy had on the colonial society is the concern of this section.

In the course of the 19th century the British implemented some uniform colonial public finance principles. Firstly, the use of imperial fiscal resources to create local colonial structures to ease access to its raw materials, accounted for as repayable loans to the colony. Secondly, strict separation between the financial accounts of the colony and the imperial state was maintained gearing colonial policy to self-sufficiency, limiting expenditure to existing revenue. Taxation of colonial society had thus become an inevitable characteristic of colonisation as a tool towards the achievement of a vertically integrated economy and colonial fiscal self-sufficiency.[190]

The taxation of the Kenya colony included both direct and indirect taxation. They adopted the existing customs revenue system. However, the levy of both direct and indirect taxation was guided by the principle of racial discrimination with preferential treatment for Europeans followed by Asians and finally Africans. The diverse racial groups present in Kenya included white Europeans, Indians, Arabs and indigenous black Africans. The tax bases for direct tax was divided into 3: Europeans, Asians and Arabs and Africans.[191] This chapter will thus discuss the general taxes that affected all members of society and the 3 racially segregated tax bases for direct taxation.

---

190   Ochieng' (1985) 102 and Daunton (1994) 17 Gladstone specifically argued for self-sustainability of Africa and taxed the colonies accordingly.

191   Europeans included all white people in the colony and included colonial administrators and settlers from UK, South Africa and Germany. Asians included Arabs and Indians including Goans and the residents of the coastal city states. Africans included all black ethnic communities resident in the East African region.

3.2.1. CREATING THE VERTICALLY INTEGRATED FISCAL ECONOMY

Shivji has described the economic colonization in Africa as the creation of a vertically integrated economy that can be broken into three. Firstly, resources (food products and industrial raw materials) from the colony exported to the imperial state. Secondly, local structures (labour reservoir, commercial, mining, quarrying, transport, construction, manufacturing, public administration and services, public utilities, agriculture, food supply) to facilitate ease of extraction were created and maintained in the colony by the imperial state. Finally, manufactured goods (food, beverages, machinery and transport equipment) were imported by the colony from the imperial state.[192]

The first step taken in creating this economy was the recognition of East Africa as a British sphere of influence by all imperial states in the early 1850s. Opening up East Africa would benefit the imperial economy immediately as British agents would handle the trade using British ships.[193] Over time, the main proponent of increasing trade in East Africa was Mackinnon. In 1877, he suggested the idea of a private company leasing the Swahili coast from the Sultan of Zanzibar and proposed that a railway should be built going into the East African hinterland using the customs revenue from the coast.[194] European imperial powers involved in the Scramble for Africa had been in continuous negotiations culminating in the Berlin Conference of 1885. This resulted in the partitioning of Africa among the imperial powers. Kenya and Uganda formed British East Africa and were recognised as part of the British sphere of influence under the protection of the British imperial state.

In 1887 Mackinnon negotiated the lease of the Swahili coast from the Sultan of Zanzibar,[195] and in 1888, Mackinnon was granted the right to form a chartered company, the Imperial British East Africa Company (IBEA). The IBEA was allowed to profit from trade

---

192   Shivji (1976) 32, 35
193   Wrigley (1978) 26
194   Munro (1987) 220
195   T (1904) 45

and collect taxes in the East African region at its own cost for a fixed fee payable to the imperial state.[196] This approach was governed by the need to ascertain the viability of improving imperial interests in the area while minimising the cost to the imperial state. The IBEA although initially successful, was facing bankruptcy by 1895 and as a result, the British declared East Africa a protectorate in 1895 marking the beginning of official British colonial rule of East Africa and Kenya.[197]

Mackinnon's recommendation of a railway financed from loans from the imperial state to be repaid by colonial customs revenue was adopted and in 1895, the British began to build the East African railway to reach present-day Uganda.[198] The railway was completed in 1901 and within the first year, an immediate effect was noted: average revenue generated of £4 per mile. In addition, the completion of the railway had saved over £300,000 in transport costs in comparison to road transport and had allowed for the transport of troops to Uganda to suppress a mutiny.[199] The building of the East African railway had cost five and a half million pounds. In addition to customs revenue from the Swahili coast, the revenue from the railway was used to balance the annual budget of the Kenya colony.[200] The existing revenue structures were expended directly on the creation of local infrastructure in order to gain access to Uganda, perceived at this point in time as the most lucrative source of raw materials in East Africa.

The fiscal policy at this point was that in creating the vertically integrated economy, there would be no systematic direct transfers of tax revenue from the British colonies to the metropolis or vice versa. In fact, fiscal transfers from the imperial state included imperial grants and colonial development funds. However, these loans or grants-in aid were to be repaid, not when the specific works become

---

196   Fieldhouse (1973) 372-383

197   Ghai and McAuslan (1970) 3

198   O'Callaghan (1900) 3, 6 This led to the hiring of labour, carpenters, blacksmiths, riveters, masons, surveyors and draughtsmen, overseers from India and locally to help build the railway.

199   *Ibid.* 17

200   Cabinet Memorandum: East African Development Loan (1925) 1

productive but when the general financial position of the colony improved.

After expenditure was incurred in replacing the IBEA and setting up the railway, the immediate concern of colonial authority was how to recover the costs. This had several components: the need to establish an administrative system that would allow for the exploitation of the natural, human and economic resources of the region[201] in order to achieve the primary aim of colonisation in the second empire: the creation and maintenance of a self-sustainable and vertically integrated economy.[202]

A)   CREATING A LABOUR FORCE THROUGH TAX

The encouragement of settlement and farming led to the need for labour to assist in large-scale cultivation in order to increase the production of raw materials. European settlers began arriving in 1902, and by 1906 there were approximately 1,814, all granted large-scale farm holdings.[203] However, apart from the coastal communities, the Africans lived on subsistence, the creation of a labour force became the next step of continuing colonisation. Sir Percy Girouard, one of the first Governors of the East African Protectorate, stated that:

> We consider that taxation is the only possible method of compelling the native to leave his reserve for... seeking work. Only in this way can the cost of living be increased for the native ...and it is on this that the supply for labour and the price of labour depends.[204]

As a result, the British first authorised the Hut Tax Regulations of 1901 by which a tax of no more than 2 rupees per annum that was levied on each African hut[205] used as a dwelling.[206] Mungeam states

---

201   Ochieng' (1985) 102

202   The railway had already proved itself in assisting in control through the transport of troops to suppress mutinies.

203   Wolff (1974) 53

204   Standard (1913) as quoted in Shivji (1976) 32

205   Each hut housed an adult male with a separate hut for each married woman and her children until they became adults and moved into their own huts.

206   In Uganda this was set as 3 rupees per hut as Uganda was regarded as a rich area. T (1904) 53 The Hut Tax was an attempt at a property tax. It was based on the assumption that the additional huts for wives and their children was a sign of increased family income due to additional family labour to farm or tend stock. However, stores

that the introduction of taxation in the Protectorate was to make the administrative areas pay for themselves.[207] By demanding tax in the form of time spent working on European farms in lieu of money, a labour market was created to assist in the creation of agricultural raw materials. The table below sets out the monetary revenue from hut tax.

Figure 3: The Levy and Increase of Hut and Poll Tax in East Africa

Year	African Population	Rate (rupees)	Total African Hut and Poll Tax Revenues (£)
1901–1902	4,000,000	2	3,328
1905–1906		2	44,541
1909–1910	3,000,000	3	105,000
1914–1915		5	175,000
1919–1920		5	279,000
1920–1921	2,549,300	10	658,000
1926		12	558,044
1930	2,930,604	12	591,424

Source: Derived from Wolff[208]

Although the initial yield from the hut tax was minimal, it forced Africans to join the labour force and European farmers to the state never remitted an equivalent amount to the hut tax. However, the growth in the amount of revenue garnered from this tax grew as more of the country came under the control of the British and thus more Africans were added to the tax base. Attempts to avoid tax resulted in the changing of culture as more than one person began to live in a single hut. In 1909, this resulted in the amendment of the levy of taxation of every hut to include taxation of every African living in a hut,[209] and the increase of tax revenue exponentially. Between 1923 and 1929, rising revenues made any large increases in national tax unnecessary.[210]

---

and other huts used for purposes other than dwellings escaped this tax and thus it was in practice a combination of a head and hut tax. In addition in some government stations one sheep was accepted in lieu of 2 rupees. See Ross (1968)145

207   Regulation no. 18 of 1901 as quoted in Mungeam (1966) 111

208   Wolff (1974) 49, 107, 117

209   Ross (1968)148

210   Brett (1973) 195

The first change to the policy on hut tax took place in 1924 when African regional administrative councils were granted the power to raise local rates to finance their services. By 1931 they were raising between 1s. and 3s. per African head in addition to the existing national tax burden. In addition, rates for different African tribes were varied based on ability to pay as a result of bad harvests, droughts, famines or epidemics and changes in income resulted in tax reductions or exemptions. Such tailor-made rates testify to certain consideration of the administration in the maintenance of the native head tax system.[211] The rate of hut tax payable was also gradually but not uniformly increased over time.[212] For example in 1938 tribes received a reduction of the standard amount of 12 shillings per capita (144 pence = £0.6). Hence, the Meru and Tharaka paid 8 shillings, the Duruma from the Digo district 6 shillings and the Turkana 3 shillings. The Maasai as a result of their continued resistance were the only tribe who paid a higher rate of 13 shillings.

B)   THE NON-NATIVE POLL TAX

Up to 1912, the only sources of revenue included customs revenue, grants-in-aid and the hut and poll tax. The only tax affecting the non-African was a 5% duty on imported goods that was raised to 10% in 1920[213] although agricultural implements, seeds and plants and livestock for breeding were tax free. Spirits were taxed at 2 rupees[214] a gallon.[215] The Kenya protectorate however succeeded in removing any need for grants from the London Treasury within two decades of its creation.[216] The estimation that by 1912 the country would be self-sufficient proved correct,[217] and in 1911-1912, a small surplus was already showing with the result that the £133,500 grant-in-aid was abolished,[218] after a final amount of £23,500 in 1913.

---

211   Frankema (2009) 23

212   Ross (1968) 147 states that the Maasai were not recognised as being part of the colony; they were taxed at 20 shillings per hut.

213   Ibid.154

214   2s. 8d.

215   Ross (1968) 146 spirit tax was increased in 1920 to 20 shillings a gallon

216   Wolff (1974) 145

217   Mungeam (1966) 259

218   Ibid. 273

By 1912, when fiscal self-sustainability was first achieved, there were several large but racially diverse populations living in the Kenya colony and assisting in the development of the economy. From this point in time until after World War II, it has been estimated that the British government rarely granted more than 1.8% of the tax revenue of a colony as a grant-in-aid. The institution of fiscal structures was based on the system of divide and rule which involved racial segregation both in terms of physical location and treatment and continuing fiscal relations. In 1912, an African poll tax of £1[219] was imposed on all adult males and this immediately yielded £9,927. Revenue increased to £11,231 in 1913 but levelled out and in 1918, £12,197 was collected.[220] In addition, with the levy of this poll tax came the objections to the fiscal legitimacy of the colonial state.

In 1926, it was insisted that the Europeans pay tax for the cost of educating their children which had previously been undertaken under general expenses of the colonial state. Despite attempts to increase indirect taxes on spirits and employers of more than 2 domestic servants, the European poll tax was increased to £3 on all adult males in 1933.[221] However the amount raised was still inadequate to pay for the education resulting in a budget deficit of £28,000 in 1933.[222]

Europeans argued that as farmers they were more affected by the depression and as a result should pay lower taxes than Asian traders.[223] In addition, the Indian colonial administration began to ask to be consulted when discussing the taxation of Asians in the colonies.[224] In order to prevent resistance the alternatives to a direct progressive tax were considered including poll tax, packaging tax, passenger tax, licensing and increase in corporation tax were instead

---

219   Report of the East African Commission (1925) 175

220   Ross (1968) 152 See also table above for periodic data on collections of hut and poll tax

221   *Ibid.* 165

222   Brett (1973) 195

223   Cabinet Memorandum: Report on Kenya (1933) 155 paragraph 9

224   Conclusions of Meeting (1933) 19-20

proposed and considered.[225] This challenge to the application of tax was unsuccessful.

3.2.2. FISCAL LEGITIMACY: NO TAXATION WITHOUT REPRESENTATION

The right to question the fiscal legitimacy of the colonial state was initially only accorded to the imperial state and its society. It was limited to the issue of continuing the policy of colonialism. From the declaration of the protectorate, the different communities living in the colony at different points in time queried the fiscal legitimacy of the colonial state. Indirect taxation in the form of customs duty was already levied along the coast and this continued. The direct tax base was implemented for the first time gradually and was split into 2: the non-native (European and Asian) and the indigenous taxpayers. As a result, this sub-section will be divided into the reactions in reference to the different tax bases.

A)   THE AFRICAN POPULATION

The legitimacy of levying taxes on the Africans was questioned first by the colonial office and the two-fold justification included: firstly, none of the African tribes being governed were original inhabitants of the country they were now occupying. Secondly, British occupation and its superior military power had protected weaker tribes[226] from raids by stronger ones.[227] The weaker tribes as a result were quicker to comply with taxation than the strong.[228] As a result, it was argued that taxation was the amount due in exchange for immunity from attack from others and the expenses of building stations, making roads, pay of Police, and cost of Patrols.[229]

This argument was supported partially by Lord Lugard who proposed that the amount of taxation paid should be regarded as a just contribution for the purposes of administration in proportion

---

225   Cabinet Memorandum: Report on Kenya (1933) 3

226   Like the Kikuyu, Kamba, Taita and Taveta

227   Like the Nandi, Kipsigis and Maasai

228   Huxley (1935) 155 discusses Nandi resistance to tax.

229   T (1904) 52-53

of wealth and the protection and benefits received by the colony from the State and therefore that the tribute or tithe must be and all other demands must be replaced by tax.[230] When Lugard's policy of indirect rule began after the 1909-1910 fiscal year, colonial resources included £13,534 from trade (not only European); £94,314 from hut tax and £138,000 from grants-in-aid.[231]

Despite Lugard's call for benefits, records show that apart from tax and labour some tribes had very little contact with the colonial administration.[232] In the early 1900s in Africa, people living near borders responded to taxation by slipping across the border to avoid tax collectors.[233] Thus, the economic impact of colonialism was mixed.[234] The tax net mainly caught those in the urban areas and those who lived a fixed lifestyle, leaving out nomads and some of the rural indigenous people especially those living along the borders.[235]

With the imposition of taxation came the organisation of Africans into various organisations in 1919 to ask for reform of the tax system.[236] These included the Young Kikuyu Association and the Young Kavirondo Association, who later made demands for the reduction of hut and poll taxes and the exclusion of women from taxation.[237] In 1921, Harry Thuku formed a more militant organisation – the East African Association – which rejected the "fundamental premises of white rule", protested against the proposed reduction in African wages, land alienation, compulsory labour recruitment, increases in hut and poll taxes, and kipande (identity

---

230   Lugard (1913-18); Lugard (1965) 206, 231, 242

231   Sorrenson (1968) 97, 249

232   *Ibid.* 279 with reference to the Luo and Luhya

233   Boahen (1987) 69

234   *Ibid.* 100

235   Meebelo (1971), a Zambian historian, documents instances of resistance including threats on the lives of messengers and district commissioners as well as the chiefs of the tribes for allowing the imposition of the hut tax. I think you should make more of this point.

236   The Young Kikuyu Association later changed its name to the East African Association in order to allow all Kenyan and East African nationalities to come together in one organisation; the Piny Owacho - Young Kavirondo Association - which was founded in December 1921 at a meeting at Lunda, Gem attended by about 8,000 people. See Singh (1969) 10-11 and Ingham (1965) 280-285

237   Boahen (1987) 85

card) laws which were introduced for "controlling movements of African labourers and for locating and identifying them." However, in 1923 the Young Kavirondo Association and the Kavirondo Central Taxpayers Association were joined together to form the Kavirondo Taxpayer's Welfare Association (KTWA), which concentrated on the volume of taxation the Kavirondo tribe produced as compared to the public funds received for welfare and agriculture.[238] The main objective of African nationalism between 1919 and 1935 was not overthrowal but reform of the colonial system.[239] However, this failed and after WW II in 1945, the issue of representation was linked to independence, with the use of fiscal tools perceived as part of the oppression of the indigenous people.

B)   THE EUROPEANS AND ASIANS

In 1911, the European population through their nominated representatives, pressed for elected representation in the law-making arm within the colony: the Legislative Council (LegCo). It was at that point made up of nominated representatives of the imperial state, the colonial administration and the Europeans. The Europeans argued that since they paid taxes they ought to have elected representatives. This demand was based on their remission of customs duties and a nominal poll tax and as a result was met with resistance within the LegCo. In 1916, the LegCo authorised a committee to investigate this concern and based on their recommendations, in 1919, elective representation was granted to the white settler community.[240]

In 1920, the LegCo passed a law requiring Europeans and Asians to pay income tax.[241] Amendments delayed the enforcement date of this legislation; a first collection for 21 months became due and payable in 1921.[242] A public meeting of Europeans took place, unanimously agreeing to oppose the tax. The meeting also resulted in the formation of the European Taxpayer's Protection League to

---

238   Ochieng' (1985) 119, Ross (1968) 236

239   Boahen (1987) 78; Singh (1969) 10-11

240   Ghai and McAuslan (1970) 45. The report also included an express recommendation that the other races would only have nominated representation.

241   Ordinance number 23 of 1920 as quoted by Dilley (1966) 47, Ross (1968) 154

242   Ross (1968) 155

ascertain the constitutionality of collecting direct tax from Europeans as long as elected members did not control the legislature.[243] The following day the LegCo suspended collection. A year later, in 1922, a motion to repeal the Income Tax Ordinance of 1920 was passed on the same day of its introduction. It was replaced with increased customs duty of 90% on cigarettes, and an increase from 10 to 30% on tea, sugar and other items.[244] The result of European action was transfer of the tax burden to indirect taxes applicable on all races particularly the Africans who were the main consumers of the goods on which additional tax was levied.

During the discussion of the 1920 Income Tax Ordinance, there was no Asian representation in the LegCo. In 1922 Asians organised a passive resistance including a refusal to register to vote or pay taxes. Although the colonial government granted an interim offer to allow for a nominated representative in the executive and legislative council, there was no evidence of the use of the position to oppose further application of taxation.[245]

As a result of the Moyne Report, income tax was considered and recommended on all regardless of race.[246] In 1935, there was brief resurgence of European resistance to the institution of income tax with a small income tax finally accepted in 1936 with the passing of the Income Tax Ordinance.[247] However, continued resistance to the payment of income tax resulted in a judicial test of its fiscal legitimacy in 1940 in *Hay v Commissioner of Income Tax*.[248] It was argued that the tax was unnecessary for the peace, order and good government of the Colony and since the LegCo did not contain a majority of elected members, it had no powers of direct taxation. On appeal the East African Court of Appeal (EACA) held that the power to make laws for the peace, order and government had been

---

243   The question of a just system of taxation and the capacity to pay as well as the nature of the work was considered.

244   Ross (1968) 156-158

245   British Empire Report (1922) and Ingham (1965) 291. Additional grievances included continual limitation to the right to own farm lands and the policy of racial segregation. Cabinet Memorandum: Position of Indians in Kenya (1924) 2

246   Lewis (2000) 133

247   Ingham (1965) 278-279

248   *Hay v Commissioner of Income Tax* (1940) EACA 7

validly delegated to the Kenya colony legislature by the King in
Council including the powers of taxation and that there was no
repugnancy with the law of England.[249]

Voting rights and franchise qualifications were differentiated
by race. European members were elected to the legislative council
in 1919 on the basis of full adult white suffrage. However, it was
not until 1924 that Indians and Arabs were allowed to have elected
representatives, and not until 1957 that Africans were allowed to
vote representatives to the central legislature. Elective representation
did not extend to the majority of the population until 1957 and
elections based on universal adult suffrage were eventually conceded
in Kenya in 1963.[250]

3.2.3. Limiting Expenditure to Sustain the Colonial Fiscal State

Various scholars for two interconnected reasons oppose the view that
imperial governments were engaged in the extraction of revenues,
by amongst other means through taxation. Firstly, it is argued that
colonial governments did not possess the power to impose taxes
straightaway. The colonial government needed to anticipate the
responses of Africans when pursuing fiscal policies. Relatively low
tax rates could provide an optimal political economic equilibrium
if they prevented social unrest and political disorder.[251] Secondly,
and related to the former argument, the bureaucratic and logistic
capacities were too limited to allow for the immediate imposition and
collection of new taxes. This forced government to choose between
maintaining a low-profile tax system (for instance, largely based on
easy collectable custom duties limited to the East African coast),
or entering into negotiations with native representatives (including
chiefs, and sultans) on the distribution of the tax burden.[252]

The colonial administration was granted control through the
superintendents of colonial finances. Oversight of the budget for

---

249   *Ibid.* 7 as discussed in Ghai and McAuslan (1970) 209

250   Subrahmanyam (2004) 7

251   See generally Austin (2008); Cooper (2002) and Davis and Huttenback (1988)

252   Austin (2008) xx; Cooper (2002) xx; Davis and Huttenback (1988) xx

the colony was careful and continuous. The Secretary of State in the imperial government was not authorized to issue grants to any colony without the express permission of Treasury. Any colony unable to meet the cost of administration, passed to the supervisory control of the Imperial British treasury. It then examined the budget of the debtor colony and mercilessly pruned expenditures until it was satisfied that all possible economies had been made. After this was ascertained, finally, it would authorize a grant-in-aid. This supervision continued until the colonial state could pay its way. By virtue of this practice, there could even be a sanctioned reduction in official salaries. Since the initial reform of taxation could only be customs revenue, the metropolitan authorities were able to indirectly ensure that, colonial governments sustained a level of commodity production and trade at least sufficient to provide a tax base to meet the recurrent cost of the local state apparatus.[253]

However, the policy of fiscal self-sufficiency also worked to limit control. It forced colonial states to rely more on locally generated tax revenue thus increasing dependence on Europeans and Africans for both production and trade instead of importing foreign labour and incurring debts. For the purpose of their own fiscal independence, colonial states had a vested interest in retaining internally as much of the revenue from the locally produced surplus product as possible, rather than having it transferred to the metropole as trading profits. This involved the colonial state directly in the contradiction between metropolitan and indigenous interests, encouraging a degree of identification with the latter. In Kenya, the result was an intensification of the linkages between the European and state and its strong stance turned state economic policy heavily towards the defence of settler interests. The expenditure of substantial metropolitan sources on colonial development after 1945 however, broke the bounds of fiscal self-sufficiency and gave the imperial metropole growing control over economic policy in the colonies.[254]

---

253   Strandes (1961) 78

254   See generally Tignor (1993)

A)   CREATING AND SUSTAINING COLONIAL FISCAL
       ADMINISTRATION

The administration had several immediate problems. Firstly, where
to set the geographical borders enclosing a fixed society or citizenry.
Although the geographical boundaries were drawn during the
Scramble for Africa,[255] the region of the East African Protectorate
was indefinite up to and beyond 1903.[256] Secondly, after the borders
were determined, the citizenry within the states that would assist in
the creation of the economy had to be convinced to comply. Thus,
the first action of the imperial state was to conquer the peoples and
bring them under the control of the state.[257]

Once the British were in physical control of the territory, the
next step was to set up a system of administration. Lord Lugard, the
main exponent of indirect rule argued for the use of the existing
administrative systems to be incorporated into the colonial tax
structure in order to obtain a maximum revenue while minimising
the costs of administration. East African exports were mainly raw
materials yielding minimal tax revenue and making it an inadequate
source of income even to maintain administration. As a result,
two steps were taken: encouraging an increase of settlement by
the British to farm and increase raw material exports to increase
customs revenue and secondly, more stringent controls of colonial
expenditure by the imperial and colonial administration.

From 1895 to 1940, Kenya and Uganda were under joint British
colonial administration. The colonial administration was peopled by
Europeans mainly while parts of the civil service such as clerical
positions were reserved for Asians. Africans were given the lowest
tier of work as well as some clerical positions. This began with a
common administration of Kenya and Uganda's EA Railways in 1902
as well as a Court of Appeal, followed by a common currency with a
currency board in 1905, a postal union in 1911, and a customs union
in 1917, a common external tariff in 1922, and free interchange

---

255   See generally Pakenham (1991)
256   Buckley (1903) 349
257   Ochieng' (1985) chapter 6

of domestic products in 1923.[258] By the interwar years, (1919–1938) between World Wars I[259] and II,[260] the administration of colonies was further ensured by the operations of the East African Currency Board, which regulated colonial money supply and convertibility of the local currency with sterling.

After the loss of World War I by Germany, British rule in East Africa widened to include Tanzania as a spoil of war. Kenya and Uganda became colonies and Tanzania became a mandated territory. From 1920 until independence Kenya, Uganda and Tanzania were jointly administered by the British colonial authority.[261] Tanzania was added to the currency board and the Court of Appeal in 1921 and to the postal union in 1933. A joint EA trade office was opened in London in 1925 and EA Air Services in 1937. In 1940 income tax services were co-ordinated between all three colonies, but Tanzania as a mandated territory was added to the EA customs union only in 1949. In addition, for the purposes of practical expediency, although the borders of present-day Kenya, Uganda and Tanzania were maintained, their administrative systems were joined in order to make it more expedient for the colonial administration.[262] This resulted in economies of scale that are said to have had a development bias towards Kenya where most industries were located while having evenly distributed benefits with Uganda and Kenya subsidising Tanzania.[263]

Capital investment by the colonial government increasingly had to be raised from private sources on the London money market, with the colony's debt situation and credit worthiness carefully supervised by the imperial state. Expenditure on supplies and capital equipment were channelled through the Crown agents for the colonies. This made certain that British Finance and industrial capital captured most of the profits available from economic activities of and within

---

258   Ghai and McAuslan (1970) 465 and Closer Union in East Africa (1931)

259   1914–1918

260   1939–1945

261   As a result, the ensuing discussion includes some historical references to either both Kenya and Uganda or all 3 countries.

262   Ghai and McAuslan (1970) 465 and Closer Union in East Africa (1931)

263   Ghai and McAuslan (1970) 471

the colonial state.[264] The Colonial state thus became the creator, regulator and controller of the capitalist economic system with the end goal of integrating the colonial economy with the metropolitan economy tailoring the former to specifically provide for the needs of and/or requirements of the latter.[265]

B)   FISCAL RE-DISTRIBUTION IN THE COLONIAL STATE

> Distant Provinces . . . must not feel aggrieved if the annual direct expenditure upon them . . . is not the equivalent of the tax they pay to Government. The stem and main branches of a tree must receive the bulk of the sap and be developed before its outlying limbs. . . . Later the bulk of the expenditure may in return be devoted to the development of the outlying Provinces.[266]

> The difficulty in Kenya finance is largely due to the fact that such taxation is absurdly inadequate.[267]

> An exact balance of contributions and benefits on a community basis acceptable from all points of view is unobtainable. Profound differences in social and economic organization and needs must be reflected by arrangements for the special but quite legitimate benefit of particular interests. Well-considered measures, for instance, to save agriculture from disaster, even though they may be directly for the benefit of a section of producers, may be fully justified in the general interest.[268]

There was no government office running an organised system of social welfare in Kenya before WW II. Services were provided by various voluntary organisations and local authorities to a limited extent.[269] Racial segregation included a racial separation of the geographical areas of residence of all races. Residential areas were divided into European only, Asian only and African only areas and the mixing of races was severely supervised and restricted. The European only areas had well-funded government schools, hospitals, clubs

---

264   Strandes (1961) 41

265   Shivji (1976) 32, 35

266   Lugard (1913-18) 165

267   Report of the East African Commission (1925) 188

268   Report of the Financial Commissioner Lord Moyne: Certain Questions in Kenya (1932) 28

269   Seeley (1987) 542

and infrastructure. The Asian areas had limited funding for schools, hospitals and infrastructure and thus also funded these institutions themselves. African welfare was most influenced by missions that provided education, health and evangelical work. In addition, some European farmers provided limited health and schools for workers and their children.

The utilisation of available revenue as already discussed was used under a policy framework that promoted the vertical integration of the economy. As a result, development within the colonial context was limited to increasing the Empire's production. This included research, medical improvement, railways, ports, and emigration and capital funds. In addition, due to the limited importance of labour, state-sponsored systems of social security[270] were never widespread. In the colonial period European administrators referred to the 'traditional solidarity' of African families and communities to regulate and avoid the expensive process for absorbing, even partially, the manifold risks of working life.[271]

During the first decades of colonial rule in Africa, an active social policy was not on the agenda of colonial officials and European entrepreneurs at all, with noted disregard of African welfare in some of the areas.[272] Benefits, it was argued should be:

---

270   The definition of the term 'social security' is problematic and each author working on the subject attempts to coin their own definition. The International Labour Office (1952 (1982)) listed eight fields of social security: medical supply, medical insurance, social insurance, old age pensions, disability pensions, surviving dependants' pensions, benefits in the case of industrial accidents and occupational disease, child allowances and legal protection of expectant and nursing mothers. See International Labour Office (1952 (1982)) 533–53. However, this definition reduces social security to legally fixed systems with an exact catalogue of obligations and periodical payments on the basis of risk-pooling, supported by public institutions. On the problems of defining social security see, among others, Woodman (1988) 69–88.

271   Due to the limited availability of financial records on the colonial period generally on the issue of social welfare and development, the improvement of social services and development will be analyzed using two main reports, the Report of the Secretary of State for the Colonies Lord Ormsby-Gore on the East African Commission (1925) (Ormsby-Gore Report) and the Report of the Financial Commissioner Lord Moyne: Certain Questions in Kenya (1932) (Moyne Report) and diverse colonial records which were available.

272   Ross (1968) 152

As small as decency allowed and the need to ensure the economic survival of the workforce would allow.[273]

Stichter aptly summarized this attitude towards both Asian and African labour in the commercial, mining and manufacturing establishments and agriculture when she stated that labour costs above day-to-day subsistence for the labourer on the job were transferred to the pre-capitalist economy.

> Such costs as retirement or social security, education, health, and the rearing of the next generation of workers, which in twentieth century core capitalist states would be met out of wages or profits, were borne by the economy of the African 'reserves', which supported the worker's wife, his children, and himself in sickness and old age. In this way, the non-monetary economy became an appendage to the new economy of estate agriculture, subsidising its low wages.[274]

This policy remained unchanged marked periodically by intermittent responses to local conditions. For example, to control labour in 1921, 24% of the total tax revenue of the department of native affairs was used to provide for registration of Africans, a service demanded by and for the benefit of employers. More often than not, grants to African and Asian services benefited European equally if not more.[275] In another instance to reduce the budget deficit by increasing agricultural production, in 1923 access to veterinary services normally for Europeans only was granted to African farmers.[276]

It is reported in the 1925 Ormsby-Gore report that the absence of social welfare and development of African areas was first questioned by both Africans and missionaries.

> It is quite natural that the more intelligent natives should ask that a fair proportion of the revenue contributed by them should be earmarked for native services ... it should be noted that, out of an estimated total expenditure of roughly £2,000,000, approximately £327,000 is for

---

273   Brett (1973) 195

274   Stichter (1982) 27–8

275   Dilley (1966) 243

276   Brett (1973) 196 The limited government support that was available went to settlers as the colonial administration looked to stimulate production through those that already had capital and skills.

the upkeep of military forces, police, and prisons. Provision is made for medical services for natives, Indians, and Europeans, costing- £133,000, about 15 per cent, of the native hut and poll taxes. It is estimated by the Treasurer of Kenya, in the absence of reliable information that 75 per cent, of the expenditure on medical services is in connection with the natives. This year (1925) it is proposed to spend £37,000 on native education, an increase of £9,000 on the previous year's estimate. We do not suggest that a great immediate increase in expenditure on native education alone is practicable, and we certainly would not suggest that less money should be devoted to the education of Indians or Europeans. More could be spent with advantage on the education of all three elements in the population.[277]

This led to the request for allocation of a proportion of the amount raised in hut and poll taxes to funds exclusively for native needs in the reserves where the taxes were collected. In addition, the report provided evidence of the quest of Africans for their betterment showed how initiatives were taking place to improve certain conditions like infrastructure.

> In Kenya, there are comparatively few roads in the native's reserves. However, in the Fort Hall area the Kikuyu natives… have already constructed 170 miles of graded roads, …The natives in this district have voluntarily proposed a head tax of one shilling towards the cost of bridging. …the Kavirondo … would be willing to construct roads needed for the economic development of their area if properly encouraged. Such roads as exist in the Kitui district of Ukamba have been made by the natives themselves without payment. The only assistance given by the Public Works Department has been the provision of a few culverts…[278]

The first act of the British to allocate money for welfare was the 1929 Colonial Development Act. They allowed free grants and loans of a maximum of £1 million primarily to relative unemployment in Britain. It could not be used for education, and possibly health too.[279] There was no intent to create a welfare state. The recommendations of the above Ormsby-Gore report were not put into effect as Kenya recorded its second deficit in 1929 as a result of locust attacks and

---

277   Report of the East African Commission (1925) 175

278   *Ibid.* 166

279   Brett 133

bad crops.[280] In addition, Amery's report to the House of Commons that £50,850 was to be spent on roads in settled areas and £332,550 in African areas, was questioned in 1929, by the KTWA who reported that £9,264 was spent on African areas and £44,968 in settled areas.[281]

In 1930, despite a budgetary deficit of £197,000 and a railway deficit of £83,000, assistance totalling £286,000 was granted to the European maize and wheat farmers as subsidies, credits and remission on railway rates and administrative charges.[282] This continued preference for the welfare of the Europeans continued into 1931 when the 1925-1938 estimates showed allocation of £37,827 to European councils while African district councils spent £7,520 annually from their own funds for roads.[283]

The depression of the 1920s resulted in the commissioning of the Moyne report where an analysis and recommendations were substantiated by a breakdown of the tax revenue and expenditure of the different tax bases as set out below.

---

280 Mungeam (1966) 281-282. In 1929, it is estimated that 50% of African taxation was used to subsidise the settler economy. See Lewis (2000) 144

281 Brett (1973) 202

282 *Ibid.* 196

283 *Ibid.* 202

Figure 4: Summary of Tax Revenue and Expenditure in 1931 (£)

	Europeans	Indians	Goans	Arabs	Natives	Indivisible	Total
Direct Taxation	42,596	39,170	3,251	18,114	530,877	–	634,008
INDIRECT TAXATION	334,477	145,213	47,346	16,992	199,181	2,345	745,554
OTHER TAXATION REVENUE	109,113	45,406	4,057	6,241	11,446	1,936	178,199
OTHER REVENUE (NOT TAXATION)	179,595	49,213	3,752	6,903	49,596	1,220,110*	1,509,169
TOTAL (£)	665,781	279,002	58,406	48,250	791,100	1,224,391	3,066,930

* Includes   Post Office   168,132
               Reimbursements   883,716

Description	Amount (£)	Detail
Indivisible Services	1,771,180.0	Vide Schedule 5.
European Services	171,247.0	n a 6.
European and Native (Indivisible) Services	2,962.0	P.W.D. Water-boring.
Asiatic Services	46,080.0	Vide Schedule 7.
Non-Native (Indivisible) Services	8,948.8	
Native Services	331,956.0	it 9.
Reimbursements and Cross Entries	883,716.0	
Total	3,216,089.8	

Source: Moyne Report Schedule 1

The report attributed Kenya's particular vulnerability to the depression to the economy's reliance almost exclusively on European farming and its sensitivity to world prices whereas government revenue derived largely from the direct taxation of Africans.[284] The report recommended firstly, that taxation should not be used to force Africans to work; secondly, that tax should be limited by capacity to pay; and finally, that Africans should get a fair return for their tax.[285] The report also recommended that a fixed sum of revenue derived from direct African taxation should be removed from LegCo control and earmarked for specific African services.[286] In light of the depression, reduced collections and the opposition from the white

---

284   Ochieng' (1985) 123, Brett (1973) 143

285   Brett (1973) 196

286   Conclusions of Meeting (1932) 14

European the earmarked fund was created.[287] Despite this argument to not distribute tax revenue, in 1935, when the local market was close to collapse the LegCo appropriated £12,500 to guarantee European farmers a minimum return on every bag of maize sold.[288]

In the late 1930s, the practice of 'externalizing' systems of social security was maintained when Lord Hailey stated:

> It is clear that by treating the native reserves as reservoirs of manpower, there is, in effect, a saving in that outlay on social services which in other circumstances might have to be incurred on behalf of industrialized labour'.[289]

Until the Second World War the few measures in the realm of social policy benefited Europeans almost exclusively.[290] The result of colonisation on the services and infrastructure of the colonial state was such that there was a bias in development in the areas where the Europeans lived and the areas they needed to access for the purposes of farming and the transportation necessary.[291] The Asians and Africans lived in areas with little or no services and infrastructure.

In contrast, during and after the WW II the vague concept of social welfare became a favoured means of expressing a new imperial commitment to colonial peoples.[292] The policy before the WW II on public outlays and social development was scant and limited relative to other programmes.[293] Metropolitan forms of social engineering were now applied more vigorously to colonial issues. A new generation of professional experts entered the stage of colonial policy. Social welfare included: implanting rural social betterment by animating civil society against social collapse; devising urban

---

287   Lewis (2000) 31-32 The reasons given for this was the end of payment of hut and poll tax communally; the undermining of the traditional society where the youth no longer assisted their families in earning a living; more time spent in collection and weak native authority that comprised chiefs and headmen that were not part of the traditional systems of authority.

288   Brett (1973) 204-205

289   Lord Hailey (1938) 710

290   Fuchs (1985) 100–3

291   Acemoglu, Johnson and Robinson (2001)

292   Lewis (2000) 147

293   Subrahmanyam (2004) 4

remedies for the incapacitated and the destitute; correcting the deviant; and training Africans to be their own policemen.

The introduction of elements of the welfare state in British colonies during the 1940s and 50s was part of what has come to be known as the 'second colonial occupation' of Africa.[294] In the tumult of the post-war years, British officials, believing that their development initiatives would make colonies more productive and ideologically more stable, sent experts to Africa to increase efficiency in the agricultural and industrial sectors and to restructure health, welfare and education policies. Great Britain launched in Africa a 'developmental colonialism', to be of immediate economic use to Britain and to help Africans attain the 'maturity' deemed necessary for independence. Thus, London allocated the sum of £50,000 from the Colonial Development and Welfare Fund for the establishment of social welfare centres based on the principle that a colony should have only those services which it could afford to maintain out of its own resources.[295]

The development concept became crucial to all participants in post-WW II politics. Development was something to be done to and for Africa, not with it.[296] Despite the new emphasis on development, social security always kept its character as a privilege, to which only a small minority had access.[297] Thus, annual United Nations reports included the phrase:

> The tribal organization provides a system of social security for the individual based on the social responsibility of the clan or family for its members.[298]

The 1952 report stated that although industrialization and urbanization would become more important, 98 per cent of the

---

294   For the origins of this term see Low and Lonsdale (1976) 12

295   Statement of Policy on Colonial Development and Welfare (1940)1375

296   For the development concept see Cooper (1997) 64–92

297   On social security systems in the West see generally Baldwin (1990); Linden, Dreyfus, Gibaud and Lucassen (1996)

298   Report to United Nations on Administration of Tanganyika for 1947 (1948) 98, this statement is repeated more or less verbatim until 1952 when the Report to United Nations on Administration of Tanganyika for 1951 (1952) 123, added 'No state services in respect of such matters as old-age pensions, maternity, health or unemployment benefits are at present provided or contemplated'.

territory's population still lived in 'tribal regions'. The colonial administration thus attempted to strengthen the efficiency and influence of traditional institutions in the field of social security.[299] Two years later the government conceded the necessity of 'some specific measures' concerning family allowances.[300] However, in his study of the problem of 'detribalization', published in 1959, the former Provincial Commissioner M. J. B. Molohan emphasized:

> Any form of compulsory state controlled provident fund scheme ... is out of the question because of the high cost of administration that would be involved.[301]

While Molohan addressed the financial and administrative burden the British were unwilling and unable to bear, others still referred to essentialist explanations. In the same year, acting governor, Gower, justified the lack of state-sponsored social security systems with reference to the specific dispositions of African societies:

> The underlying philosophy, that social security is not the responsibility of the individual or of his family, is alien to Africa.[302]

3.2.4. CREATING THE POST-COLONIAL FISCAL STATE (1960-1964)

In 1961, the budget was in deficit and the provisions for services were an expenditure above the revenue resources of the state and as a result needed to be curtailed if the budget was to balance.[303] The hut tax was providing £1.1 million, one-fifth of local revenues from the African district councils and 3% of total receipts. Graduated personal tax yielded £1.6 million and was 4% of total receipts and income tax amounted to £5.4 million. Rebates on customs and consumption tax to white farmers amounted to £500,000 annually.[304]

299 Report to United Nations on Administration of Tanganyika for 1952 (1953) 147

300 Report to United Nations on Administration of Tanganyika for 1954 (1955) 67. However, the report did not set out what kind of measures the government was thinking about.

301 Molohan (1959) 67

302 Gower to Secretary of State for the Colonies (1959)

303 The economic development of Kenya: report of a mission organized by the IBRD at the request of the Government of Kenya and the United Kingdom (1963) 283-284.

304 *Ibid.* 285-291

In African areas the £5 million expenditure consisted of 44% primary education; 10% roads; 8% location councils. 40% of expenditure was expected from government grants while 40% came from poll tax, cesses on produce and payments for services provided (dispensaries, house rent, beer halls, markets and slaughterhouses).[305] Allocations to improve the welfare of people remained racially divided both in collection of hut tax and in distribution for health, education and other social services. Development records show that in the years 1957–1962, less than 10% of allocated revenue to social services was development expenditure whereas the bulk of expenditure was to maintain the provision of the existing services which were mainly for the Europeans.[306]

The British imperial government during colonisation had established an infrastructure of roads and rail, built schools and hospitals and government buildings. It left in place an infrastructure that was partially shared by Kenya, Uganda and Tanzania, which had for the 10 years before independence been administered jointly.[307] Part of the complications of independence included how these were to be shared. The result of negotiations between the incoming indigenous government and the British colonial office was that all three countries were to have access to the infrastructure and the benefits were to be re-distributed based on negotiated shares.[308] Thus, revenue and expenditure was collected at the regional level and shared in terms of proportions freely negotiated before independence.

However, before independence could be granted, Kenya, Uganda and Tanzania's shared administration of services which included tax collection and distribution had to be agreed upon. As part of pre-independence negotiations the three states agreed to continue the shared administration to share common services including a tax system.[309] In 1961, all the shared services were brought under the East African Common Services Organisation (EACSO). The

---

305   *Ibid.* 294–295
306   *Ibid.* 275
307   This included communication, transport and money
308   Ghai and McAuslan (1970) chapter 12
309   Mueller (1997) 102

indigenous political leaders of the three East African colonies were given the free right to negotiate the terms of the share of services.[310] Revenue collection powers were given to EACSO with the right to fix amounts of revenue being assigned to the regions on the principle of derivation from revenue on specific items, and population on others. The rates of customs and excise duty or taxation were to be determined by national parliaments on the recommendation of the Central Federal Government after consultation of the three states. A formula on the shares of revenue for distribution included Kenya keeping 59% of all collections. 35% went to Uganda and Tanzania, and the extra 6% re-distributed to the countries based on the infrastructure advantage that Kenya had. Taxation from licensing of vehicles and drivers though determined by parliament were collected by and formed part of the revenue of the three regional authorities. The regional authorities also had certain independent powers of taxation including graduated personal tax, poll tax (up to a maximum decided upon by Parliament), land tax, entertainment tax, and royalties for minerals.[311]

Not all citizens within the state had equal access to all the services and one condition of the attainment of independence was maintaining the rights of those already granted before independence, in certain categories of social services such as pension benefits.[312] This provision was, however, immediately withdrawn on the grounds of lack of resources for the rest of the population. Since the majority had never had access to any of these services in the past and in many cases were not aware of the existence of these benefits in the rural areas, their provision and subsequent withdrawal did not register with the population as being the loss of a benefit directly related to the payment of taxes.

---

310   The services included railways, harbours, posts and telecommunications, civil aviation, collection of customs, excise and taxes, statistics and research. Ghai and McAuslan (1970) 474

311   *Ibid*. 203-204

312   Republic of Kenya. The Constitution of the Republic of Kenya ((1988) 1992) Chapter VIII provided that social security was only available to all colonial administrators and civil servants working in government and a limited section of Asian civil service personnel.

Development before independence was along racial lines and thus the physical infrastructure in place on the ground upon independence was enough to cater for the Europeans present in Kenya at the time, which amounted to approximately 10% of the total Kenyan population.[313] However, through independence and the end of British Colonial rule, the independence Constitution declared the right of equality of access to all state services and the termination of the pre-existing colour bar or apartheid policy. The policy of the colonial office had included the provision of social welfare services, in particular education, health and unemployment and pension benefits for some categories of the public service, but only for racial minorities.[314]

The pre-independence negotiations resulted in an agreement by the British government to grant independence, which was subject to several conditions. Firstly, like many other newly independent colonies, Kenya was required to adopt a quasi-federal form of government operating under its first written Constitution based on the decentralised[315] and multi-party[316] Westminster-style of governance.[317] Secondly, all colonial legislation, international treaties

---

313   Himbara (1994) 472

314   Dilley (1966) 246

315   Government administrative levels or layers included 7 provinces, 52 districts, and a multitude of areas. However, towns/cities/municipalities also had a mayor's office. All these administrative levels fell under the Ministry of Local Government or Internal Affairs.

316   Kenya became independent under the ruling party, the Kenya African National Union (KANU) and with two main opposition parties. Political platforms were not however as crystallized as in other emerging nations. The political platform of KANU was described as African socialism, but the economy that had been inherited was strongly capitalistic. The opposition, while it existed, was based more on the fear of marginalisation of minority ethnic communities or tribes and therefore stressed the protection of their interests as their main platform. Ndegwa (1997) 604.

        However, the turn of political events led to the abolition of the political parties as they all joined forces and later, by constitutional amendment, Kenya became a single-party state as a unitary government. Republic of Kenya. The Constitution of the Republic of Kenya ((1988) 1992) Section 2A (now repealed by Legal Notice 12 of 1991 section 2).

317   Singh (1965) The imperial British state had and to date still has an unwritten Constitution and as a result, the concept of a written Constitution was completely alien to the pre-independence history of Kenya. The Constitution of the Republic of Kenya that was adopted was and is based on the Westminster model of governance with a decentralised form of governance, two houses of parliament and based on a federal system. However, constitutional amendments soon after independence

and agreements that the Crown had undertaken on behalf of the Kenya colony were to be adopted without question by the newly independent state and parliament.[318] Thirdly, that the Constitution would compulsorily contain provisions designed to protect the minority interests of the white population including a Bill of Rights that thus only included civil and political rights, pension rights protections as well as other social welfare provisions that were then the colonial policy in effect at independence. Finally, at the practical juncture Kenya did not apply extensive changes to the inherited administrative and economic structures,[319] which were inherited from the colonial period and was left virtually unshaken by the process of democratization that had been the political pre-occupation of the independence movement since 1954.[320]

From a fiscal perspective, Kenya's Constitution, includes an elaborate set of provisions, together with a set of legislation that comprehensively provides for all areas of tax law. Kenya has a detailed legal framework that governs raising government revenues and allocation and use of public resources. This framework is grounded in Part VII of the Constitution and other laws, financial regulations and procedures. Every fiscal measure, whether dealing with mobilisation of revenues or public expenditures, is catered for by a specific law, including those on extra-budgetary activities. The principal law on Public Finance is the Constitution, with more specific provisions in the Exchequer and Audit Act, the Paymaster-General Act, the Government Contracts Act, the Internal Loans Act, and the External Loans Act. All these laws provide for accounting, auditing and disclosures, as well as division of responsibilities.

---

immediately abolished the federal system and centralising power and vesting it in the office of the President.

318   However, the only exception to this was the request by the new government for re-negotiation of all Double Taxation agreements. This resulted in re-negotiation of the six double taxation agreements that the Crown had negotiated for the colony. Irish (1974) 299 note 24.

319   See generally Leys (1975)

320   See generally Okoth-Ogendo (1972)

3.3.   CONCLUSION

At independence, Kenya could be considered a non-aligned fledgling democracy with severely limited human rights and social welfare provisions and a mixed economy reflecting neo-colonial state tendencies. Fiscally, the state could be placed as consisting of a mixture of a primitive, tribute and tax state, so that Kenya may be placed within the Ormrod-Bonney model of the developmental stages of the fiscal state.[321] Kenya experienced sixty-six years of autocracy tempered by limited elections, followed by two years of democratisation, ending with six months of responsible government prior to independence.

The colonial period in Kenya (1895-1963) was a period of gross violations of non-white human rights, as they are understood today. Within the realm of the traditional civil and political rights, lands were seized; Kenyans were subjected to forced labour; Kenyans who resisted colonialism were killed or imprisoned; there was no right to vote; taxation was without representation; resources were exploited by the colonial power; the right to associate was denied and cultural rights were violated. The colonial power established an apartheid system (then called "colour bar") that discriminated based on race.

Discriminative direct taxes were used as an important tool to support the development of the market economy as well as to centralize the public budget. Although the revenue from native head or hut taxes was rather modest in absolute terms, the relative contribution of such taxes to the colonial state coffers often outweighed the contributions of taxes targeted at the non-native residents. Due to the enormous income differentials between Africans and non-native European or Asian residents, the expenses incurred on the salaries of state administrators were relatively high. The burden of these expenses rested mainly on the African.

If Backhaus' argument that needs outweighing resources amount to a fiscal crisis then the Kenya colony was managed on the basis of a constant fiscal crisis. The tax bargain that existed in colonial Kenya was based on inequality. Unequal distribution of resources,

---

321   See the Ormrod-Bonney model 33

unequally collected from different tax bases. Taxpayers were racially segregated and the distribution and use of revenue to improve well-being was allocated to physical areas based on the occupancy of the different races. The inequality in treatment of society on the grounds of race infringed the rights of some while selectively granting others.

The three separate tax bases may have felt differently about the manner of the levy of their taxes and the lack of commensurate re-distribution except when decided upon locally. Despite the redistribution of revenue from natives to non-natives, the absolute levels of revenue were still far too low to create the right conditions for a sustainable constructive role of the post-colonial state in post-colonial economic development which at independence was 5% of GDP.[322] Thus the independent Kenyan state in 1963 can be best described as a rudimentary tax state predominantly in the urban centres with elements of tribute and primitive states in the rural areas.

---

322   Ndulu and Mwega (1994) 109

CHAPTER 4

LEGITIMISING THE KENYAN POST-COLONIAL FISCAL STATE

This chapter will continue with the line of inquiry that began in the previous chapter: an exploration of the fiscal history of Kenya with reference to the typology of the fiscal state. The preceding chapter already established that the imperial and colonial state policy ensured that the link between tax expenditure and tax revenue was crystallised regarding only one part of the tax base, the Europeans. Belated and mixed attempts by colonial authorities towards the end of colonisation to try to link the benefits of taxation for the Africans and Asians were limited and largely unsuccessful. The results of attempts by certain parts of the Africans to agitate for the link between the taxes paid and expenditure to improve well-being was also mixed. Upon independence, taxation was perceived as a force of oppression and domination. This chapter will explore the Kenyan post-colonial fiscal state in order to establish whether this partial, fragile and tenuous link between tax revenue and expenditure was maintained and whether there has been progression towards fiscal legitimacy. The colonial period thus had two decisive legacies: economic underdevelopment and the policy inheritance.[323]

Any discussion on the fiscal relations between the state and society must begin with a discussion of the basis on which Kenya taxes its citizens: its fiscal system. The fiscal system is the tabulation of the tax bargain. It reflects the compromise achieved between the state and society. It has been termed by Moore as the fiscal social contract.[324] While the Constitution and legislation sets out the state's duties and responsibilities towards its citizens generally, fiscal policy sets out the application of the tax bargain as understood by the state and accepted by the society through the election of a particular political party. Politically and economically the state adopted and maintained the existing structures and attempted to slip into the

323   Fahnbulleh (2006) 46
324   Moore (2004) 299

civil service gaps of Kenyan citizens to maintain what under the colonial regime was a racially structured but class based society.[325]

If the Constitution, legislation and policies reflect the ideals pursued by the state, then the other side of the discussion in this chapter rests on the society's part in the state-society relationship. This can be measured in several ways to show what the societal perceptions may be. Firstly, the success or failure of the fiscal system being implemented based on the achievement of the aims and goals. Secondly, the overall improvement of well-being and finally, the reaction of citizens to implementation of the laws and policies through evasion, avoidance and resistance to the laws and policies. However, there is limited availability of information on societal response as regards comprehensive statistical data. This chapter will thus proceed on the basis of available information which includes the success or failure of policies and the public response to the use and administration of fiscal resources of the state, their effectiveness, efficiency, fairness and justness and the accountability, transparency and responsibility with which the governance of the state is conducted with reference to the characteristics in the OB model and where the Kenyan post-colonial fiscal state can be placed in relation to them.

The nature of Kenya's unfolding fiscal crisis and the obstacles to gaining fiscal legitimacy is similar to those of many post-colonial fiscal states, to which Kenya is no exception. This includes low tax revenues, mismanagement of resources (foreign aid, debt, tax and profit from government business), inadequate allocations to welfare and development, inadequate accountability, transparency and responsibility and low societal participation. The Kenyan state has been aware of these difficulties and has attempted to remedy the fiscal crisis in a variety of ways since independence. There are limited surveys since independence to allow for a comprehensive analysis of societal perception and therefore the fiscal legitimacy of the post-colonial state. This chapter will refer to the constitutional, legislative and policy changes both in theory and their practical application. The key characteristics that will be discussed in this

---

325   Ochieng and Maxon (1992) 264

chapter will include tax revenue, tax expenditure, governance, administration, participation, corruption, clientelism, patronage and how they illuminate the evolving tax bargain between the state and society and their effect on fiscal legitimacy. All of these characteristics form part of the governance of the fiscal state. The roots of fiscal legitimacy can be broken down into representation; the fiscal contract, accountability and politics.

The attempts made to reverse the fiscal crisis can be divided into three main periods. Firstly, the immediate post-independence period – this was the era of President Kenyatta, whose leadership was characterised by strong authoritarian and single party rule with sporadic policy changes mainly as a reaction to changing economic circumstances both nationally, regionally and internationally and severely limited societal participation (1964-1980). Secondly, the era of President Moi is divided into two. He initially continued authoritarian and single party rule but this was tempered by the realisation of the debt abyss into which the developing world was disappearing into and thus spearheaded a change through the introduction of loan conditionalities that were then applied across the developing world without much reference to societal conditions and circumstances with the inclusion of the voice of creditors (1981-1992). Moi subsequently bowed to international pressure and reduced authoritarian rule, introduced multiparty politics and limited presidential terms. Fiscally the role of international actors grew and they controlled the policies implemented during this period. (1993-2003). Finally, the election of Kenya's third President, Mwai Kibaki, coupled with the realisation of the international lending institutions that the imposed loan conditionalities were proving unsuccessful. Fiscal policies moved partially towards concentration on home-grown strategies for resource collection and distribution involving greater participation that ran and continue to run parallel to the reform policies applied since independence, under the direction of different members of the international community (2003 to date).[326]

---

326   See appendices 3-13 255-268

4.1.   THE ERA OF PIECEMEAL REFORMS (1964–1980)

Legislative elections in 1963 resulted in a KANU victory followed by the declaration of independence. These elections were for the first time in Kenya's history general and open to all people in the state: Europeans, Africans and Asians – all members of the society were equally free to stand up for political posts. Universal adult suffrage marked the beginning of increased societal participation. However, the growth in participation was subsequently curtailed when Kenya was declared a republic in 1964 and became a *de facto* one party state. Participation of political leaders in the state went through increased stress during this era with the assassination of political leaders, banning of all political parties apart from KANU and the detention of political leaders. Kenyatta was re-elected for three terms unopposed until his death in 1978.

The independent government of Kenya practiced a policy of cautious spending in order to reduce reliance on British grants and government expenditure was limited to available resources. However, despite independence, British aid continued to flow. There were concerns, about the economy, but there was an initial boom as prices of agricultural products like coffee were rising.

The first post-independence strategy was set out in Kenya's first planning document entitled 'African Socialism and its Application to Planning in Kenya'.[327] Its main stated aim was to guarantee every citizen full and equal political rights, a firm basis for rapid economic growth. It was stated specifically that the economic approach of the government would be ensuring Africanisation of the economy, education, employment, welfare and public service but not jeopardising growth.[328] Amongst other things, this planning document declared that the Government would concentrate investment in places where it was likely to maximise returns, which would subsequently be redistributed to the rest of the country.[329] This approach concentrated resources in the same places as the

---

327   African Socialism and its Application to Planning in Kenya (1965)

328   See generally Himbara (1994)

329   African Socialism and its Application to Planning in Kenya (1965) 1

colonial state had done, at the expense of opening up the rest of the country.

The Africanisation policy included encouraging of African business and employment and enterprise. This included a preference in hiring of Africans in the civil service. This positive policy of discrimination to encourage employment of Africans soon converted into nepotism and tribalism in the choice of employees in addition to over-employment which resulted in bloating of the civil service. Encouraging of African business, it has been noted, was centred on the geographical areas that were occupied by the communities who had political representation and leadership. During this first era of independence under Kenyatta the Kikuyu benefited the most.[330] Here is another characteristic of the primitive fiscal state.

During the first decade of Independence, the Kenyan government maintained an impressive record of macroeconomic management. A cautious financial policy was pursued which saw inflation and external debt kept within manageable levels and avoided major balance of payments disequilibrium.[331] The government was able to reverse the fiscal position that it had inherited at Independence. It turned the deficit in the recurrent budget into a sizeable surplus, increased its development expenditure sevenfold, and reduced its relative dependence on foreign aid. Government recurrent revenue grew at an impressive average annual rate of 15 per cent between 1965 and 1973. Total tax revenue increased from K£39.8 million in 1964/5 to K£265.9 million in 1976/7. This was the result of an increase in direct taxes from K£14 million to K£108 million and an increase in indirect taxes from K£39.8 million to K£265.9 million, helped in large part by the introduction of a sales tax. The government financed 80 per cent of its total (recurrent and development) budget out of recurrent revenue.

From 1963 to 1972, there was an average annual growth rate of 6.8%; low inflation and a viable balance of payments with steadily increasing reserves (there was a small balance of payments deficit the year the EA Customs Union was created (1967) and in 1971). This

---

330   Kimenyi and Mbaku (2004) 127

331   Moyi and Ronge (2006) 7

was due to increased public sector employment and the increase in the value of exports like coffee. By the mid-1970s, government revenue accounted for 23 per cent of GDP, an exceptionally high ratio for the developing world. Thus, although recurrent expenditure increased by 11 per cent per annum, the Kenyan government's good revenue performance enabled it to meet its expanding recurrent expenditure whilst making a substantial contribution to development expenditure. Up to 1970-1, the Government did not have recourse to borrowing from the Central Bank, instead for much of this period it had a positive outstanding balance with the Central Bank.[332]

The downwards trend in economy began between 1967 and 1969[333] with inflation of 8.9% and an increase in the share of direct taxes to total revenue of 48%.[334] The reasons for this have been explained as the decrease in export trade, minimal external pressures, and the tapping of previously idle resources easily utilized. The lowering of income tax allowances coupled with rising employment mainly in the civil service, which had also resulted in more payers of direct income tax. Although, the early independence years saw record economy growth rates, they seemed to have induced irresponsible management of state resources as well as regional inequalities. For example, the rapid growth of the civil service could only be explained on political grounds, rather than on the grounds of need inspired by the efficient production of services.[335] Meanwhile, parts of the country that had been left out of the market economy continued to lag behind. The critical characteristics that pushed the state away from fiscal legitimacy and towards a fiscal crisis included: firstly, mismanagement of limited resources; secondly, limited improvement in welfare; thirdly, failure to engage with the participation of society.

No attempt was made to engage society in participation in the re-distribution of state resources. Instead the encouraging of self-

---

332   See generally Legovini (2002)

333   Tom Mboya, KANU Secretary General, was assassinated, Luo-Kikuyu enmity escalated, KPU was banned and its principal leaders including Odinga and 7 other party representatives were detained.

334   See generally Economic Survey (1969)

335   See generally Macgregor and Schuftan (1998)

help coupled with voluntary assistance from charities, civil society and philanthropic individuals. The use of paternalistic attitude, corruption, clientelism and limited re-distribution led to the eventual failure to create or develop fiscal legitimacy.

In the 1960s there were limited resources available for development. The rapid economic growth compounded unemployment, rural–urban migration and widened social and economic inequalities. As a result self-help and 'harambee' were encouraged. In 1964/65 gross financial aid counted for 87% of development revenue.[336] It revitalised community development and encouraged collective effort and self-reliance. It has been estimated that harambee between 1967 and 1973 contributed 11.4% of National Development Expenditure.[337]

However, how the re-distribution as regards social welfare was to be undertaken remained 'vague'.[338] Social welfare services also inherited from the colonial era were adopted with their meaning 'to rehabilitate maladjusted and socially disorderly individuals and to reduce and prevent social problems'.[339] Remedial care was thus the main concern of social welfare. Since independence in 1963, Kenya has had a predominantly general tax-funded health system, but gradually introduced a series of health financing policy changes.[340] Life expectancy increased from 38 years in 1960 to 47 years in 1978 despite a GNP per capita increase from USD 222 to USD 280.[341] Primary education was declared free for all in 1964 but its implementation was limited by the available fiscal resources and by 1980 only the first 4 years of primary education were free with parents continuing to pay for books, stationery and teaching materials.[342] In addition, the access to this resource was affected by ethnic bias and was based on a practice of inequality and clientelism.[343]

---

336   Holtham and Hazlewood (1976) 52

337   Mbithi and Rasmusson (1977) 14

338   Seeley (1987) 541

339   Kenya National Development Plan 1984–88 (1983) 172

340   See generally Dahlgren (1991)

341   See generally World Bank (1981)

342   Nkinyangi (1982) 202

343   Alwy and Schech (2004)

Competition for resources became competition for favours as the client-patron relationship developed along tribal lines and towards central government and the office of the President.[344]

The 1966-1970 National Development Plan established the basic structure for urban and regional planning at the provincial and district levels, leading to the distribution of technical personnel. Key among the policy initiatives from the period were the Integrated Rural Development Programme, Area Based Integrated Development Planning, the framework of urbanization and spatial redistribution of infrastructure and other development facilities, and services through the hierarchical Growth Centres Policy. Others included district planning, the Rural Urban Balance Strategy and the District Focus for Rural Development Strategy. The integrated area based development planning approach emphasised the active involvement of the local community. The District Development Committees were established with economic, regional and project planning mandates. Also introduced was the Local Authority Development Programme (LADP) for investment priorities incorporated into the District Development Plan (DDP).

Despite these written policies on societal participation, economists like Oyugi argue that during the first years of Kenya's independence, prior to 1970, Kenya's budget process lacked consultation and was merely an accounting exercise on revenue and spending. In 1970 the Programme Review and Forward Budget (PR&FB) was introduced to: firstly, provide concrete budget constraints; secondly, establish costs of programs and process of reviewing priorities; and finally establish criteria for reviewing performance and ensure linkage between budgets and planning.[345]

In 1970/71, the Minister of Finance changed the policy of cautious spending and began an expansionary policy 'to utilize resources that were lying idle'.[346] The first oil crisis of 1973 coincided with the introduction of a sales tax. As a result there was still a resultant budget deficit of KSh. 442 million in 1974, a change from

---

344   Grindle (1996) 65

345   See generally Oyugi (2005)

346   In 1970 there was a 170% increase in expenditure resulting in subsequent deficits.

1973 when there had been an overall balance of payments surplus of Kenya £s 234 million. In the 1975/76, budget speech it was noted that the average import prices in 1974 had increased by 64% without including the 42% rise in oil prices. Export prices however only rose by 30%. This resulted in an additional Kenya pound 75 million[347] finance shortfall. The deficit now grew. Resulting fiscal reforms included a 20% withholding tax on non-resident entrepreneurs, capital allowance restricted to rural investment, a new tax on the sale of property, taxes on shares, and the sale of land and a custom tariff of 10% on a range of previously duty free goods.

In 1977 came the collapse of the EA federation and customs union as the treaty proved difficult to maintain. This was attributed to the failure to agree on the division of the surplus revenue and share of facilities. The coffee boom that year added to the revenue and resulted in an immediate surplus of 249 million shillings. A substantial windfall occurred to private agents resulting in an increased demand for imports. The collapse of the East African Community (EAC) in 1977, however, required money to form corporations and buy out others.[348] The limited availability of resources led to the commencement of government involvement in business especially in relation to the previously jointly owned and shared railways and harbours, the telecommunications and post.[349] This entry into business signalled a change in government revenue sources and led to additional resources to the post-colonial fiscal state. These events led to a Balance of Payments (BOP) deficit in 1978[350] by which point the rise in coffee prices had stalled.[351]

With the second oil crisis of 1979,[352] import prices were on the decline and the availability of domestic credit, lower returns from agriculture and commerce led to a large drop in revenue. The state

---

347   The Kenyan pound was set at 20 Kenya shillings per pound.

348   See generally Bevan, Collier and Gunning (1990) these debts were finally paid off by the Kenya government as recently as 1994.

349   Grosh (1991) 13

350   Kenyatta died in August and was replaced by his Vice President Moi

351   Temporary terms of trade windfall usually accrue to government revenue. In the Kenyan case, export taxes being negligible, this accrued to private individuals. Despite this, there was a surplus.

352   In November, Moi won the national elections running unopposed

response was to decrease Personal Income Tax from 36% to 29% and increase sales tax from 10% to 15% with the result of an increase of the overall tax share of manufacturing sales, import duty and excise duty from 50% (1976/77) to 59% (1979/80).[353]

The reforms carried out during the first decade and a half of Kenya's independence dealt with taxation as and when there was a need. Fiscal policy was pragmatic – there was no reform or restructuring of the tax or budgetary system itself. This stemmed from the government trying to sort out problems as they arose without any long-term policy considerations. As a result, there were at first, ad hoc measures that because of increasing governmental expenditure and growth of economic structures that resulted in complicated, contradictory and cumbersome structures. Secondly, a trade policy was developed with an emphasis on reduction of trade barriers that led to the need to tax the citizens more heavily than before but at the same time trying to continually add onto the tax base. Thirdly, the resulting recession of the 1980s began with the oil crisis of the 1970s that led to long-term critical problems.[354] The persistence of deficits in the late 1970s have been attributed to the uncontrolled public expenditure and a possibly inelastic tax system.[355]

4.2.   TAX MODERNIZATION PROGRAMMES (1980-1992)

With the death of Kenyatta in 1978, Vice-president Moi took over the presidency until 1979 when he ran and won the seat as a sole candidate. Moi's presidency began with fiscal crisis in the wake of the end of the coffee boom, severe droughts and the second oil shock. He, however, adopted a general policy of following in the footsteps of Kenyatta and among other results was the continuing of the already existing corruption, clientelism and patronage politics of the 'big man'.[356] He also began the era of IMF loans with loan conditionalities. In 1982 Parliament declared KANU as the sole legal political party and there was stronger press censorship,

---

353   See generally Bevan, Collier and Gunning (1990)

354   Burgess and Stern (1993) 805

355   Moyi and Ronge (2006) 7

356   Murunga (2007) 125

increased political censorship and an attempted military coup with increased detentions. Additional state actions included closure of the University of Nairobi, the rise of left-wing opposition, constant re-shuffling, dismissal and forced resignation of political appointees from both government positions and KANU for criticising the state. This continued until 1992 when public pressure punctuated by riots and demonstrations and international pressure including withholding of loan and a refusal of further loans forced legislative changes allowing multiparty elections and free presidential elections.

After 16 years of independence there was no real fiscal reform. Kenya was a fairly closed economy, with the government controlling prices, interest rates and foreign exchange transactions. The downward spiral of the Kenyan economy from 1979 led to increased loan requests being put into the Breton Woods institutions. These institutions granted loans with attached loan conditionalities. As a result, this period was marked by legislative and policy reform of fiscal law at the behest of these institutions. These policy reforms included reforms to encourage investment, decreasing welfare provisions in order to increase revenue to pay off debts.

Import licensing was liberalized in 1980/81 and the government acquired 60% of the total increase in domestic credit.[357] However, a financial crisis in 1982/83[358] resulted in a shortfall in recurrent revenue. Inflation had been rising while the Balance of Payments had worsened with Gross Domestic Product (GDP) declining. In May 1980, the government projected a reduced growth rate between 1979 and 1983.[359] The expansionary policy had resulted in large amounts of money being spent on education, social services, agriculture and security. Government then pursued a policy of import substitution, which was used to rationalize high import

---

357   Working Paper on Government Expenditures in Kenya (1989)

358   There was also a political crisis at this time with the National Assembly declaring KANU as the sole legal party, an increase in press censorship and political detentions. Moi was re-elected for his second term as president with only 48% of the electorate casting ballots and this was followed by an attempted coup to overthrow the government with the subsequent arrest of Odinga as being responsible and subsequently placed under house arrest.

359   Sessional Paper no 4 "Economic Prospects and Policies" (1980). see appendix 7 262

duties. Globalisation proponents argue that in the end these policies resulted in the protection of inefficient industries.[360]

Policy has been geared towards wages and salaries in all sectors and away from non-wage goods. In its effort to remedy the lack of educational opportunities during the colonial period, the state recognized the importance of expanding opportunities in this sector. By the early 1980s, however, public sector expansion was extensive.[361] The government's heavy involvement in the market became increasingly outdated and primarily served the interests of narrow and kleptocratic elite. As a result, the state became a massive drain on investment and consumption and progressively lost its ability to provide the services it promised. Inflation rose from less than 4 percent in the early 1970s to 10 percent by 1981, and 22 percent by 1982.[362] When a fiscal crisis set in, the state strenuously tried to avoid externally imposed adjustment that would have limited its ability to deliver on promised entitlements.[363] It finally buckled under pressure, however, as the crisis was exacerbated by continued mismanagement, growing incompetence, and corruption.

Education was to be considered a social right and was underscored by early guarantees and efforts toward free and compulsory schooling up to grade four and, by the early 1980s, through seventh grade. Similarly, the state underwrote higher education by providing tuition waivers and living stipends that helped many who would otherwise not have been able to attend universities or other institutions of higher learning. The state's priority on education was reflected in its annual budget allotment of 40 percent (or 6 percent of GDP) to public education. Of this, 57 percent was spent on primary schooling, while 20 percent was directed at university education.[364]

The health sector reflected similar trends. Real spending on health increased from 81 in 1977 to 114 in 1981 to 81 in 1986 (in

---

360   See generally Bevan, Collier and Gunning (1990)
361   Swamy (1994) 198
362   *Ibid.* 199
363   *Ibid.* 193
364   *Ibid.* 227

1985 Kshs).[365] In the 1980s health expenditure averaged around 2 percent of GDP and registered impressive gains in health indices. For example, between independence and 1980, life expectancy rose from forty-two to fifty-eight years, while child mortality rates fell by more than half, from 200 deaths per 1,000 births to 83.[366] In 1980, although 20.5% of total expenditure was spent on education, the relative population growth between 1980 and 1990 was more than increase in expenditure. The allocation was not enough to even maintain recurrent expenses and thus very little was actually available for developing the education structures.[367] In 1989 and 1990 the government changed the policy to increase resources in health.[368] In 1990 there were widespread protests which resulted in the removal of outpatient registration fees. Outpatient attendance dropped by 50% and increased by 41% after the removal of fees. Treatment fees were reintroduced in 1992 linked to effective available treatment and with better exemption rules.[369]

Between 1980 and 1985 there was a GDP of 2.5% p.a. and concerns were raised about the productivity of government investments. The concerns were about inadequacy of provision for operations and maintenance of existing projects and a bias towards new programs; that had led to the build-up of white elephant projects. In the context of a fiscal crisis, the fifth development plan was launched in 1984[370] with major changes in revenue composition as part of the WB and IMF conditionalities. To stimulate industrial efficiency and competitiveness in export markets, tariffs and protectionism of domestic industries would be reduced. This culminated in the reduction of overall customs duty while increasing sales tax.[371] This was the commencement of trade liberalization policies, which are a main part of the SAPs. Secondly, there was a heavier reliance on cost sharing as a means of financing government services. While SAPs

---

365   Bruton, Hill and Banerji (1996) 153

366   Bradshaw and Wallace (1996) 69–70

367   Bruton, Hill and Banerji (1996)150–153

368   *Ibid.*14

369   See generally Collins, Quick, Musau, Kraushaar and Hussein (1996)

370   There was a drought and a food crisis in Kenya at this point

371   In 1984 the drug import duty was reduced by 12%, income tax brackets were increased from 1,500 to 1,800 and budget rationalization policies were given prominence..

were initially a reforms package for countries willing to implement them, they soon became the pre-condition for any donor assistance. Essentially, the reforms required governments to liberalise their economies, opening them up to local and foreign competition while also cutting down public sector employment and subsidies to reduce the government's spending burden. The government's wage bill would reduce, as would its overall expenditure burden since it would cease to finance free or subsidised health care, education and staple foods.

In 1986, the government implemented a new sessional paper[372] which explored methods of increasing tax collection to 24% of GDP by 1999/2000. The resulting policy favoured savings and investment and attempted to make tax revenue more responsive to changes in GDP. It proposed strengthening the involvement of the private and informal sectors and the community in the process of economic development and planning. It also resulted in the introduction of the Rural Trade and Production Centres to strengthen the implementation of the rural/urban balance strategy by emphasising the strengthening of rural-urban relationships and resource hinterlands.[373]

In 1986 and 1988 parliament enacted constitutional amendments limiting the independence of the judiciary and removing the security and tenure of the Attorney General, the Controller and Auditor General, the judges of the High Court and the Court of Appeal. Parliament, which at this time was under the control of the executive arm of the government, did not resist these amendments. The control of parliament and the judiciary meant that the office of the president was in a position to manipulate the functions of the two branches of the government. Both Parliament and the Judiciary ceased to have the constitutional rights to control the excesses of the Executive. When the Controller and Auditor General questioned why a state-owned corporation engaged the services of a private lawyer in this particular case,[374] his office became the object of executive branch criticism. Moi interpreted both of these actions as

---

372   Sessional Paper No. 1/86 on Economic Management for Renewed Growth (1986)

373   *Ibid.*

374   Maina (1996) 67

direct threats to his leadership and thus pressured parliament to enact the amendments to give him more authority over the judiciary and the audit department.[375] The police had, through Act 14 of 1988, the prerogative to detain the critiques of the regime for fourteen days while coercing them into submission. By this time parliament was functioning largely as a rubber stamp of policies initiated by the presidency.[376] This resulted in a compromise to the transparency, accountability and responsibility functions of the general governance and budgetary process.

Despite these changes in 1987 there was an improvement of exchequer receipts. The government aimed at placing a greater burden of tax structures on consumption in order to encourage savings and promote investments making sales tax the most significant contributor. In 1989, the sealing of loopholes on tax remission, improved climate, high world coffee and tea prices, increased domestic and international demand, trade liberalization and budget rationalisation boosted economic performance.[377]

In 1989, user fees, or 'cost-sharing' were introduced.[378] In 1989 severe budget constraints led to the introduction of user fees for outpatients and inpatients at government health facilities with exemptions for children under 5 years. User fees were abolished for outpatient care in 1990, after widespread protests and inspired by concerns about social justice, but re-introduced in 1992 because of budgetary constraints. Until recently, these fees have remained, with their impact on access to health care the subject of several empirical studies.[379]

Budget Rationalization Programme (BRP) was then introduced in mid 1980s to improve allocation of resources and link budgeting

---

375   Constitutional (Amendment) Act (1986)

376   Adar and Munyae (2001)

377   See appendix 6 261

378   See generally Dahlgren (1991)

379   See generally Mbugua, Bloom and Segall (1995); Mwabu, Mwanzia and Liambila (1995) 4; Moses, Manji, Bradley, Nagelkerke, Malisa and Plummer (1992) 5; Bitrán and Giedion (2003) 6; Collins, Quick, Musau, Kraushaar and Hussein (1996) and Xu, James, Carrin and Muchiri (2006).

with development priorities.[380] There was however no participation or consultation of society in budgetary decisions. However, by late 1980s it was realised that the Budget Rationalisation Programme could not itself achieve a higher level of strategic investment planning, a basis for forward budget and annual budget capital spending. The early 1990s was marked by falling tax revenues,[381] which were possibly compounded by the failure of the Structural Adjustment Plans (SAPs) by the World Bank and the IMF. The Public Investment Program (PIP) was introduced in the 1990s to strengthen the forward budget by providing a more comprehensive instrument for planning and prioritization of public spending in three categories– 'core', 'high priority' and 'others'[382]. It also aimed at strengthening the project cycle, introducing revenue forecasting and aid coordination in budgeting. The financing of the objectives was considered in terms of debt sustainability. Tax reform also began in earnest with the replacement of sales tax with Value Added Tax.[383]

From 1990 to the elections of 1992, Kenya was racked with political unrest including increased opposition to one-party rule. Multi-party rule was allowed in 1991 followed by elections in 1992 involving violence, exacerbating ethnic tensions and the arrest of political prisoners. Economically, the government inflated the money supply by 76% to finance their electoral campaign. Fears of the political leaders of an expected loss of power triggered the beginning of grand corruption and financial frauds like the Goldenberg fiscal scam,[384] using loopholes in the law to extract money from the state before elections in 1992. This resulted in an increase in the share of recurrent expenditure to over 70% of government revenue, leaving little or no space for societal welfare or development.[385]

---

380   See generally Peterson (2003)

381   See appendix 6

382   See generally Oyugi (2005)

383   Karingi and Wanjala (2005) 8

384   The total amount of illegal funds are estimated as between USD 3bn and USD 4bn, equivalent to about a third of Kenya's annual economic output. It is estimated that Kenya lost 10% of its GDP through this scandal. See Warutere (2005) 1

385   See appendix 8 263

4.3. DECENTRALISATION, PARTICIPATION AND EARMARKING (1993–2003)

President Moi was sworn in as President for two 5-year terms in 1993. This decade continued to be a period of slow growth, reduced donor aid[386] and a continual BOP problem. Tax reforms focused on raising revenue to meet specific economic policies. Pressure from the IMF and World Bank resulted in liberalisation and relocation of tax on imports, with the move being counter-balanced by increased tax on domestic transactions for revenue generation. The sixth National Development Plan recommended reduction of the budget deficit by increasing revenue through improved tax administration, reform in the tax structure as well as cost sharing.

Between 1976 and 1992, physical planning either retrogressed or stagnated, with the use of informal Part Development Plans (PDPs) to addressing localised needs. Although emphasis shifted to project oriented planning approaches, the development control machinery virtually collapsed in the face of political interference through clientelism and patronage. From the early 1990s, strategic planning was introduced, immediately associated with the Nakuru Strategic Structure Plan, which was centred on the implementation of the Agenda 21 Programme focusing on strategic development of the town in relation to the national, regional and citywide growth contexts. Emphasis was on community participation, environmental compatibility and implementation, to facilitate more efficient and sustainable planning and urban development. The approach required further refinement for extensive application.[387] The highlighting of inefficiency in public spending provided a possible rationale for decentralization of resource management. This resulted in earmarking and the creation of the Secondary School Education

---

386   See appendix 9 264

387   See generally Brown, Quiblier and United Nations. Environment Programme (1994) and Kenya Institute of Policy Research and Analysis (2006b). In 1982, the Local Authority Development Programme (LADP) was introduced in order to enable local authorities to draw out practical investment programmes in line with national development goals. However this was unsuccessful.

Bursary Fund launched in 1993/94[388] and the Road Maintenance Levy Fund in 1994.[389]

In 1995 as part of further loan conditionalities, administrative reform in revenue collection arm of the government was de-linked from the Ministry of Finance and the Kenya Revenue Authority (KRA) was created as a single purpose autonomous executive agency in line with the New Public Management framework to minimise political interference. The KRA was created with five overlapping accountability structures mandated by legislation and parliamentary scrutiny. These structures include frequent internal audits reports from the internal Controller General to the KRA Board; the CAG and to the Ministry of Finance, with annual reports from the Ministry to Parliament.[390] KRA has consistently exceeded revenue targets despite the slowing down of the economy.[391] Although statistics on corruption are often questionable, the available data suggest that it accounts for a significant proportion of economic activity. For example, in Kenya, "questionable" public expenditures noted by the Controller and Auditor General in 1997 amounted to 7.6 percent of GDP.

---

388   The Kenyan independence objective of creating an educated labour pool to substitute the departing colonial labour force saw the Government introduce a means-tested bursary scheme enabling qualified children from African households to continue with education. While the scheme's resources dwindled with the economic stagnation of the 1980s, a revitalised Secondary School Education Bursary Fund (SEBF) was re-launched in 1993/94 to ensure access for children from poor households while enhancing retention and completion rates. Its special focus would be orphans, children from slums, arid and semi-arid lands and girls, allocations depending on the number of schools and students in a constituency, and its poverty index. Nkinyangi (1982)

389   The restructuring of the Kenyan economy through the 1990s produced minimal tangible beneficial returns, the Government's poor service delivery capacity being evident in a deteriorating road infrastructure, for example. Reforms pushed for levies on road users, a 1994 Act of Parliament establishing the *Road Maintenance Levy Fund* (RMLF) targeting roads under the ministry, Kenya Wildlife Services and district roads committees. Levies were originally always collected at toll stations across the country, until mismanagement of RMLF revenues led to the 1999 establishment of the Kenya Roads Board to manage revenues collected as levies on fuel purchases. Sixty per cent of the revenues maintain international, national and primary roads, while 24% and 16% respectively go to secondary and rural roads. See generally Wasike (2001)

390   See generally Taliercio (2004)

391   Wahome (2009)

The institutional context of urban planning and development did not realize much improvement in terms of both the capacity of local authorities to effectively plan and manage urban development and the legal instruments available to facilitate effective control and guidance. The Local Government Act of 1963 was inadequate and the Physical Planning Act of 1996 was introduced and had far-reaching changes in the types and levels of plans to be prepared. In addition, further earmarking of levies was implemented in 1998 and 1999 through the Rural Electrification Programme Levy Fund (1998; but active from the late 1970s)[392]; Local Authority Transfer Fund (1999)[393] and District/Constituency HIV/AIDS fund (1999)[394] in response to the crisis facing the state in the sectors of electrification, petroleum and HIV/AIDS.

The continuing undermining of the accountability, transparency and responsibility of both national and regional governance resulted in the commencement of pockets of resistance to tax collection. Collective resistance against government taxation demands

---

392   The recognition of the potential role of electricity in rural development, especially in opening up enterprise opportunities, led the Government to launch a rural electrification scheme in 1973. Its exclusive management by power utility, Kenya Power and Lighting Company, resulted in the mismanagement as corruption and theft of resources as well as overemployment resulted in a drain of the scarce Government-provided resources. In 1998, the initiative was restructured into the *Rural Electrification Programme Levy Fund* (REPLF), created by sections 129 and 130 of the Electric Power Act (Act 11 of 1997). The Act imposed a 5% levy on all electricity consumption which the Government and other sources would augment to improve the rural targeting of the network, focusing on market centres and public institutions, amongst other areas.

393   Involvement of communities in local development has been a challenge for over four decades of Kenya's development. Odhiambo notes that the lack of participation of residents of local areas in service delivery and management has been highlighted as one of the factors contributing to poor service delivery. However, the various past decentralisation programmes, except the Local Government Reform Programme, did not put a framework for participation in place. The LGRP, through LATF/LASDAP, put in place a framework which has begun changing local development, although a lot of improvement is still required in the area of community participation. See generally Odhiambo, Mitullah and Akivaga (2006)

394   During the same year, the Government declared HIV/AIDS a 'national disaster' requiring a more focused attention leading to a Presidential Order in Legal Notice No. 170. The National AIDS Control Council was established to streamline the pandemic's management, leading to AIDS Control Units in all ministries, administration levels and constituencies. This led to the 1999 establishment of the District/Constituency HIV/AIDS Fund which channels care and support resources from the President's office to grassroots organisations fighting the scourge.

was almost non-existent since independence due to not only a previously oppressive political regime but also the lack of freedom of opinion. The first real resistance to a government levy took place when a residents Association representing the affluent residential area of Karen-Langata sued the Nairobi City Council for failure to supply the Association with budgetary records detailing how their tax revenue was being spent. The Association complained that garbage was not collected, roads had deteriorated, water supplies were unreliable and sewage pipes frequently burst and remained unattended. The Association demanded accountability for the Ksh. 803 million (USD 13.3 million) in annual service charges the Nairobi City Council collected from the ratepayers all of whom were members of the Association.[395] The High Court forced the Nairobi City Council to set up a joint fund with the Association and levy rates against its residents only through that fund. However, this initiative has not been undertaken by any other residential areas in the city.

Towards the end of the 1990s, the Government introduced the Medium Term Expenditure Framework (MTEF) budgeting system[396] and the Poverty Reduction Strategy Paper (PRSP) planning system. A medium term expenditure framework (MTEF) approach to budgeting was adopted for the first time for the 2000/2001 budget. Although this and other developments, such as programme-based planning and the use of a Poverty Reduction Strategy Paper have not been captured in legislation, they have a legal foundation – albeit a weaker one – based on guidelines. Poor forecasting, however, has been noted as part of the problems in budgetary planning, leading to poor quality of development projects partly due to internal "earmarking" which are then aggravated by unexpected business cycles.[397] Despite all these policies, social expenditure, which included expenditure on health, education and housing never added up to more than 10% of GDP since independence.[398]

---

395   Anon (2008)

396   See appendix 11

397   See generally Kiringai and West (2002) who state that revenue forecasts were also not made public, making it significantly harder to monitor the revenue side of the budget.

398   See appendix 10

It is expected that the MTEF would alleviate some of these problems both on the revenue and expenditure side. However, this will only be possible when it is developed as an all-inclusive process, with legally mandated participation by civil society, and full information disclosures through all the stages of the budget process. Under the MTEF, the future impact of current policies and new projects would be valued, and opportunity costs identified to facilitate trade-offs, which if properly used could lead to better consideration of the policy-based spending, provided the expenditure estimates are accurately framed and reliable resources were appropriated and executed as planned. Although the MTEF has brought in some civil society and private interest groups, at present this is only by invitation. The participants are neither legally entitled to be consulted, nor is the government bound to accept their ideas, as the process is operating based on patronage, which is not sustainable.

In 2000, as a result of calls for the reform and overhaul of government, a Constitutional Review process began that was said to have resulted in a 1 billion shilling expense by 2004. But, thus, far this has not resulted in a constitution.[399] CGD Policy Briefs for instance documented 475 billion Kenya shillings lost by the government between 1991 and 1997 through corruption, neglect, wastage and a "don't care" attitude of public officers. Analyzing the annual reports of the Controller and Auditor General (C&AG) covering the period between 1990/1991 and 1996/1997 also shows wasteful expenditure, undelivered goods and services, irregular payments, undeclared/uncollected revenue among others.[400]

Legislature at this point was given wider powers that included the right to introduce money bills, amend them, set their own salary and the parliamentary budget with proposals pending for judicial

---

399　In October 2000, the Government of Kenya passed The Constitution of Kenya Review Act (2000) mandating a Constitutional Review Commission to spearhead a constitutional review process which would culminate in a National Constitutional Conference. The review process was suspended in the run-up to the December 2002 general elections and was re-convened by the NARC government under President Kibaki. The National Constitutional Conference adopted Republic of Kenya: Draft Constitution of Kenya (2004) on March 15, 2004.

400　Center for Governance and Democracy (CGD) (2001)

review of their actions and the power to ratify the budget.[401] Thus, the status quo remains in place: an oppressive legislative system that gives too much discretion to parliament and government on fiscal matters, combined with a citizenry that remains generally inactive as concerns the use or misuse of their tax money.[402]

4.4.   DEVELOPMENT AND SOCIETAL PARTICIPATION (2003 TO DATE)

The Kenyan economy has recorded varying degrees of growth since the commencement of the presidency of Kibaki in 2003, which began with a declaration at the presidential inauguration that primary school education would be free. In 2004, the healthcare user fee system was significantly altered when health care at government dispensary and health centres were made free for all citizens, after a minimal registration fee in health facilities.

The economy had grown only by 1.1% in 2002. A growth momentum began in 2003 which grew in 2006 to 6.4% and in 2007 to 7%. However, the growth trend was disrupted by violence and uncertainties before and after the general and presidential elections of December 2007, and in 2008-2009 by the global financial crisis. Strong revenue collection meanwhile cut the budget deficit by 4.1 % of GDP in 2008/2009. It was expected that in 2009, the economy would grow at 3%.[403] However, these positive estimates remain clouded by continuing state mismanagement as Central Bank growth rates and inflation rates do not seem to tally with on the ground experiences.

Kenya's PRSP was incorporated into the government's strategy for reviving the economy after the poor growth years of the previous government, the *Economic Recovery Strategy for Wealth and Employment Creation 2003 – 2007*.[404] The PRSP required governments to specifically incorporate their strategies responding to citizens' views on how the poverty affecting them could be managed, into

---

401   Levy and Kpundeh (2004) 226

402   See generally Akech (2000)

403   Nyambura-Mwaura (2009)

404   Kenya Economic Recovery Strategy for Wealth and Employment Creation 2003-2007 (2003)

future appeals for development assistance from the World Bank/ IMF and other development partners. It is in the context of these concerns with poverty that the Government also introduced two decentralised funds in 2003, the Constituency Development Fund[405] and Free Primary Education Fund.[406] The PRSP required MPs to ascertain citizens' priorities, which would then be fed into policy through parliament and the MTEF subsequently locks into available financial resources.

However, the MTEF focuses on macro-economic issues at the expense of social sector issues. Budgeting would require that the MTEF process be also locked into welfare targets such as resources required, reducing child and maternal mortality, to provide safe drinking water, amongst others. The SB approach uses district observatories to identify priorities and mainstream spending through local institutions, such as CBOs, and regional authorities, giving the people themselves a chance to initiate the budget and sustain it. District observatories also monitor expenditure and budget implementation and could be very useful in monitoring the integration of decentralised funds into mainstream development plans.[407] In addition, the government added on Public Sector Hearings the first of which was held in 2005 where the Minister of Finance in April held a series of public and open meetings in order to hear the concerns of citizens as regards the use of fiscal resources.

In 2003 after declaring a government with no tolerance for corruption, international donors insisted on the creation of the Kenya Anti-Corruption Authority. It was created and despite constitutional and legislative impediments by 2009, 498 investigations had been completed and forwarded to the Attorney General. It had recovered corruptly acquired assets valued at Ksh 4.5 billion and conducted

---

405   This decentralised fund is discussed fully in chapter 6.

406   The second education fund covered Free Primary Education (FPE). Founded on NARC's election promise rather than any substantive law, FPE has since been incorporated into the Education ministry's KESSP 2005-2010 and Sessional Paper No. 1 of 2006. The scheme has been lucky to attract donor financing, receiving nearly USD 5bn for capital investment in its first operational year. FPE allocations per child are pre-determined by the Education ministry, and have been set at Kshs 1,020 per child since 2003, even though it has not always been possible to meet this figure, or even on time.

407   See generally Swallow (2005)

seven covert investigations leading to disruptions of corruption valued approximately at Ksh 4.66 billion.[408]

Despite these positive policy initiatives in 2003, government mismanagement included the use of USD 425,000 to purchase a home for the late Vice President's widow, and another USD 587,000 to pay off his private debts. In 2004, the state effectively wasted USD 137 million when it scrapped a police communications networking project four weeks before completion. They then announced plans to initiate essentially the same project for a cost of USD 187 million. As of April 2004, new task forces had cost the taxpayer USD 8.1 million.[409]

In 2004, the former head of the Kenya Anti-Corruption Authority, John Githongo, uncovered evidence that a nonexistent company called Anglo Leasing was awarded several huge government contracts. The scandal reached the highest levels of the Kenyan cabinet and cost the country as much as USD 1 billion. The Attorney-General must approve any prosecutions, however, and he declined to prosecute the case. The United Kingdom wanted to investigate Anglo Leasing itself, but the Attorney-General prevented its fraud office from moving forward. Kenyan lawyers and civil society members who advocate for good governance agreed that judicial reform was imperative.

Compliance surveys by KIPPRA, KRA and Ministry of Finance indicate that 51% of taxpayers view the corporate tax rates as high, while 29.8% view them as being fair. In addition, about 85.9% of taxpayers view PAYE rates being either very high or high. About 62.5% of taxpayers hire paid accountants to prepare VAT returns while 64.9% hire paid consultants to prepare the IT returns.[410] Research shows that compliance to VAT and income tax is 55 per cent and 30 per cent, respectively.[411] This implies that it should be possible to reduce the current taxpayers' burden by raising

---

408   Press Release: Achievements in Investigations (2009)

409   Kagari (2004)

410   Moyi and Ronge (2006) 26; see generally Kenya Institute of Public Policy Research and Analysis (2004)

411   Karingi and Wanjala (2005) 21

the compliance rate. In other words, it is possible to reduce the VAT rate from its current level of 16 per cent without any government revenue shortfall by increasing compliance. The same applies to CIT: even if the rate is reduced from 30 per cent to 25, a revenue-neutral position can be achieved by raising income taxation compliance.

Low compliance is mainly an administrative issue related to KRA, and their costly administrative structure itself contributes to the problem. For instance, a taxpayer in Kenya can be audited three times (for VAT, income tax, excise tax) but yet still be dealing with KRA only. Furthermore, if liable to a levy, the taxpayer may also be audited by government ministries. The tax-by-tax organization of KRA needs to be revisited. Best international practices suggest that revenue administration be organized according to function, so that audits are conducted as a single operation, and not by the type of tax.[412]

A successful area of tax advocacy by women's groups targeted VAT reductions on necessities that in Kenya include food and medical products. In Kenya, there was already a breaking ground action by women and women's rights organisations asking for a reduction of the price of sanitary pads in 2004 by removal of the 16% VAT levy because this was a necessity. The result of the call was the President ordering that the sanitary pads be zero rated immediately. The pads have remained zero rated ever since[413].

The W Nairobi W! Campaign[414], launched in 2004, and based in the Nairobi slum of Korogocho has so far made appeals to international donor agencies, namely the Italian Co-operation who now fund the Korogocho Slum Upgrading Programme working together with the Kenyan Government. Improving service delivery was pegged on the availability of external financing, with strict monitoring requirements. Campaigns and petitions to the city council and the national government failed due to lack of both political will and demonstrated taxpayer representation.

---

412   *Ibid.*
413   See generally Adongo and Rop (2004)
414   International Alliance of Inhabitants (2009)

The planning tended to be, however, skewed to the expenditure side within the government, while revenue forecasting is left to specialists at the KRA and the Ministry of Finance. In 2006, VAT collected was 25% of total revenue. The long-term development strategy, Vision 2030, whose implementation began in June 2007, is similarly built on the three pillars of achieving higher growth, rising to 10% by 2012; achieving Equity and Poverty reduction, and governance. Kenya's development strategy since 2003 has been export-led and private sector-driven. This means that the focus of the strategy is to create a conducive environment for private sector development and maintain macroeconomic stability.

The Kenya Bribery Index 2007 by Transparency International reported twice as many bribes paid in 2006 as compared to the previous year. In 2007, the National Taxpayers Association was founded by a group of CSOs with the mandate of creating a citizen's report card to ascertain societal requirements in order to allow lobbying for fiscal resources to focus on improvement of the delivery of services to the people including health, education and security. In addition, to improve governance by improving citizen-government accountability as well as citizen–citizen accountability.[415] The NTA also had a mandate to monitor the CDF, which allowed for citizens' participation albeit to a limited extent. The CDF is the case study of this thesis and the subject of analysis on both the issues of participation, welfare and accountability and will be discussed in more detail in Chapter 6. The CDF linked the revenue to the expenditure for the first time in Kenya's history and required that it be distributed for the purposes of development. This fund is a culmination at a micro level of the operation of government and its link to society, and the fiscal legitimacy of this fund like many of the other devolved funds connects back towards the fiscal legitimacy of the state. However, this fund like the others has also been faced with many challenges and is currently under scrutiny by the state and citizens.

---

415   National Taxpayer's Association (2006)

4.5. THE 2010 CONSTITUTION OF THE REPUBLIC OF KENYA

On 27 August 2010, Kenya promulgated a new Constitution that also overhauled its finance provisions. Although currently the legislation in place remains the same, Kenya is at the cusp of creating an entirely new legislative regime that will change the manner in which tax is collected and re-distributed.

4.6. CONCLUSION

The Kenyan post-colonial fiscal state has encountered difficulties that have limited the development of the characteristics discussed in the OB model. These include limited resources, poor management and governance as well as the lack of accountability, transparency and responsibility to the citizens of the state. In addition, the most critical need of society, the improvement of its well-being, has been neglected. The Kenyan state as a result has characteristics of the tax state.

In order to truly achieve the level of the fiscal state, there is a need to address well-being and social welfare and improve it. However, not only is the state faced with limited resources in the form of low collections of taxes, poor accountability and governance, a very low proportion of taxes are spent on development initiatives and welfare. Finally, taxes remain in force as an oppressive tool of governance and this obstacle is further crippled by inadequate accountability for spending decisions and little or no public participation in the decisions on collection and re-distribution of tax.

Currently, Kenya like many post-colonial developing countries is grappling with how to improve the living standards and well-being of people within their limited resources. There has been little legislative reform until the most recent period from 2003 onwards and no constitutional fiscal reform. The development strategies and reforms instigated over the years by both internal and external actors seem to have brought some changes in improvement of certain services and improved revenues intermittently, but Kenya has in no way progressively improved the living standards of its citizens. As a result one can conclude that the movement from the tax to the fiscal state has not been realised.

However, since 2003 with the introduction of the MTEF and the PRSPs, culminating in the setting up of the National Taxpayer's Association, there seems to be an increase in not only the awareness of taxpayer rights but also the need to improve the awareness. Citizen awareness especially in urban areas seems to be progressively increasing as well as taxpayer actions. How this can be maintained and whether a better control or relationship can be developed between the citizens and the state forms the basis of the subsequent chapters which will enquire into human rights.

The people perceive the state as demanding taxes without actually providing adequate or any commensurate services seen by the sporadic taxpayer suits, however, these are mired with a set of difficulties including the lack of independence of the Kenyan judiciary. The failure of both the state and citizens to understand each other has led to the failure to demand rights. The absence of guidelines on citizens' requirements as well as checks on government discretionary power has led to an impasse in the development of the fiscal state and the improvement of the welfare state provisions of the Kenyan post-colonial fiscal state. This in turn has led to a crisis of the fiscal post-colonial developing state as it plunges further into debt and aid-dependency. Thus it may be now time for the re-analysis of the developing country and its 'fiscal' state and consider an alternative to the current defective accountability, transparency and responsibility in state tax policy taking all of the country specific and unique criteria in consideration, and perhaps looking at an alternative approach to address the problems that seem to be persistent obstacles to the attempt to realise the improved social welfare and well-being which in turn will improve the fiscal legitimacy of the Kenyan state today.

PART 2

HUMAN RIGHTS AND STATE FISCAL RESOURCES

CHAPTER 5

REALISING HUMAN RIGHTS THROUGH TAXATION

In the previous chapters the discussion and analysis drew out the obstacles faced by the Kenyan post-colonial fiscal state in achieving improved well-being. The various legislative and policy initiatives undertaken and pursued in Kenya thus far have not achieved their goals of improved well-being; raised living standards; development and poverty alleviation. One of the biggest obstacles to achievement of the fiscal state identified in the preceding chapter is that of accountability of fiscal resources.

With traditional fiscal policies seeming to be unsuccessful, this thesis will proceed on the basis that a possible solution may lie in a multidisciplinary approach. Tax academicians and scholars have not traditionally approached the analysis of tax law and policy from a multidisciplinary perspective and there is no literature on a multidisciplinary approach to tax law using human rights or vice versa. Tax scholars make no reference to human rights with the recent exception of an article by Mumford who discussed rights of fathers and taxes utilising fiscal sociology.[416] Similarly, human rights scholars have also largely ignored the issue of fiscal requirements to the realisation of human rights and this has been referred to most recently by Alston in a two-page discussion.[417]

This chapter will discuss a possible solution to the fiscal crisis and the need to improve fiscal legitimacy of Kenyan post-colonial state from a multidisciplinary perspective of tax and human rights. From the perspective of society, this can be achieved by increasing the standard of living and well-being of society through visibly accountable re-distribution of the state's fiscal resources. The chapter will posit and explore the idea that the application of human rights law and policy in the re-distribution of the state's fiscal resources will

---

416   See generally Mumford (2008)
417   Steiner, Alston and Goodman (2007) 305-306

not only improve well-being and accountability but also improve the fiscal legitimacy of the state.

As a result, the approach undertaken in this chapter has a two-fold impact. Not only may the utilisation of human rights as a policy in taxation solve the issue of the legitimacy of the fiscal state through improved fiscal accountability, but it may also possibly answer the dilemma of the realisation of human rights. Providing improved welfare using state resources will be discussed from the perspective of the expenditure characteristic in the OB model. Human rights will be considered as an element in the characteristics of the typology of the fiscal state to chart the development of the post-colonial fiscal state and guide its development to the ultimate fiscal achievement, the improvement and maintenance of the well-being and social welfare of society as envisaged by Schumpeter. The proposition of the application of human rights law will be argued based on the critiques to the Schumpeterian model of the welfare state as applied in the context of the post-colonial fiscal state as set out in the preceding chapter.

In order to do this, this chapter will discuss why human rights may solve the legitimacy issue for tax and simultaneously tax may solve the realisation dilemma in human rights. It will analyse the genesis, background and continuing development of the realisation of human rights from the perspective of a state's fiscal resources and how they can and do impact upon the legitimacy of the fiscal state. The first part of this chapter will discuss the nature of human rights and how they impact on welfare, making them a possible alternative approach to fiscal expenditure. The second part will analyse the state and its obligations in respect of the human rights treaties it has ratified and the obstacles to the use of human rights in fiscal re-distribution policies. The final part will discuss the continuing development in human rights being spearheaded by post-colonial states that have developed welfare, accountability and governance provisions specifically impacting tax law and policy and which if used may improve fiscal legitimacy.

The lens with which the following analysis will be undertaken is with reference to over 100 years of the Kenyan post-colonial fiscal state discussed in the preceding chapters as well as the historical background and evolution of human rights law today. Thus the discussion of the application of human rights that follows stems directly from the context of the Kenyan post-colonial fiscal state. As the focus of this study is Africa and Kenya, this chapter will emphasize developing states, Africa and the Kenyan approach towards human rights obligations and the question of their fiscal realisation. It will limit discussion to the international and regional treaties and conventions that Kenya is state party to and the efforts that Kenya has made in achieving these rights and obligations. Thus, the international stand that Kenya has taken as well as the practical internal application of human rights that the Kenyan state is following in its resource allocation will be broadly referred to using human rights benchmarks and principles.

5.1.   THE PARALLELS BETWEEN WELL-BEING, SOCIAL WELFARE AND HUMAN RIGHTS

Social welfare and well-being were conceptualised and discussed in chapter 1 and the challenges to its realisation were seen in the context of the Kenyan state in chapters 2 and 3. The preceding chapter placed the Kenyan post-colonial state today predominantly in the stage of the tax state. The concept of social welfare is the main goal in Schumpeter's discourse of transitioning the tax state to the fiscal state. This section will thus attempt to ascertain whether the fiscal policies geared towards social welfare can be also geared towards human rights, and thus whether there are similarities and parallels to be drawn between these concepts in order to apply fiscal policies in the achievement or realisation of human rights. There are several issues to be considered in drawing this parallel: they are the similarities and differences in firstly, the content of welfare and human rights; secondly, the obligations that both these concepts place on the state and finally, the fiscal burden involved in their realisation.

5.1.1.   Conceptualising Social Welfare, Well-being and Human Rights

Social welfare in fiscal systems has been considered in Chapter 1 and can best be summarised as the provision of goods and services that improve the well-being of individuals and groups within society. Social welfare objectives include among others, direct spending for income on security, housing, health care, education, employment and training, and social services. Society perceives states that provide social welfare as providing guarantees for a minimum standard of living, protecting citizens from loss of income beyond their control, especially retirement, sickness, disability or unemployment including public assistance and social insurance, serving both the poor and the middle class.[418]

In addition, social welfare scholars most notably T. H. Marshall set out a model of the evolution of the rights of citizens in the Western world, using the UK as the case study. He argued that civil rights developed first followed by political rights and finally, economic or social rights was introduced gradually in the nineteenth and twentieth centuries.[419] There is thus a comparable division created in the development of the rights of man or welfare rights into three stages.

The post-war human rights movement used the concept of the indivisibility of fundamental rights and freedoms to justify the development of social welfare provisions by liberal governments.[420] One question that arises constantly for welfare state scholars is that if the arguments are to stand, then, are not human rights part of the welfare state itself, or alternatively is welfare not part of human rights? Some authors see welfare as a basic human right to be considered alongside life, liberty and property.[421] Louis Henkin, while commenting on the welfare state in the United States in the mid-1990s, stated that the welfare state and all other rights are so deeply

---

418   See generally Pampel and Williamson (1989); Marmor, Mashaw and Harvey (1990) and Meeting the Challenge to Fiscal Legitimacy through Well-Being

419   See generally Marshall (1950)

420   Mclaughlin and Baker (2007) 55

421   Plant (1986) 22

entrenched in the society that they have near-constitutional status, and that Americans have begun to think and speak of social security and other benefits as an entitlement and right.[422] Onora O'Neill argues that it is impossible to proclaim universality of rights in goods and services with reference to welfare rights without connecting the right-holder to an obligation-bearer, leaving the content obscure. She goes on to argue that the absence of institutionalisation of the right to development renders it useless.[423]

Welfare rights are seen by some to be different from the classical rights of life, liberty and property in the nature of the content. Classical rights are said to be rights to freedom of action whereas welfare rights are rights to goods. Liberty rights are seen as those that govern individual interactions, though they do not guarantee success, while welfare rights are the right to have goods and services provided by others if one could not earn them themselves. In addition, liberty rights require a resource outlay that involves or includes security issues in order mainly to uphold laws. The implementation of welfare rights is seen to involve huge capital outlay and use of tax money. Finally, it is also argued that the implementation of liberty rights does not require resources in that the ability of people to forbear from doing certain activities does not result in a function of wealth. There is no universal and non-arbitrary standard for distinguishing need from luxury and thus defining the content of welfare rights. This is dependent upon the relative wealth of a society.[424]

> You cannot have a right unless it can be claimed or demanded or insisted upon, indeed claimed effectively or enforceably. ...rights thus are performative-dependent, their operative reality being their claimability; a right one could not merely be 'imperfect' – it would be a vacuous attribute.[425]

This statement is what funds and fuels the distinction that remains and that which is maintained by some social welfare scholars to keep human rights in a separate category. They argue that what society claims as a right may be contradicted by its substance or

---

422   Henkin (1984) as quoted in Steiner and Alston (2000) 251
423   O'Neill (1996)131-32
424   Kelley (2000)259
425   Stoljar (1984) 3-4

administration. Thus the issue of equality of right is used to exclude social welfare benefits from the 'rights' category by some human rights scholars.[426]

There are three main core texts that are the source of all discourse on human rights: the UDHR, ICCPR and ICESCR. All these texts do not specifically contain a definition of human rights; however they state that the purpose of human rights is to enhance human dignity.[427] Broadly speaking, as a result, human rights are the concrete expression of values that are designed to enhance human dignity. Contemporary thought is what gives these values the form of rights bestowed on individuals and groups.

Some scholars regard the absence of a definition of human rights as an impediment to its realisation. However, Donnelly regarded it as a sign of its continually evolving content which reflects the relationship of society within itself and with the state.[428] This approach will be adopted in this thesis as it allows one to draw into human rights the existing concepts of welfare and well-being. Human rights and human dignity can thus be perceived as the modern-day interpretation of social welfare as espoused by Schumpeter and economic and welfare scholars. This then allows the discussion of welfare and human rights to proceed as one with the improvement of human rights of people part of the ultimate expenditure aim of the development of a state into a fiscal state.

From the initial broad starting point in the UDHR, ICCPR and ICESCR the content of human rights obligations have developed very significantly. The content of the these texts list out human rights to include: the right to life, liberty and security of the person; freedom from slavery and servitude; freedom from torture or cruel, inhuman and degrading treatment; to recognition everywhere as a person before the law; equality before the law and without any discrimination to equal protection of the law; effective remedy by the competent national tribunals; arbitrary arrest, detention or exile; full equality to a

---

426   See generally Sampford and Galligan (1986)1-19

427   United Nations General Assembly. Universal Declaration of Human Rights (1948) article 1

428   Donnelly (2003) 1

fair and public hearing by an independent and impartial tribunal; right to be presumed innocent until proved guilty; protection of the law against such interference or attacks; right to freedom of movement and residence; right to seek and to enjoy in other countries asylum; right to a nationality; right to marry and to found a family; right to own property; right to freedom of thought, conscience and religion; freedom of opinion and expression; right to freedom of peaceful assembly and association; right to take part in the government;[429] right of equal access to public service in his country; right to social security; right to work, right to rest and leisure, right to a standard of living adequate for the health and well-being, right to education; right freely to participate in the cultural life of the community.[430]

Regionally African states formed the African Union and have negotiated and created a regional human rights treaty, the ACHPR.[431] This treaty includes all of the rights listed above except for the right to social welfare and additionally recognises both individual and peoples rights, family protection by the state,[432] guarantees peoples the right to equality,[433] the right to self-determination,[434] to freely dispose of their wealth and national resources,[435] the right to development,[436] the right to peace and security[437] and the right to a generally satisfactory environment.[438]

---

429   Whereas all these rights are in the UDHR those listed thus far are only in the ICCPR and not the ICESCR.

430   Although the entire set of listed rights are found in the United Nations General Assembly. Universal Declaration of Human Rights (1948) articles 1–27, the latter half from the right of equal access to public services are the content of the ICESCR.

431   A Charter is not legally binding, but it is worthwhile referring to as it constitutes the expression, at the highest level, of a democratically established consensus on what is considered as the catalogue of fundamental rights for all. The recognition of the African Charter is based on its application, use and the weight of its recommendations which are mere recommendations and not enforceable.

432   Organisation of the African Unity. African Charter of Human and Peoples' Rights (1982) article 18

433   *Ibid.* article 19

434   *Ibid.* article 20

435   *Ibid.* article 21

436   *Ibid.* article 22

437   *Ibid.* article 23

438   Organisation of the African Unity. African Charter of Human and Peoples' Rights (1982) article 24

Over the years the content, purpose, applicability, realisation and enforcement of human rights continues to be questioned, evolve and grow. Today, additional international instruments have been developed with the recognition of more states internationally that have added their voices to the discourse of international human rights law. The framework for international human rights law allows for additions to the list of rights to be included in the content of human rights through additional treaties, covenants, declarations and resolutions. These newer rights added onto the continually evolving list of rights include the right to development, peace and a healthy environment.[439] It also makes provision for states to deviate from these rights through a system of reservations to the international treaties.[440]

Domestically, a state chooses what will form the list of human rights of its citizens by signing and ratifying a treaty or refusing to do so. Today, most states of the world have signed and ratified these treaties.[441] Some states have either not signed or ratified both these treaties,[442] while certain states like the USA and South Africa have abstained from ratifying the ICESCR.[443] Kenya became a member of the United Nations in 1963 after it gained independence and adopted the UDHR. Its international human rights treaty status remained the same until 1976 when Kenya signed and acceded

---

439   Henkin (1987) 198

440   In addition, in practice, national deviations are not really permitted. The UN Committees don't allow differences in interpretation between states, and from the HRC's general comment 24 it would seem that most of the reservations that try to change the content of the obligations are actually not valid.

441   United Nations (2004). The ICCPR was concluded in 1966 and has been ratified by 152 states, 45 states however are not yet party to this treaty and 8 states have signed it but have not as yet ratified it. The ICESCR has been ratified by 146 states, 51 states are not yet party to the treaty, and 8 states have signed it but have not as yet ratified it.

442   The following states have signed but not ratified both treaties: China, Comoros, Cuba, Guinea-Bissau, Laos, Nauru, Pakistan and São Tomé and Príncipe. States that have neither signed nor ratified it include Antigua and Barmuda, Bahamas, Bhutan, Brunei, Burma (Myanmar), Fiji, Kiribati, Malaysia, Marshall Islands, Micronesia, Oman, Palau, Qatar, Saint Kitts and Nevis, Saint Lucia, Saudi Arabia, Singapore, Solomon Islands, Tonga, United Arab Emirates, Vanuatu and Vatican City (through the Holy See).

443   States that have neither signed nor ratified the ICESCR but have signed and ratified the ICCPR include Andorra, Haiti, Mozambique, Nauru, South Africa, United States of America.

to both the international covenants[444], the International Covenant on Economic, Social and Cultural Rights (ICESCR)[445] and the International Covenant on Civil and Political Rights (ICCPR).[446] To date, Kenya has signed and ratified 7 of the 9 core international human rights treaties[447] in addition to several other treaties.[448] Regionally, Kenya is party to the 1986 African Charter on Human and Peoples' Rights (ACHPR)[449] in addition to several other regional treaties and protocols.[450] Kenya has not registered any reservations to any of the international human rights treaties, declarations, charters, covenants or protocols to which it is a party. As a result, Kenya has shown that by ratifying these treaties it has accepted that its citizens are entitled to all the rights listed above.

---

444 These covenants or treaties are internationally legally binding.

445 Ratified on 3/1/76 with a reservation to article 10(2). Office of the United Nations High Commissioner for Human Rights (2004)

446 Ratified 23/3/76 without reservation. Office of the United Nations High Commissioner for Human Rights. Ratification Status of the ICCPR (2004)

447 The International Convention on the Elimination of All Forms of Racial Discrimination ratified 13 Sept. 2001; Convention on the Elimination of All Forms of Discrimination against Women ratified 24 August 1984; Convention against Torture and Other Cruel, In-human or Degrading Treatment or Punishment ratified 21 Feb. 1990; Convention on the Rights of the Child ratified 30 July 1990; International Convention on the Protection of the Rights of all Migrant Workers and Members of Their Families not ratified; Convention on the Rights of Persons with Disabilities ratified 19 May 2008; International Convention for the Protection of All Persons from Enforced Disappearance signed 6 Feb. 2007, not ratified

448 Kenya also has ratified the Optional Protocols to the Children's Rights Convention on the rights of children in armed conflict and on the prohibition of child trafficking, prostitution and pornography. In June 2005, Kenya ratified the Rome Statute for the International Criminal Court. Kenya has so far not ratified the Optional Protocols to the human rights treaties which enable individuals to submit complaints to the UN treaty bodies.

449 These regional treaties support the implementation of human rights on the regional level, and often reflect additional human rights concerns particular to specific cultural contexts.

450 Ratified the Convention Governing Specific Aspects of Refugee Problems in Africa, and the African Charter on the Rights and Welfare of the Child. By ratification of the Protocol to the ACHPR on the Establishment of an African Court on Human and Peoples' Rights (African Court) in 2005 Kenya has accepted the jurisdiction of the African Court but not on individual complaints. The Maputo Protocol to the ACHPR on the Rights of Women in Africa has not yet been ratified by Kenya.

5.1.2. THE STATE OBLIGATIONS UNDER SOCIAL WELFARE AND HUMAN RIGHTS

By deciding to apply a particular policy or pass a certain law and adopt a treaty a state evinces an intention to desist from or carry out certain actions. The parallels between well-being and human rights are already clearly seen in the immediately preceding sub-section and they use different terms but encompass the same broad areas: the improvement of the living standards of their citizens.

Historically, well-being and social welfare were and are policies applied by governments domestically through their domestic political process as a result of the society electing leaders who intend to apply certain policies. Over the years this policy has been adopted by many states both with and without reference to their particular political leanings. For example, the UK, which is a capitalist state also applies social welfare policies and provides among other services, state subsidised education and health services. Human rights on the other hand have developed internationally and are subsequently applied within the domestic state.

As a result, although these concepts all address broadly the same content, the concept of well-being developed first in time followed by social welfare and finally human rights. With their continuing development the obstacles and solutions are also continually being addressed. The first challenge to the achievement of social welfare and a challenge that continues to face human rights is their realisation: limited resources.

The first Constitution to address the issue of resources was the French Declaration of 1789. It recognised the transfer of the responsibility for security to the state in exchange for money in its articles 13 and 14:

> 13. A common **contribution** is essential **for** the **maintenance** of the **public forces** and for the cost of **administration.** This should be equitably distributed among all the citizens in proportion to their means.

> 14. **All the citizens have a right to** decide, either personally or by their representatives, as to the necessity of the public contribution;

to grant this freely; to know to what uses it is put; and to **fix the proportion, the mode of assessment and of collection and the duration of the taxes**.[451]

Following from this, the Constitution of France of 1793 declared:

> Society owes subsistence to its unfortunate citizens either by giving them work or assuring them the means to exist if they are incapable of work.[452]

From a historical perspective, it can be argued that the French tax state was first codified here through the recognition of the link between resources and welfare or human rights in its Constitution. The citizens were granted the right to control the state's resources and at the same time were granted the right to work and the constitutional authorisation to set up what were the rudimentary beginnings of modern social welfare.

Industrialisation was the next point in history when the concept of resources allocated to rights was recognised. Large-scale production and labour resulted in the mistreatment of workers by the factory owners. This led to an outcry and the creation of workers' rights. The 'rights of man' were extended to include the male working classes. The states going through industrialisation went through labour activism and trade unions demanded better treatment of people.[453] With time this translated into government policy changes and the development of civil and political rights. It is out of the context of class struggle and exploitation that the second generation rights developed and socio-economic rights now emerged.[454]

Despite this groundbreaking step in linking rights to resources in the French Constitution, this development did not spread to other states. Instead the world was split on the basis of class, race, gender as well as other historical factors that led to the neglect of the need to fund the improvement of the well-being of the society using its

---

451   Declaration of the Rights of Man (1789) 1
452   Constitution of the Republic of France (1793)
453   Mill (1963) 366
454   Lauren (2003) 53-55

available resources, and political and civil rights took precedence over the socio-economic rights.

The period from World Wars I and II was the period when human rights were institutionalised through firstly, the creation of the League of Nations, the International Labour Organisation and the United Nations and secondly, through the granting of self-determination to colonies.[455] It is in this background of the development of states that one discovers the commencement of negotiations on human rights. In 1948 after World War II, of the 51 founding members[456] of the United Nations only 32 states were involved in the actual debates surrounding the creation of the Universal Declaration of Human Rights (UDHR).[457] A major step was then taken in the elaboration of the general principles of the UDHR in two Covenants: the ICCPR[458] and the ICESCR.[459]

The UDHR, ICCPR and ICESCR were all affected by several factors. Firstly, like all other international documents, they are politically negotiated documents and a compromise not only in principles but in the use of deliberately vague terminology in their phrasing.[460] Although the document that results from the negotiations is one with legally binding obligations, the process of negotiations involving many states having diverging ideas and philosophies resulted inevitably in a broad and unspecific text.[461]

---

455   Weston (1992)

456   Argentina, Australia, Belgium, Bolivia, Brazil, Byelorussian Soviet Socialist Republic, Canada, Chile, China, Colombia, Costa Rica, Cuba, Czechoslovakia, Denmark, Dominican Republic, Ecuador, Egypt, El Salvador, Ethiopia, France, Greece, Guatemala, Haiti, Honduras, India, Iran, Iraq, Lebanon, Liberia, Luxembourg, Mexico, Netherlands, New Zealand, Nicaragua, Norway, Panama, Paraguay, Peru, Philippine Republic, Poland, Saudi Arabia, Syria, Turkey, Ukrainian Soviet Socialist Republic, Union of South Africa, Union of Soviet Socialist Republics, United Kingdom, United States, Uruguay, Venezuela, Yugoslavia.

457   United Nations (2009)

458   United Nations General Assembly. International Covenant on Civil and Political Rights (1966)

459   United Nations General Assembly. International Covenant on Economic, Social and Cultural Rights (1966)

460   Alfredsson and Eide (1999) 49-52

461   Lauren (2003) 9-11

Secondly, in 1948, when the UDHR was negotiated it was a product of the culmination of the two world wars, a period of limited fiscal resources for all states, as well as the political and philosophical divide between the capitalistic and communist philosophies.[462] Donnelly argues the content of any document must be read in its historical and political context at the time of negotiation.[463] Although the UDHR itself did not recognise the ideological divide, this did result in its provisions being limited to a 'mere' declaration. The declaration was drawn up on the basis of natural law which considers the principles as expressing inherent rights.

Thirdly, the issue of realisation was also not fully explored, instead after lengthy discussions; it was left to the state under the provision of state sovereignty.[464] This divide manifested itself clearly when the negotiations of the ICESCR and the ICCPR reached a stalemate due to the different political stands of capitalist states that only wanted to give preference to civil and political rights and communist states that preferred economic and social rights.

It was only in 1965 when the newly recognised states including Kenya continued the push for the creation of internationally recognised human rights instruments which they perceived as both a method of protecting their recently achieved independence and a recognition of the equality of all people, that the texts of the ICCPR and ICESCR were finally agreed upon.[465] However, the ideological divide between capitalist and communist states could not be overcome and the result was two separate treaties. Although a group of 19 states actually urged that the UN Commission on human rights give higher priority to economic, social and cultural rights, they settled to urging states through the HRC that equal

---

462 Alfredsson and Eide (1999) 29. This divide today can itself be seen to be in an identity crisis with the end of the Cold War. Smith (1997) 6

463 Donnelly (2003) 1. This is now considered well settled in human rights circles. See generally Zeleza and McConnaughay (2004).

464 Alfredsson and Eide (1999) 6

465 The activity of the newly independent states led to the introduction first of the Declaration on the Granting of Independence to Colonial Countries and Peoples in 1960 and later in 1965 the Declaration on the Elimination of all Forms of Racial Discrimination. Lauren (2003) 242-244. By 1966 the UN had 122 member states.

budgetary and human resources be devoted to each of the two sets of rights.[466]

5.2.   THE HUMAN RIGHTS OBLIGATIONS ON A STATE

Once a state becomes a signatory to the diverse treaties, it takes on the duty to protect, promote and respect human rights. This duty has been set out from the commencing clause of the UN Charter,[467] later in the Tehran Declaration[468] and the Vienna Declaration[469] and most recently in 2004 by a General Assembly Resolution[470] through General Comment 31 where it was stated at paragraph 5 that:

> The obligations of the Covenant in general and article 2 in particular are binding on every State Party as a whole. All branches of government ... are in a position to engage the responsibility of the State Party.[471]

The above comment places the realisation of rights on the government. There was no further step taken to concretise what fiscal implications a statement of this nature entails. Instead, the international community avoided reference to the issue of resources, especially domestic resources like tax revenue and its allocation on the grounds of the sovereignty of nations and the importance of allowing states to pursue their own economic policies. General Assembly resolutions reaffirmed that states should not interfere in the domestic policies of other countries.[472]

---

466   See UN Doc. E/CN.4/1999/120, paragraph 103(b) as discussed in Steiner and Alston (2000) 250

467   United Nations. Charter of the United Nations (1945) article 55

468   United Nations General Assembly. Proclamation of Tehran (1968)

469   United Nations General Assembly. Vienna Declaration and Program of Action: World Conference on Human Rights (1993). The 1993 Vienna Declaration that has been adopted by over 170 states.

470   General Assembly resolutions to be non-binding. Articles 10 and 14 of the UN Charter refer to General Assembly as "recommendations"; the recommendatory nature of General Assembly resolutions has repeatedly been stressed by the International Court of Justice. However, some General Assembly resolutions dealing with matters internal to the United Nations, such as budgetary decisions or instructions to lower-ranking organs, are clearly binding on their addressees.

471   United Nations General Assembly. Nature of the General Legal Obligation Imposed on States Parties to the Covenant (2004)

472   Examples include United Nations General Assembly. Declaration on Friendly Relations between States (1970) and United Nations; United Nations General Assembly. Resolution on the Permanency of Sovereignty over Natural Resources (1962)

A further analysis into the specificity of terminology regarding resource allocation, within the international arena leads to the use of the terms the 'limitation to resources' or resource 'constraints'. These terms are used repeatedly almost as a refrain while espousing 'progressive realization' of human rights 'obligations'.[473] These terms are used to allow the delimitation and exclusion by states from the human rights obligation of undertaking their obligations.

Under human rights law, the state has the primary responsibility to respect, protect and fulfil the human rights of all those in its territory. The conventions, declarations, resolutions and comments together all set out the minimum standards that states agree to be bound by. However, the method used to meet these standards is seen as a matter of state concern. By participating in the international human rights framework, states agree to undertake that their Constitutions, laws, policies, and budgets reflect these legal obligations and those policies will be applied in order that they move towards achieving these minimum standards.[474]

Rights, therefore, only become more than mere declarations if they confer power on bodies whose decisions are legally binding. Thus the people who do not live in a state having effective remedies in reality have no legally enforceable rights.[475] Any and all legal rights exist in reality only when and if they have budgetary costs. In the claims to grant the right to free education, for example, this will only take place in reality and on the ground in the country if there are adequate resources to build schools near communities that require this service. In the Kenyan case as discussed in the preceding chapter free education was set out as a right upon independence but only in 2003 did the government actually make it fiscally and legally possible.

Discourse on the state's obligation to respect, fulfil and protect human rights has led to the division of human rights into the immediately realisable civil and political rights and the progressively

---

473   Human Rights Committee (1990)

474   See generally Twomey (2007)

475   European Union. European Convention on Human Rights (1953) article 13 states that rights are reliably enforced when subscribing states treat them as domestic law.

realisable economic, social and cultural rights. It was initially perceived that civil and political rights were negative and did not require state intervention or fiscal resources whereas economic, social and cultural rights were a fiscal burden and on the basis of limited resources required progressive realisation. The choice to provide the latter rights was left to the political leanings of states. As a result states that felt that economic and social rights were not their main responsibility did not sign and ratify the ICESCR. The US believes in the self-funding of most services, whereas states like Russia, following communist and socialist ideology, attempted to provide these services and so were willing to sign and ratify the ICESCR. In addition, traditional human rights scholars argued that the implementation of welfare rights involved a large outlay of resources, while the implementation of liberty rights do not require resources in that they are obligations on the state to refrain from certain activities. The realisation of economic and social rights was left entirely dependent upon the relative wealth of a society.[476]

The Committee on Economic, Social and Cultural Rights set out this distinction best in General Comment number 3:

> The principal obligation of result reflected in article 2 (1) is to take steps "with a view to achieving **progressively** the full realization of the rights recognized" in the Covenant. The term "**progressive realization**" is often used to describe the intent of this phrase. The concept of progressive realization constitutes a recognition of the fact that full realization of all economic, social and cultural rights will generally not be able to be achieved in a short period of time. In this sense **the obligation differs significantly** from that contained in article 2 of the ICCPR which embodies an **immediate obligation** to respect and ensure all of the relevant rights. Nevertheless, the fact that realization over time, or in other words progressively, is foreseen under the Covenant should not be misinterpreted as depriving the obligation of all meaningful content. It is on the one hand a necessary flexibility device, reflecting the realities of the real world and the difficulties involved for any country in ensuring full realization of economic, social and cultural rights. On the other hand, the phrase must be read in the light of the overall objective, indeed the raison d'être, of the Covenant which is to **establish clear obligations for States**

parties in respect of the full realization of the rights in question. It thus imposes an obligation to **move as expeditiously and effectively** as possible towards that goal. Moreover, **any deliberately retrogressive measures** in that regard would require the most careful consideration and would need to be **fully justified** by reference to the totality of the rights provided for in the Covenant and in the context of the **full use of the maximum available resources**.[477]

It is argued by scholars and affirmed by the United Nations, that there is no division of civil and political rights from economic and social rights. However, the treaties make the separation. Conceptually they are both the same and equal.[478] Despite this, the analysis of the terms 'progressive realisation' and 'immediate' is what divides civil and political rights from economic, social and cultural rights at its very root. It has been argued by Philip Alston that the use of these terms renders the obligation devoid of meaningful content.[479] Despite rights being termed as obligations, no state deals with them as obligations. Even if a state fails to 'fully utilise its resources' there is no enforcement mechanism of the United Nations at any level that can compel fulfilment. Sanctions have taken place in the past for failure to meet human rights obligations that have resulted in legislative changes but there have been no reflected changes in fiscal behaviour.[480]

When the final version of the ICESCR was adopted, it was celebrated as being the first comprehensive international human rights instrument to be legally binding on state parties.[481] However some states, for example, New Zealand, entered reservations when ratifying it citing resource scarcity.[482] The lack of international enforceability which also recognises the inherently limited resources at the disposal of a state is found in numerous examples. State action

---

477   Human Rights Committee (1990) 17 paragraph 9 (emphasis mine)

478   United Nations General Assembly. Alternative Approaches and Ways and Means within the United Nations System for Improving the Effective Enjoyment of Human Rights and Fundamental Freedoms: (1977) 150–151

479   Steiner and Alston (2000) 247

480   Ignatieff, Gutmann and Appiah (2003) 42

481   E/CN.4/SR (1987) (statement by Mr Smirnov, USSR) in McCorquodale and Baderin (2007) 9

482   New Zealand. Core Document Forming Part of the Reports of States Parties: New Zealand (2006)

to the term immediate fulfilment is evidenced by their submissions to the United Nations and its constituent bodies. Thus, despite that fact that there are tiers of achievement in human rights, no state can claim to have achieved complete and immediate achievement of human rights or even civil and political rights, if the use of the term immediate is to be understood and addressed. Among other reasons, this includes resource constraints.

There are two steps to the realisation of human rights. The first is their adoption in the Constitution, legislation and policy of the state, and the second is the actual allocation of fiscal resources to the human rights that remain as yet unrealised and require resources.

5.2.1. THE DOMESTIC LEGAL AND POLICY FRAMEWORK

Until 2010, Kenya's independence Constitution remained in place.[483] The text of the Kenyan Bill of Rights before 2010 remained predominantly as it was at independence, almost identical to the original European Convention of Human Rights with certain exceptions.[484] The human rights expressed by the Bill of Rights are almost purely civil and political. It does not recognise socio-economic rights.[485] The material welfare of the individual, which is crucial to human life and dignity, is left out. In addition amendments to the Constitution since independence have added further limits regarding: derogation of rights during emergencies by restricting the rights of movement of resident non–citizens,[486] removal of the right to form trade unions,[487] extension of the period of detention of those charged with capital punishment,[488] removal of the right to compensation for compulsory acquisition of property out of

---

483   Although there was a Constitutional Review process that had been ongoing since 2000, it resulted in a rejection of the new draft Constitution in a national referendum. The process stalled but restarted and was finally completed in August of 2010 with the promulgation of a new Constitution.

484   There is no right to marry and found a family as in article 12 ECHR and gender discrimination as in article 14 was excluded with a narrower interpretation of the right to privacy. However there was inclusion of the right to movement and residence and the protection of private property.

485   Ghai (1999) 196

486   Constitution of Kenya (Amendment) Act No. 14 of 1965

487   Constitution of Kenya (Amendment) Act No. 16 of 1966

488   Constitution of Kenya (Amendment) Act No. 4 of 1988

the country.[489]However, the current bill of rights under the 2010 Constitution has been celebrated as being the most comprehensive one in the world today.

As a signatory to the ICESCR and the ICCPR as well as other human rights treaties, Kenya has responsibilities to make reports to the Committees and over the years Kenya's reporting has varied between diligence and laxity in fulfilling these obligations.[490] Since 2003 nationally, there have been endeavours to improve the human rights situation of the country that includes not only the policies and practice of government but also the review of the entire Constitution including its Bill of Rights. However, the status of human rights and the monitoring of their observance in Kenya have been fraught with controversy and subjected to extensive debate.[491]

Kenya in 2006 submitted its candidature as a member of the UN Human Rights Council.[492] Although the candidature was subsequently withdrawn Kenya made pledges documented in the

---

489   Constitution of Kenya (Amendment) Act No. 13 of 1977

490   Kenya's State Reports and Concluding Observations include the ICERD no report submitted, last report due in Oct. 2006; ICCPR Concluding Observation (2005) last report due in April 2008; ICESCR last report 2006 Concluding Observation (2008); (2007) CEDAW last report 2006; CAT initial report due in 1998, submitted June 2007 Concluding Observations (2008); CRC 2007 last report 2005.

491   For a thorough discussion on the development of the state intent to apply human rights from pre-independence to 1999 refer to Ghai (1999)

492   United Nations (2006) The Commission on Human Rights, is a Charter-based mechanism, as is its replacement, the Human Rights Council (HRC). Whereas the HRC was a political forum where states debated all human rights concerns, the Human Rights Committee (HRCOM) is a treaty-based mechanism. The HRCom is a UN body of 18 experts that meets three times a year to consider the five-yearly reports submitted by UN member states on their compliance with the ICCPR. The Committee is one of eight UN-linked human rights treaty bodies. States that have signed the First Optional Protocol (currently 111 countries) have agreed to allow persons within the member states to obtain an opinion from the Committee regarding violations of that Covenant. For those countries, the HRCom can thus function as a mechanism for the international redress of human rights abuses, publishes its interpretation of the content of human rights provisions, in the form of General Comments on thematic issues. It remains disputed whether the HRCOM is in principle non-binding final views qualify as decisions of a quasi-judicial body or simply constitute authoritative interpretations on the merits of the cases brought before them for the members of the Optional Protocol of the ICCPR. The members of the HRCom must be of high moral character and recognized competence in the field of human rights, are elected by the member states but on an individual basis, not as representatives of their countries. They serve four-year terms, with one-half of their number elected every second year at the UNGA.

aide memoire it presented to the UN where it pledged to promote and strengthen human rights nationally and internationally by improving both civil, political as well as economic and social rights within the nation, one of the first pledges being to open up the country to full participation of all citizens.[493]

By ratifying human rights treaties, Kenya has shown the intent to accept certain state obligations. One obligation is that human rights are understood as obligations on the state, limitations on how state power should be exercised, and hence a form of check on state power. A second obligation is to issue or amend domestic legislation to be consistent with human rights.[494] Another obligation relates to the consideration of human rights in policies, strategies, budgeting, and, more generally, administration. All governmental bodies are bound to respect human rights and to protect individuals from violations by third parties, all the treaties and conventions that affect most states as well as specifically those treaties that Kenya is a party to. The state is thus the pivot which balances the available limited resources and its distribution and is the basis for any form of rights-based development.[495] Human rights standards therefore provide the link between taxing and spending in an equitable manner.

In addition, the specificity of references to the fiscal realisation will also refer to the guidelines that are applicable in terms of declarations, general assembly resolutions[496] as well as general comments which as a member state of the United Nations, Kenya has chosen to apply human rights within the Kenyan society. The intent of the state to abide by human rights is evidenced by the ratification, accession

---

493   Aide Memoire: Kenya's Candidature to the Human Rights Council (2006)

494   See generally Wanjala (1993). However, as Kenya is a monist state, the signing and ratification of international treaties makes them enforceable as domestic law despite the absence of a subsequent constitutional amendment.

495   Grugel and Piper (2009) 94

496   Voting in the UNGA on important questions – recommendations on peace and security; election of members to organs; admission, suspension, and expulsion of members; budgetary matters – is by a two-thirds majority of those present and voting. Other questions are decided by majority vote. Each member country has one vote. Apart from approval of budgetary matters, including adoption of a scale of assessment, UNGA resolutions are not binding on the members. The UNGA may make recommendations on any matters within the scope of the UN, except matters of peace and security under Security Council consideration.

and domestication of these rights together with the representations that the state has made both internationally and domestically. As a result, these human rights policies, principles and provisions and guidelines will be referred to as the laws which govern the state-society relationship in the use of the fiscal resources that the society remits to the state. They are internationally recognised, and more importantly for the purposes of taxation, constitutionally enshrined, domestically applicable and enforceable laws.

5.2.2. THE OBSTACLE TO REALISATION: ALLOCATION OF LIMITED RESOURCES

All rights cost some money, although some may cost more than others. Rights cannot be protected or enforced without public funding and support.[497] Rights can practically become more than mere declarations only if they confer power on bodies whose decisions are legally binding. A legal right exists in fiscal reality, only when and if it has budgeted costs.[498]

In dealing with economic and social rights that require progressive realisation the UN and its constituent bodies continue to recognise the resource limitations of states. The earliest reference to resources that the United Nations has made was in the discussion on the right to life and nuclear weapons when the Human Rights Committee stated that:

> While remaining deeply concerned by the toll of human life taken by conventional weapons in armed conflicts, the Committee has noted that, during successive sessions of the General Assembly, **representatives from all geographical regions have expressed their growing concern** at the development and proliferation of increasingly awesome weapons of mass destruction, which not only threaten human life but also **absorb resources that could otherwise be used for vital economic and social purposes**, particularly for the benefit of developing countries, and thereby for promoting and securing the enjoyment of human rights for all.[499]

---

497   Holmes and Sunstein (1999) 18-20

498   *Ibid.* 19

499   Human Rights Committee. General Comment No. 14: Nuclear weapons and the right to life (Article. 6) (1984) emphasis mine

Political will when targeted as the reason for the failure to realise a right is quickly countered with the fiscal limitations argument. In 1993, the Committee on Economic, Social and Cultural Rights, noted in the case of Kenya, that any reform measures must be accompanied by the adoption of targeted programmes designed to protect specifically the vulnerable groups and members of society, and that the Government of Kenya had demonstrated very little awareness or willingness in this regard. However, the Kenyan government cited a lack of financial resources as justification for the comprehensive neglect of such protective measures.[500] State sovereignty over its limited resources has been cited not only by Kenya but by many developing and developed states to justify the inability to realise human rights. For example, in 2004, Bosnia and Herzegovina also reported that lack of resources was an obstacle to the realisation of the right to health and the Committee accepted this from both states as a justification.[501]

Using the argument of the aspirational nature of rights justifies its open-ended formulation to all an infinite possibilities of protections, and with it an infinite cost implication.[502] However, within the state citizens assume that public officials whether at national, municipal or local level, will routinely locate public resources and use them to salvage or boost the value of the society's rights. These rights will only have a budgetary allocation if their precise nature and scope are legally stipulated, interpreted and recognised by law. For example, despite the continual existence of crime, citizens feel relatively secure that they will receive personal or physical security and that police will be paid salaries to maintain security.[503] Pogge adds that although reference commences in the national level with the Constitution and the laws, the vigilance of citizens and their participation is required.[504]

---

500 Committee on Economic, Social and Cultural Rights. Concluding observations of the Committee on Economic, Social and Cultural Rights: Kenya (1993)

501 United Nations. Core Document Forming Part of the Reports of States Parties: Bosnia and Herzegovina (2004)

502 Holmes and Sunstein (1999) 120

503 *Ibid.* 14

504 Pogge (2008) 68

In 2005, Bolivia stated that 'poverty and economic adjustment limit **resources**'[505] in their discussion on the limitations to the implementation of the rights of the child and the argument was accepted to allow for progressive realisation and simply, urged to allocate more resources.[506] In 2006, Hungary was asked by the committee on torture to provide in its next periodic report information about the **allocation of adequate resources** to ensure the effective functioning of programmes.[507]

Even in the case of the immediately realisable civil and political rights, the UN and its constituent bodies recognise resource limitations. For example, in 2003, Mexico, in reference to the freedom from torture, stated that great efforts had been made to eradicate torture, but that cases continued to occur due to a lack of training for police officers, a problem that was more acute in public attorneys' offices where **resources were scarce**.[508]

However, the international community does recognise that the term 'progressive realisation' is used as an escape clause, and as a result there is a movement towards a system of indicators to measure progress in realisation.[509] Many Africans argue that, economic rights should take preference over civil and political rights in their poverty stricken, underdeveloped countries.[510] Today, the World Bank is also approaching development from the angle of basic needs.[511]

Thus, one can see clearly, that civil and political rights need resources just as much as other rights. The Human Rights Committee is making statements more and more towards realisation of not only

---

505   United Nations. Core Document Forming Part of the Reports of States Parties: Bolivia (2005)

506   Committee on the Rights of the Child. Consideration of Reports Submitted by States Parties Under Article 44 of The Convention: Concluding observations: Bolivia (2005)

507   Committee Against Torture. Consideration of Reports Submitted by States Parties Under Article 19 of the Convention: Conclusions and Recommendations of the Committee Against Torture: Hungary (2006) 17

508   Human Rights Committee (2003) 48

509   World Conference on Human Rights. Vienna Declaration and Programme of Action (1993)

510   See generally Nyerere (1969)

511   See generally Streeten (1980); Javed Burki and Ul Haq (1981)

civil and political but also economic, social and cultural rights. They recognised that civil and political rights can never be attained unless all basic necessities of life are available to everyone.[512]

5.2.3. THE DOMESTIC REALISATION OF HUMAN RIGHTS

At the domestic level there remains a balance of power between the state and the judiciary in the decision on how to distribute resources. The political intent of the state is the only impetus that can lead to the realisation of human rights domestically. Although in developing states this includes foreign development aid, the purpose of this thesis is to discuss how the fiscal legitimacy of the state can be improved using human rights. The only way this can be realised is if the state itself is actually using its fiscal resources to improve the human rights of the society.

The Committee on Economic, Social and Cultural Rights has stated that one argument used by states is that matters involving the allocation of resources should be left to the political authorities rather than the courts.[513] Thus, only if a government has adequate funding can provision be made for the right to be maintained. The South African Constitutional Court has heard cases on the right to housing[514] and medical care.[515] However, in all 3 cases the decision was that the resources allocated for these issues were limited to the government budget and the court could not rule on how government policy distributes government revenue annually, a direct reflection of the HRC approach.[516] The arguments presented in these cases are critical to this thesis as the link between state resources was again left to the political will and the limited resources available to the state. The difference between what was being

---

512   Commission on Human Rights. The Right to Development (1977)

513   Human Rights Committee (1990); Committee on Economic, Social and Cultural Rights. General comment No. 9 The domestic application of the Covenant: Substantive Issues Arising In the Implementation of the International Covenant on Economic, Social and Cultural Rights (1998) 58 paragraph 10

514   South Africa v Grootboom (2000) (Grootboom case)

515   Treatment Action Campaign v Minister of Health (2002) (TAC case) See also Soobramoney v Minister of Health (KwaZulu-Natal) (1997) (Soobramoney case)

516   See generally Soobramoney v Minister of Health (KwaZulu-Natal) (1997); South Africa v Grootboom (2000); Treatment Action Campaign v Minister of Health (2002)

requested in these cases and the proposal of this thesis, is that the accountability function in human rights that allocates resources for development if progressive and clearly shown to the society would perhaps increase the understanding of the people whether in the TAC on the limited availability of certain medicines. In the other two cases of Grootboom and Soobramoney that referred to the right to housing policy considerations by the state that showed how future allocations of state resources were to take place and a tabling of housing as a future budget expenditure would also go a long way in relieving the pressure of citizens on the state to provide housing as it would show that other citizens are also benefitting.

The US Supreme Court has stated on several occasions that the government's interest and therefore the public's interest is in conserving scarce resources and is a factor that must be weighed. An individual's safeguard may be outweighed by cost over the specific action. Thus the cost of protection may also come out of the available resources for a social welfare programme. The court held that there must be a hearing before the ending of any welfare benefits.[517]

5.3. Linking Tax to Human Rights to Legitimise the Fiscal State

It is the contention of this thesis that despite the arguments posed by human rights policy makers, scholars and practitioners in dividing the rights into categories of divergent types for purposes of implementation or enforcement, they have undermined their fiscal realisation. In addition, it is argued that the view that the United Nations treats both these sets of rights equally is becoming increasingly difficult to support 'when the institutional arrangements for implementing the former were clearly inferior to those relating to the latter.'[518] To realise human rights, the fiscal requirements for each and every single right and its enforceability as a result will require that all rights be addressed together.

It is recognised that as with the discourse on human rights, the discourse around the right to development being the most recent is

---

517   *Mathews v Eldridge* (1976); *Goldberg v Kelly* (1970) and *Goss v Lopez* (1975)
518   Alston (1987) 357

also not well settled, neither is it universally accepted. In addition, this right has not been granted equal status with the rest of the human rights set out under the UDHR, ICCPR and ICESCR. However, it affirms and strengthens certain characteristics of human rights that are pertinent to a reading of human rights as the obstacle that must be overcome in order to achieve development and human rights and as a result achieve the level of the fiscal state. These include the affirmation that human rights are indivisible, and interdependent; that respect for some rights does not justify violation of others, it blended individual rights, collective rights, responsibilities with opinions and values to participate, contribute to and enjoy economic, social, cultural and political development and finally the devotion of resources especially for developing countries.[519]

A new approach has come about with the rise in importance of the right to development which has been developed and crystallised through the DRD. It is the one right that has made a link between the right and the resources required to fund it.[520] The second critical part of the right to development was the recognition of the right of people to participate in its realisation. The provision granted the right of all people to participate, contribute to and enjoy economic, social, cultural and political development in which all human rights and freedoms can be realised.[521]

5.3.1.   THE RIGHT TO DEVELOPMENT AND RESOURCES

As early as the 1950s, the UN as a whole recognised the need for development.[522] The basis of concern of the United Nations in development rested on article 55 of the UN Charter which states that:

> With a view to the creation of conditions of stability and well-being which are necessary for peaceful and friendly relations among nations based on respect for the principle of equal rights and self-determination of peoples, the United Nations shall promote:

---

519   Henkin (1987) 199

520   Smith (1997) 7

521   Tlakula (2004) 110

522   Smith (2007) 342

a. **higher standards of living**, full employment, and **conditions of economic and social progress** and **development;**[523]

Initially, this article was drafted through the continual and consistent use of the term, 'raising of the standard of living'.[524] The text, however, went on to recognise, the fact that domestic financial resources together with the then current international flows of income were inadequate to attain the desired level of economic development.[525] This was a recognition that in the era of the emancipation of peoples and the end of colonisation, the solution to the world's problems, was not based on the dictates of a monetary system or an economic growth oriented approach to development, but a new order and view of development and the preconditions for development through which peace and human rights may be realistically achieved.[526] This marked the entry of the post-colonial states to the international arena of human rights. Although the imperial states were part of the development and creation of international human rights law, the developing states constitutionally guaranteed human rights law as part of their independence negotiations. Freedom fighters and leaders in colonies clamouring for independence referred to the UDHR in the quest for independence but this was mainly reflected in constitutional provisions thus did affect the discourse but did not result in a new human rights tradition.[527]

With the entry of a large number of previously oppressed states to the fold of the United Nations there was an added impetus to protect rights. This led to the introduction first of the Declaration on the Granting of Independence to Colonial Countries and Peoples in 1960 followed later in 1965 by the Declaration on the Elimination

---

523   United Nations. Charter of the United Nations (1945)

524   United Nations General Assembly. Reports on World Economic Conditions and Trends (1947); United Nations General Assembly. Implementation of Recommendations on Economic and Social Matters (1947); United Nations General Assembly. Economic Development of Underdeveloped Countries (1948)

525   United Nations General Assembly. Financing of Economic Development of Underdeveloped Countries (1950)

526   See generally O'Rawe (1999)

527   Imperialism and human rights: colonial discourses of rights and liberties in ... By Bonny Ibhawoh 161 Kenyan independence was in 1964 and despite accepting all international treaties, the 1966 ICCPR and ICESCR were adopted through the free will of the independent post-colonial state.

of all Forms of Racial Discrimination. This also resulted in the change in the stalemate between the states previously attempting to convert the UDHR into a covenant,[528] and in 1966 the UDHR was finally converted into two covenants, the ICCPR and the ICESCR.

However, the question of realisation of human rights came into the forefront and in 1968 at the first world conference on human rights. The conference concluded that the achievement of lasting progress in the implementation of human rights was dependent upon the sound and effective national and international policies of economic and social **development**.[529] This was followed by the 1976 World Employment Conference, where a link was made between absolute poverty and basic need.[530] This was the beginning of the recognition of the need for states to implement policies aimed towards development not only within their respective states but that there was also a responsibility for states to develop policies on assisting each other.

In 1977, the United Nations Commission on Human Rights proclaimed the existence of the right to development.[531] The right itself was eventually formulated in 1986 in the Declaration on the Right to Development (DRD).[532] The DRD sets out critical obligations in its articles.

> States have the right and the duty to formulate appropriate national development policies that aim at the constant improvement of the well-being of the entire population and of all individuals, on the basis of their active, free and meaningful participation in development and in the fair distribution of the benefits resulting therefrom.[533]

This entails three important basic principles. Firstly, that it is the primary responsibility of states to apply policies aimed at improving

---

528   Lauren (2003) 240-244

529   United Nations. The Proclamation of Tehran in Final Act of the International Conference on Human Rights (1968) in Alston, Robinson and New York University. Center for Human Rights and Global Justice (2005). This Declaration was unanimously adopted by the United Nations General Assembly. Proclamation of Tehran (1968).

530   Director General (1976)

531   Commission on Human Rights. The Right to Development (1977)

532   United Nations General Assembly. Declaration on the Right to Development (1986)

533   *Ibid.* article 3

the well-being of the population, secondly, that the human person is the central subject and should be the active participant and finally, that there should be distribution of benefits.

In addition the DRD went one step further and placed the responsibility of the realisation of the right to development not only on individual states in consideration of their populations but also on states collectively for all peoples.

> States have the duty to take steps, individually and collectively, to formulate international development policies with a view to facilitating the full realization of the right to development[534]

One important development that is marked by these two provisions was that the DRD through these articles clearly articulates that it is the state's obligation to implement the right. Thus, the realisation of the right to development requires states to link resource allocation to human rights. However, despite this big step forward in the development of human rights and the increasing crystallisation of its constituent characteristics, the right to development to date has received a lot of criticism from many countries in the world and despite efforts recently to have the right recognised as a full right equal to those set out in the ICCPR and ICESCR, this has not taken place due to several challenges to its realisation that remain unsettled including who the right holder is as well as the perceived fiscal responsibility that will be placed on any state in order to realise it for human beings worldwide.[535] This is perhaps also based on the failure of the state and society to see the right as an obligation on the state to manage resources in an accountable way.

If state intent is to be ascertained it is important to note that the only international treaty that expressly recognises the right to development is the African Charter of Human and Peoples Rights, which came into effect in 1984, and binds it member states.[536] This

---

534 *Ibid.* article 4

535 See generally Smith (2004) for his discussion on why the United States continues to oppose its adoption.

536 Committee on Economic, Social and Cultural Rights. General comment No. 9 The domestic application of the Covenant: Substantive Issues Arising In the Implementation of the International Covenant on Economic, Social and Cultural Rights (1998).

has resulted in the inclusion of this right in more recently drafted Constitutions like that of Benin including it in their bill of rights.[537]

In 1995 the world embraced the significance of well-being and development for all. However, states have neither absorbed this right into their Constitutions nor have they with a few exceptions, declared this as a human right.[538] From the perspective of the Schumpeter's typology of fiscal states, the fiscal state's levels of development achieved include provision of a diverse array of social welfare benefits to their citizens and as a result the state perceives no additional rational in adding a constitutional provision for an issue already well settled in state-society relations. However, for the post-colonial fiscal state, this need for the recognition of the developmental needs of their citizens is necessary in order to provide better guidelines for the resource uses of the state.

Despite these criticisms, the need for international co-operation was recognised and the existence of state obligations to co-operate in order to realise the right to development, there developed various instruments allowing for co-operation. These included international economic co-operation in the form of overseas development assistance or foreign aid;[539] access to markets through trade liberalisation;[540] incentives to increase investment

---

537   Every human being has a right to the development and full expansion of his person in his material, temporal and intellectual dimensions, provided that he does not violate the rights of others nor infringe upon constitutional order and good manners. Republic of Benin. Constitution of the Republic of Benin (1990)

538   United Nations (1995) introduction

539   Foreign aid remains the most important instrument of international co-operation, because it can be used at the discretion of authorities to pursue certain policies. In addition, there is on record, a voluntary commitment by industrialised countries to provide at minimum 0.7% of GDP as foreign aid. This proportion has however never been reached but instead has hovered around 0.32/0.33% for over 15 years. Sengupta (2000) 571, Committee on the Convention on the Rigths of the Child. General Comment No 5: General Measures of Implementation for the Convention on the Rights of the Child (2003) paragraph 61.

540   The need to spur development is not new and although the move towards the creation of the right to development is seen as a relatively new human right, the need to alleviate poverty, raise standards of living, ensure full employment and allow the use of the world's resources for sustainable development are all fairly well settled parts of human rights. All these terms are found not only in human rights documents but also the preamble World Trade Organisation. Marrakesh Agreement Establishing the World Trade Organization (1994) preamble. The mixed impact of trade and globalisation is a continuing area of discourse to date, see generally Payne (2009)

flows and technology transfer; bilateral and multilateral assistance to implement structural adjustments and economic reforms; debt forgiveness[541] and assisting countries to meet financial crises.[542] However, these strategies have come under heavy criticism as being oriented towards economic growth and financial considerations which usually indirectly result in human rights violations.[543]

There has also been the development of measures with which states can analyse their realisation of human rights. These include the use of approaches like Amartya Sen's capability approach,[544] development indicators[545] and the Millennium Development Goals[546] which set benchmarks that allow for the realisation of human rights while taking into consideration the resource constraints that states face. In addition, global organizations that are formally or informally linked to other organizations, agencies, and governments around the world, such as the United Nations and the World Bank, view citizens' participation in claiming their rights and budgetary design

---

541　Sengupta has argued that states should cooperate with each other in ensuring development and eliminating the obstacles to development. That progress towards realisation of the right to development requires effective national development policies and a favourable international economic environment. Finally that the international community should make all efforts to alleviate problems such as the external debt burden of states in order to supplement efforts of the governments of developing states. See generally Sengupta (2003a)

542　Sengupta (2000) 570-571

543　United Nations. Global Consultation on the Right to Development as a Human Right (1990)

544　This is currently being extrapolated and re-interpreted to apply to all human rights see generally Carpenter (2009)

545　This is a measure of progress of nations developed allowing for cross-country comparative context. However, despite a large amount of growing literature on this issue, it has been focussed mainly on the distributional or equity aspect of development without recognition of changes at the source base. However, equity without efficiency is not sustainable over time. There is thus the need to look into the optimal use not only of distribution but also collection of resources. The need to integrate efficiency into the index is a case of attempting to integrate welfare and production economics. See generally Arcelus, Sharma and Srinivasan (2005)

546　The Millennium Development Goals are the current global and quantified targets for addressing extreme poverty in its many dimensions—income, poverty, hunger, disease, lack of adequate shelter and exclusion—while promoting gender equality, education, and environmental sustainability. They are also basic human rights—the rights of each person on the planet to health, education, shelter, and security as pledged in the Universal Declaration of Human Rights and expounded by the UN Millennium Declaration Project (2005) 1. See generally Schmidt-Traub (2009) for the most recent discussion on how to achieve the MDGs.

practices as a crucial part of their responsibility to improve their well-being.[547] In addition, more recent endeavours have begun within the United Nations to analysing how fiscal policies and budgets can be converted in order to realise human rights.[548] Scholars are now beginning to recognise not only the importance of the link of tax to human rights but Alston in one footnote of his most recent edition has expressed the possibility of using Schumpeter's fiscal sociology as drawing together the lines of this debate.[549]

While recognising these objections at the international level to this development in the characteristic of rights, this thesis addresses the domestic capacity and capability of state and its tax revenue. As a result this historical evolution in the right to development created a position which allows this thesis to move forward into the discussion of the diverse characteristics of the state that impede in the domestic realisation of human rights using the limited resources available at the disposal of the state.

5.3.2.   ACTIVE FREE AND MEANINGFUL PARTICIPATION

Participation is understood by development practitioners and theorists as the de-professionalization in all domains of life- schooling, health care, transportation, planning – in order to make 'ordinary people' responsible for their own well-being.[550] Friere best explains this issue by stating that the supreme touchstone of development is whether people who were previously treated as mere objects known and acted upon, can now actively know and act upon, thereby becoming subjects of their own social destiny. Thus the movement from a culture of silence they become active subjects of knowledge and action and construct their human history and engage in development.[551] However, the most practical definition is

---

547   There is now an entire World Bank department dedicated to participation and citizen engagement. Basok and Ilcan (2006); World Bank (2009)

548   United Nations International Children's Fund (2007)

549   Steiner, Alston and Goodman (2007) 305

550   Illich (1975); Illich (1978); Illich (1983). See also Naik (1975); Naik (1977); Naik, Naik and Banerji (1977)

551   Freire (1970); Freire (1970); Freire and Freire (1973) See also Goulet (1989)

that espoused by Marshall Wolfe and the United Nations Research Institute for Social Development that states:

> Participation is the organised efforts to increase control over resources and regulative institutions in given social situations, on the part of groups and movements hitherto excluded from such control.[552]

The use of the term 'respect of citizens' can be used synonymously as 'active, free and meaningful participation'; which implies the voicing of and taking of account of the opinion of the people in the political process with reference to their right to development. However, it thus calls into question the current provisions within governmental structures of the representation already in place.

Four arguments support the rise of public participation: postmodern discourse theory; disillusionment with bureaucracy; the search for the democratic ideal and the need for participation in developing countries.[553] When development and participation are discussed together, participation is seen as having three functions. Firstly, it guarantees the treatment of government of the powerless people. Secondly, it is an instrument for mobilizing, organising and promoting action by the people themselves. Finally, it is a channel through which local communities gain access to macro areas of decision making. These functions liberate people and give them a set of goods that can be both fulfilled and are practical. This can be implemented further than development issues as evidenced by the immediate effect of readily available resources at grassroots level.

The ACHPR's concept of African historical values and traditions removes intermediary groups within the participation context. The Lome III Convention also recognised the role of grassroots communities and self-help organisations as mediating structures. Finally, the African Alternative Framework to Structural Adjustment Programmes for Socio-Economic Recovery and Transformation conceptualises a genuine and active partnership between Government and the people through their various institutions at national, local and grassroots level.[554]

---

552   Wolfe and Development (1983)2

553   Moynihan (2007)

554   United Nations Centre for Human Rights (1991) 37 paragraph 116

The right to participate in decision making has a basis in UN Human rights instruments,[555] and expert studies[556] as well as instruments in economics[557] and development strategy.[558] Development is seen as being special/specific thus strategies must be developed by the people themselves and adapted to meet local conditions and needs.[559] This makes participation the primary mechanism for identifying appropriate goals and criteria.[560] In this case, the right to development becomes not as much a right to improve material conditions, but the right to have a voice in and share control over the economic environment[561] but within the limitation imposed by budgetary constraints and state legislative procedures.[562]

As already stressed earlier the state's duty is to formulate development policies on the basis of 'active, free and meaningful participation'.[563] This term is linked to the concepts of 'equality of opportunity in access to basic resources' and 'fair distribution of income'.[564] Linking tax revenue to tax expenditure through human rights is best expressed here within the right to development and its

---

555   United Nations General Assembly. International Covenant on Civil and Political Rights (1966) article 25 (rights to elect representatives and take part in the conduct of civil affairs); United Nations General Assembly. Declaration on Social Progress and Development (1969) (seeking active participation of all members of society, individually or through associations, in defining and in achieving the common goals of development) and article 15 (effective participation in a democratic system)

556   See generally Ganji (1969); Ferrero (1983) and General (1985)

557   United Nations General Assembly. Charter of Economic Rights and Duties of States (1974)

558   United Nations. Declaration of Principles and Programme of Action of the World Employment Conference (1976) (participation of the people in making decisions which affect them through organisations of their own choice); United Nations. Report of the World Conference on Agrarian Reform and Rural Development (UN Doc. A/54/485) (1979) (participation is a basic human right and (is) also essential for realignment of political power in favour of disadvantaged groups).

559   United Nations. Global Consultation on the Right to Development as a Human Right (1990) 155-156

560   *Ibid.* paragraphs150 and 179.

561   Barsh (1991) at 329

562   See generally Fukuda-Parr, Lawson-Remer and Randolph (2008) for the most recent method developed for measuring progressive realisation of human rights.

563   United Nations General Assembly. Declaration on the Right to Development (1986) articles 1(1) and 8(2)

564   *Ibid.* article 8(1).

link to its resource requirements. Participation is a tool that can be used to ensure accountability, responsibility and transparency as well as efficiency and effectiveness in the context of limited resources.

The Global Consultation on the Right to Development[565] went a step forward and agreed that participation must be active and involve genuine power.[566] It set out conditions for democratic participation as including a fair distribution of economic and political power among all sectors of a national society[567] and genuine ownership or control of productive resources like land, financial capital and technology.[568] Factors to evaluate participatory processes include representation and accountability of decision making bodies, decentralization of decision-making; public access to information; and the responsiveness of decision makers to public opinion.[569] All these provisions are important both for the right to development as well as all other human rights and the need to link the resource allocation of tax in its collection and distribution is a direct manifestation of the peoples' region specific needs. However, one must not lose sight of the overall bigger development picture and needs that can only be put into effect by the state itself.

Within the developing country context, participation is seen to foster good governance. Proponents point to corruption, opaque resource allocation, the failure to deliver basic services and a power structure that does not allow non-elites an opportunity to have their voice heard. At an overall level, participation is said to promote transparency, increase social justice and help individuals become better citizens.

---

565   United Nations. Global Consultation on the Right to Development as a Human Right (1990)

566   *Ibid*. paragraph147.

567   United Nations. Global Consultation on the Right to Development as a Human Right (1990) paragraph 148

568   *Ibid*. paragraph 150 (which is a rejection of the welfare state) see also paragraphs 174–176.

569   *Ibid*. paragraph178

5.4.   CONCLUSION

This chapter recognises the divisions and the challenges posed by the realisation of human rights. It also recognises that the state intent of the post-colonial fiscal state has remained constant with the states continually and consistently adapting and expanding the definition and characteristics of human rights. The initial division to the realisation of the human rights and the objections to the widening of the provisions have been posed by the fiscal states and not the post-colonial developing fiscal states. This is in itself adequate vocalisation of the intent of states and their obligations to be bound by the treaties.

The question that remains to be answered is whether the state's intent to be bound by the human rights law that it has been involved in creating and carving out at international level is being implemented at domestic level through its utilisation of fiscal resources.

The linkage of rights to resources from the point of view of the fiscal state must recognise the evolving nature of the definition and content of human rights to be contextually specific, to the post-colonial fiscal state, and state intent is evinced by the signing of the international covenants which despite not being translated to the regional level is as a result of the political compromise reached with other African states and finally the inherent characteristic of the right to development to include all rights overrides the division of rights and the limitations of placing preference on certain rights over others.

In addition, human rights are held to be inalienable in the sense that they exist inherently and are a benchmark. They are used by individuals and states as well as non-state actors as standards of justification and criticism, whether or not they are recognized and implemented by the legal system or officials of a country.[570] Their recognition and enforcement is sometimes characterised as humane, charitable, beneficent, or as an entitlement.[571] However, this translates into the continual problem in the application and enforcement of

---

570   Nickel (1987) 561-2

571   Donnelly (1982) 391

human rights; how to decide upon the minimum level of each right and how to quantify it in terms of resource allocation. This argument is also the basis upon which many states rest their position in avoiding allocation of resources to human rights. The broad nature of the treaties in question leaves the fiscal practicalities open for interpretation. This is an area of future research though.

Thus, there are several possible explanations for the limited discussion on national fiscal resources and the realisation of human rights within a state. Firstly, that management of resources is seen as something inherently domestic – whereas human rights are generally recognised as part of the international sphere. Secondly, that natural law sees human rights as inherent and therefore doesn't concern itself with the practicalities of how they are to be implemented. Finally, the historical development of human rights in Europe moved firstly from recognition of civil and political rights that were seen as traditionally negative rights having no real resource implications to economic, social and cultural rights which had resource implications but were left to the domestic jurisdiction of states and are very recent.

Dichter argues that development in Africa has failed because it targeted the wrong things in the wrong way. That the key to successful development includes the fostering of institutions, attitudes and laws in enhancing human resources. The Blair Commission declared:

> Africa's history over the last 50 years has been blighted by two areas of weakness. These have been capacity-the ability to design and deliver policies and accountability-how well a state answers to its people.[572]

---

572   Commission for Africa (2005) 12

CHAPTER 6

LINKING HUMAN RIGHTS TO TAXATION THROUGH PARTICIPATION: BUDGETING FOR DEVELOPMENT

Developing countries like Brazil and India began rudimentary and home-grown approaches to participation in the budgeting process. This chapter delves into the growth and evolution of the process of participation in budgeting in the main place of its origin-Porto Alegre (PA), Brazil and the alternative format found in Kerala, India. An account of the historical evolution is followed by a critical analysis of the manner in which the practicality of the approach answers the research questions as to how to link tax revenue to tax expenditure using human rights principles that embody or include the use of participation as envisaged by the right to development.

The core discussion in this chapter centres on whether or not the case studies of participatory budgeting in India and Brazil show that human rights principles were utilised in any way directly or indirectly. In addition, this chapter will address the issues of firstly, whether the respective societies approve of the distribution of taxation revenue and how this approval is obtained or ascertained; in other words, whether PB has assisted in legitimating the fiscal state. Secondly, whether the economy is benefiting and there is an improvement in the effectiveness of the government in its use of revenue. Thirdly, whether budgeting is being more effectively carried out where it is not entrusted solely to the government. Finally, the approval of the citizen must be both qualified and quantified and thus the last issue is whether the linking of fiscal decentralisation with the recognition of human rights and participatory rights together is one way in which government may legitimise it today in order to fulfil peoples' needs and thus realise human rights, development and poverty alleviation. These needs in turn become prioritised by the people, for the people give them a sense of ownership of the process, recognition of their concerns and add to the legitimacy of their citizenship.

The current crisis of both the fiscal and welfare states as discussed in Chapter 1 has resulted in popular unease with the growth of government and the acknowledgement of the discretionary authority of bureaucracies. These in turn have given rise to a search for alternative models of democratic accountability and control.[573] There is also a worldwide shift to post-modern values including a distrust of formal institutions such as government and political parties and a desire for more participatory democracies[574] which has resulted in fiscal decentralisation and PB. The needs of the people and the approach through which PB takes place, as well as its level of impact, affects several dimensions at the theoretical and practical levels within the state. The breakdown of the application of PB as set out below will thus bring to light the mechanisms already in place that recognise; allow recognition of; and fail, avoid and/or refuse to recognise human rights. It will also delve into the changes or considerations that may be contextually required in order to support and absorb recognition and realisation of human rights principles.

6.1.   PARTICIPATORY BUDGETING (PB) IN BRAZIL: PA

The origin of PB as it is generally understood today is inextricably linked to PA and Brazil. Brazil's demographic, historical, legal, political and economic context is therefore critical to understanding its origin and development.[575] The South and South East of Brazil are the poorer regions of the country while the North, North East and Central West are considered fairly wealthy with comparatively middle to high income.[576] Brazil's population today is a combination of native Americans, European settlers, the descendants of Portuguese colonists as well as African slaves.[577]

From the 16th to the 19th centuries, Brazil was a colony of Portugal. In 1822, the country declared its independence from Portugal and became a constitutional monarchy. Slavery was abolished by royal decree in 1888 and this was swiftly followed by a military coup

---

573   Simonsen and Robbins (2000) xvii

574   See generally Ingelhart (1997)

575   Cabannes (2004) 29

576   Camargo and Ferreira (2000) 11-12

577   See generally Intute (2008), Perz, Warren and Kennedy (2008)

in 1889 which then established a republican government.[578] The country remained nominally a democratic republic, except for three periods of overt dictatorship (1930–1934; 1937–1945 and 1964–1985).[579] A main governance characteristic of this last period of military rule (1964-1985) was centralization, inherited from the colonial era.[580] An interesting exception to the normal model of military rule was that Brazilian politics allowed for the existence of two political parties, the National Alliance for Renovation, that was supported by the regime and the existence of a single opposition party, the Party of the Brazilian Democratic Movement.[581] Apart from strategic cities like state capitals and major ports, the military government allowed relatively fair mayoral elections.[582]

Although Brazil inherited its social welfare system during Portuguese colonisation mainly in health and social security,[583] welfare was not legislated until the 1920s and 1930s. By the 1960s, social welfare had developed into a system that scholars term as 'simultaneously selective, heterogeneous and fragmented.' This system covered not only virtually all the country's public sector working population, but it had liberal entitlement conditions and generous benefits with mature pension schemes.[584]

The emancipation of the African slaves in Brazilian history was couched and perceived by both the released slaves and by citizens in general as a privilege, not a right and the end of colonisation was seen as an extension of this privilege. This perception, it is argued by Sales, has now extended to the selective application of social welfare rights and assisted in reinforcing clientelism and patronage ties. Wampler posits that this developed a culture of donation where rights were seen to have been given to the masses and this was linked to the culture of patronage, in that the political elites extended these

---

578   Davis, Finan and Peck (1977) 135

579   See generally Prado (1967)

580   See generally Lockhart and Schwartz (1983)

581   Guidry (2003) 89

582   Shah (2007) 93

583   Midgley (1986) 127

584   Dixon and Scheurell (2002) 241

rights based on employment or bureaucracy.[585] The recognition of human rights was limited in this era of Brazilian history. Although Brazil was one of the 51 founder members of the United Nations in 1945 and a member of all the specialised agencies,[586] there was apart from the limited social welfare provisions, no recognition of human rights in its constitutional and legislative framework, and Brazil was not a signatory to either the ICCPR or the ICESCR.

The political changes that culminated in the creation of PB began from the mid-1960s onwards. The beginnings of decentralisation emerged in 1964 when the Federal Republic of Brazil created three relatively autonomous layers of government: central government, 26 state governments, and a final layer of more than 5,500 municipalities.[587] There was as a result administrative decentralisation. However, the decentralisation reforms did not extend to changes in fiscal powers. This resulted in the allocation of more revenue at municipal and local levels over time, with the same set of responsibilities; while the responsibilities of the central federal government remained constant if not greater and as a result had less disposable income.[588] During this final period of military rule and immediately after, Brazil could be considered a tax state.[589]

Towards the end of military rule in 1983, studies show that 10% of the population held 46.2% of the nation's wealth while the poorest 20% held 2.4% of the national wealth.[590] Thus, the poor were dismally poor and the rich controlled the economy completely. In the 1980s there was also a widening of the social welfare system to include housing, health, welfare and social security. Despite this there remained selectiveness in its application and rights only extended to certain classes of workers. By the 1980s, only small groups of unionized workers had social rights but the majority of the population did not have access to any of these social welfare benefits.[591] This

---

585   Wampler (2007) 22

586   Brazil and the United Nations (2008)

587   Baiocchi (2005); Ministry of Finance Brazil, (2008)

588   Souza (2005) 2

589   29

590   World Bank (1992)

591   Wampler (2007) 23, Baiocchi (2005) 9

system was the first to be afflicted by financial disequilibrium due to high costs and insufficient revenue. An ageing population (meaning a lower ratio of contributors to pensioners), resulted in depleted reserves, coupled with existing payroll contributions which were so high that they could not be further increased, such that the state had to subsidize the system.[592] The welfare financing policy in the late 1990s evolved into a pay-as-you-go financial method with social insurance, together with health care and social assistance being based on this system.[593]

By 1970 and 1980 Brazil was also characterised by the appearance of new civic associations and social movements, grassroots church activism and new unionism, that politicised the question of access to services such as the cost of living, housing rights and transportation.[594] The government in 1979 abolished single party politics and in 1980 the Worker's Party (WP) was formed with an agenda of internal democracy, openness, decentralisation, and aligning class struggle with citizenship. It included a mixed membership of union workers, leftist, progressive Christian activists, representatives from social movements and intellectuals.[595] These groups began the call for participatory democracy and based their agenda on the phrase 'the right to have rights'.[596]

Dagnino and Alvarez argue that this 'right' is a necessity. Before one can consider one's human rights, one must address whether one has the 'right' to have them.[597] They argue that this includes three necessary points. Firstly, a notion of citizenship encompassing this right. Secondly, that these 'new' or informed citizens define their rights. Finally, to have the right to participate in the definition and development of the state's political system. However my interviews in Brazil elicited diverse responses to the value of this slogan. Several explanations for it were suggested. One was that it was to raise the awareness of people that they have the right to ask the state and

---

592   Mesa-Lago (1997) 502-503

593   Paiva (2008) 2

594   Baiocchi (2005) 10

595   Guidry (2003) 90

596   Baiocchi (2005) 11

597   See generally Alvarez and Dagnino (1998)

public institutions for their rights, but referring to consumer rights not human rights.[598] Others suggested that it expressed the feeling that social revolution in Brazil must be done through radicalisation of democracy;[599] to show the presence of government in life;[600] to make clear that the market promotes social inclusion and the state policy and activities should perform social inclusion of these people left outside by the market;[601] and to show representation.[602] However, although there were divergent views on why the campaign began, and the implications of this slogan, there was agreement that ideas of human rights were not a factor in the commencement of PB in PA.[603]

In 1988, nationwide grassroots campaigning resulted in the redrafting of the Constitution. The new 'Citizens' Constitution[604] included for the first time, a strong and extensive bill of rights. The 1988 Constitution also codified decentralisation[605] and defined Brazilian municipalities as federal entities, including them constitutionally as part of the federal system and in addition to this administrative specificity also delineated their fiscal responsibilities. The Constitution established which taxes may be created, which level of government (union, states or municipalities) was competent for each tax, the limitations on the taxing power, and the way that revenues must be shared.[606] The mayors were thus allowed to use their new constitutional authority to institute reforms and innovate in areas critical to sound municipal governance, and they were given additional fiscal resources to carry them out.[607] The 1988 Constitution also allowed for the transfer of fiscal resources through inter-governmental finance and many municipalities have been able

---

598   Luis Renato Vedovato Interview 11 (2009)

599   Raphael Moya Interview 12 (2009)

600   Luis Alberto Interview 9 (2009)

601   Taxiete Interview 10 (2009)

602   Christiano Carvalho Interview 8 (2009)

603   *Ibid*; Luis Alberto Interview 9 (2009); Luis Renato Vedovato Interview 11 (2009); Raphael Moya Interview 12 (2009); Taxiete Interview 10 (2009)

604   The Federal Constitution of Brazil (1988)

605   Wampler (2007) 8

606   The Federal Constitution of Brazil (1988) articles 145–162

607   Mona Serageldin et al. (2005)

to improve their financial situation, in particular the state capitals. These transfers of resources determined by the 1988 Constitution were phased in over time and were finally completed in 1993.[608]

6.1.1. THE EVOLUTION OF PARTICIPATORY BUDGETING IN PA

Goldfrank states that the first recorded use of the PB process is said to have been in the late 1970s and 1980s in the municipal Brazilian governments of Lages,[609] Boa Esperanca[610] and Pelotas[611] all of which were then controlled by the Party of the Brazilian Democratic Movement.[612] However, at this point the form of participation in the budget was limited to mere consultation of specific citizens or groups on their opinions without any guarantee of follow through in the decision making process.[613]

The Workers Party (WP), which had played a key role in the opposition to the dictatorship, won the mayoral elections of PA in 1988, and was eager to implement its own brand of socialism. A decision was made, despite dissension within the party, not to implement state socialism, but instead a program was launched to invite participation.

The WP set out four key reasons for the conceptualisation of PB. Firstly, direct citizen participation and oversight; secondly, transparency to prevent corruption; thirdly, improvement in services with reference to aiding the poor; and finally, development of citizenship and education on rights.[614] There was no reference to human rights directly or through education of citizens on their rights either as international principles or domestic legislation. Arguably the only reference to human rights was the express inclusion of women and minorities, and the development of themes in resource allocation.

---

608   Souza (2001) 163

609   See generally Lesbaupin (2000)

610   See generally Baiocchi (2001)

611   See generally Goldfrank and Schneider (2006)

612   Souza (2001) 160-161

613   Harnecker (1999) 7-8 and Goldfrank (2007) 93.

614   See generally Goldfrank (2002)

The process involved primarily participatory planning and management of the distribution of allocated fiscal resources, and partnerships with private enterprise and NGOs for economic and social development initiatives.[615] The resulting model that evolved was developed by the then offices of the mayor and assistant mayor of PA.[616] The neighbourhood groups[617] thus joined together in PA where the Workers Party won its first elections, to enter the state civic structure and their rights agenda resulted in the calls for participation. PA began to implement PB as a municipal policy, with no central government or legislative backing.[618]

At this time, although PA was the capital of the wealthiest state of Brazil (Rio Grande do Sul), one third of its citizens lived in shanty towns or slums, and the city as a whole faced a budget shortfall so severe, it was unclear how to best spend the funds available.[619] The PB concept took a while to take off and according to the analysts of this history, the reasons appear to have been: an initial lack of financial resources; a government structure in disarray; and a lack of mobilization of the poor.[620] On this last point, the civic organizations that existed either had a history of protest and confrontation with the government or were dominated by clientelistic practices. This was dealt with in PA by the strong role played by local government in contracting community organizers to positions within the administration.

The mayor's representatives would visit unmobilized neighbourhoods, seeking out new leaders and disseminating information on the PB process. Participation was sought from factory workers as well as the "popular classes" more generally, including women's groups and civil society organizations. This built upon the Workers Party's desire to break from more traditional worker party

---

615   Mesa-Lago (1997) 502–503
616   Harnecker (1999) 7
617   See generally Baierle (1998); Baiocchi (2002).
618   Baiocchi (2005) 11
619   Chavez (2004) 161, Baiocchi (2003) 48
620   Souza (2001) 165; Avritzer (1993); Abers (1996); Santos (1998); Abers (2000); Wampler (2000); Avritzer (2002); Baiocchi (2003); Cabannes (2004); Wampler (2004); Astorga, Berges and Fitzgerald (2005); Baiocchi (2005); Wampler (2007)

models that privileged factory (usually male) labour as the subject for revolutionary change, and create post-authoritarian democratic politics. After consultation with these various constituencies, the mayor issued a decree establishing the Participatory Budget.[621]

In Brazil today, the participatory budget is both consultative and deliberative. The classically elected city council is held legally accountable for the adoption of the budget, but the local government is bound to respect the compromises reached with the Council of PB (COP) elected every year. The participatory budget process follows an all-year-round cycle. The COP is staffed with administrative council members who are appointed for unpaid, one-year mandates (with the possibility of one renewal); the PB Councillors are not representatives in the same sense as elected officials. They are subject to strict controls and their function is limited to assuring that priorities defined by the citizens are actually taken into consideration in the final budget. If they overstep the boundaries of this restricted role, they can be dismissed. The population has and maintains a real autonomy in the process and represents a countervailing power to the state administration.[622]

At its inception, citizen participation was allowed in only 2% of the total budget; and the municipal legislature allocated the rest.[623] In this early phase, the process prioritized those most underserved. Upon the completion of its first year, there was a dramatic improvement to basic services like sanitation, health and education to the poorest and most marginalized.[624] Participation was extended in 1999 to debate and decision over roughly 15% of the budget (investment and related operations).[625] Since 1999 it has been further extended to the COP debating and influencing the total municipal budget (investments, taxes, debts, municipal employee's incomes).[626]

---

621   Chavez (2004) 57-70

622   See generally Fung and Wright (2003)

623   Baiocchi (2003) 50

624   See generally Chavez (2004)

625   See generally Baiocchi (2003)

626   See generally Wampler (2000)

6.1.2.   THE PA MODEL: PARTICIPATION IN THE BUDGETING PROCESS

The process begins in March of each year just before the first round of formal assemblies to gather demands of individual citizens and mobilize the community to select regional delegates. The municipality is not involved in these intra-community discussions with district-level assemblies in each of the city's 16 districts that can amount to over 1,000 participants. These meetings are held to elect delegates as well as to review the previous year's projects. Since this first step of PB was implemented at municipal level, there were no legislated rules specifically written out for the PB process, the municipality was left free to create the political space for participation as it deemed fit. In PA, these rules evolved into for example, 3 minute periods for each speaker and after 10 people speak, government leaders make clarifications and comments. After these 10 participants have spoken there is an informal vote on whether to allow additional speakers or not. Thus, the rules have evolved and continue to evolve based on current practice, and norms of behaviour that guide the process and interaction of the participants.[627] However, these rules are subject to the level of interests and involvement of the participants in the PB, if there are inadequate numbers of participants there will be little or no effect, feedback or reflection of needs in the municipal budgets.

The first round of meetings between the citizens and the executive follows in April, when the mayor and his staff attend. Delegates are elected based on a diminishing margin formula of 1 for 10 for the first 100 participants; 1 for 20 for the next 150; 1 for 30 for the next 150 and 1 for 40 for any additional participants. Civic societies are responsible for choosing their own representatives.[628] The attendance of trade union representatives in the COP was also specifically created in Brazil and the other citizen participants perceived this as a positive factor.[629]

Between the first and the second rounds (March to June), informal preparatory meetings are held to discuss demands for

---

627   Wampler (2007) 10

628   Baiocchi (2003) 48

629   See generally Wampler (2000)

investment in sectors as presented by the various community associations (unions, cooperatives, mothers' clubs, among others). The delegates attend two types of meetings. Firstly, they meet at district level, weekly or bimonthly, to learn about technical issues as well as to decide on district needs. Delegates here can number between 40 and 60 people. Secondly, all the delegates in the city are split into 5 thematic groups; transportation; education, leisure and culture; health and social welfare; economic development and taxation; and city organization and urban development.[630] Each thematic group meets to deliberate on city-wide projects. Attendees at these meetings include ministry representatives who explain participants' roles and any issues that concern them. Demands are ranked on an ascending scale of 1 to 5 by the participants. These are then aggregated by the executive together with points earned through two other criteria: firstly, need – measured by how much of access a region has had to a particular service, and secondly, population size. Maximum points that can thus be attained is fifteen: 5 points if a region has had less than 20% access to a service, if it has more than 120,000 inhabitants, and 5 if people rank it top on their list of demands. Each specific project selected by the PB participants receives a tracking number that enables municipal bureaucrats to inform any interested party about the project's current status.

After the delegates decide upon projects, at a second plenary meeting they elect councillors to represent them at the Municipal Council level. Councillors are elected on the basis of two per district and two per thematic area after which their duties are considered discharged for the year. This COP is a 44-member committee: two councillors (and two substitutes) are elected from all 16 regions (32 delegates), from all the 5 themes (10 delegates), in addition to a member each from the civil servants' trade-union and an umbrella organization of neighbourhood communities (2 delegates).

The second round takes place in July when councillors pass on the projects and priorities to the Municipal Council of the Budget. This council meets biweekly over several months. It is made up of the representatives from the district and thematic group with the

---

630   World Bank (2003e)

mayor's administration. They then reconcile demands with available resources, propose and approve a municipal budget in conjunction with members of the administration. This group also amends the scope and rules of the process itself. Changes have included increasing the scope of PB, broadening the powers of the Municipal Council to cover personnel expenses, as well as changing the criteria of district resource allocation.

Between September and December, the COP follows the debates in the Chamber and lobbies intensely, while working on a detailed investment plan that lays down all specific public works and corresponding amounts to be allocated to each region. The executive drives the COP process by coordinating the meetings, setting the agenda, having its departments present information before allowing interventions from the Councillors to seek clarifications. In the end, resources are divided through a weighting system that combines the subjective preferences of citizens with the objective quantitative criteria. PA's municipal budget is much closer to a real budget than the "black box"[631] that budgets tend to be at other levels of government.

Brazil's fiscal year coincides with the calendar year[632] as a result, in January, the municipal legislature votes on the budget, which is usually approved without modification. After PB participants select projects, the implementation process is mainly administrative.[633] As the projects are implemented, street committees monitor their progress. Near the year's end, participants re-draw the rules of the process for the following year based on their experience.[634] This flexibility in the rules and development in them to suit the situation as well as the leeway given to the citizens in PA has translated into the overall success of the process. The participatory budget is thus

---

631   An accurate budget makes it easier for citizens to understand the budget process and to work to include their own items. Under these conditions, items included in the budget enjoy a much higher likelihood of being implemented than under the more familiar "black box" method. This also gives all factions the opportunity to know what the government is actually doing.

632   Marquetti (2005) 4

633   See generally Wampler (2004)

634   See generally Baiocchi (2003)

based on rules that are elaborated and modified in the course of the participative process and can be revised annually.

Citizens thus took over many functions usually reserved for bureaucrats: setting city-wide spending priorities, planning investments, and reviewing payrolls, as well as setting the rules for the PB process itself and monitoring its outcomes. Since the 1990s PA has assumed responsibility for most social-service provision and infrastructure investments and citizens are able to exert significant control over transportation, education, public health, and public works.

The municipal administration implements the public works they select in a timely and transparent manner. Implementation is at the discretion of the mayor, because line items in the budget do not necessarily have to be implemented. In PA, decisions made through PB have become binding decisions, as the municipal administrations have implemented projects selected by PB participants. By honouring the decisions made in PB, the government signals to the population that important public policy decisions are now made in this institutional sphere. This shifts decision making processes away from the private spheres of the government and into the PB meetings. The municipal administration has taken a third step that has increased horizontal accountability and public trust by submitting its own policy initiatives for approval by PB participants. Without formal approval in the citizens' forum, the government's specific public works initiatives could not be included in the municipal budget and therefore could not be implemented. This step represents a fundamental change in Brazilian policy-making, because PA's government must publicly defend its specific projects and submit these projects to a project-specific vote.[635]

At this level, the responsibility for decisions on the budget rests with the City COP consisting of two district delegates from PA's 16 districts plus their sub-district, as well as representatives of local government, municipal employees, unions, and neighbourhood associations. PA's PB has made extensive efforts to create a new

---

635   See generally Wampler (2004)

public arena for deliberation and negotiation.[636] Citizens are mobilized for a series of local, regional, thematic, and municipal meetings that enable them to interact with each other as well as with public officials. This allows interested and engaged citizens to maintain pressure on the mayoral administration. It also allows mayoral administrations that support PB participants' demands to argue for the "inversion of priorities" based on the participation of increasing numbers of citizens.

PA's PB took the municipal council out of the decision making process by having citizens make all budgetary decisions that fall within the purview of "discretionary spending." This undermined horizontal accountability, because one branch of government (the municipal council) received a smaller, weaker role in the budgetary process. PB still has not been legally constituted, which means that it is technically and legally part of the municipal administration (mayor's office). While successive WP mayors in PA have gone to considerable lengths to ensure that citizens in public venues make most budgetary decisions, final legal authority still rests with the mayor's office.

The experiment in PA was the turning point for PB possibly due to both its success and also since it is the place where the practice of PB is most consolidated today. PA developed the rules which then spread to the rest of the country and by 2004, more than 250 Brazilian municipalities had adopted PB.[637] By 2008, however, the PA experiment began to change as the new mayor of PA did not belong to the WP and was not as keen on their social agenda and now only 1% of the city's budget is debated in PB.[638]

6.1.3. THE EVOLUTION OF THE PA MODEL IN BRAZIL

After PA's success, the WP[639] in Brazil progressively experimented with citizen budget councils in 12 out of the 36 municipalities that

---

636   See generally Avritzer (2002);Avritzer (2002)

637   See generally Baiocchi (2005)

638   Fox (6 July 2009)

639   Brazil at this point in time was one of the only countries that simultaneously allowed an opposition party to exist, gave significant spending responsibilities to municipalities and had relatively fair mayoral elections.

it won in 1988-92.[640] Of the 12 initial case studies on PB, Wampler considers that the results were mixed and while two were quite successful (PA, Ipatinga); two were clearly failures (Blumenau and Rio Claro).[641] However, no municipality has managed to mirror the PA process.

Nevertheless, with each successive municipal election term, as the WP in Brazil progressively won more municipal mayoral seats, more cities attempted to apply the PA model. In 1993-96 there were 53 mayors, and 36 municipalities under PB; 1999-2000, 115 mayors, 140 municipalities under PB and in 2001-04, 187 mayors with 300 municipalities under PB.[642] PB has now spanned three consecutive presidential terms and is being applied across all political ideologies in Brazil including the municipal strongholds of the Party of the Liberal Front, which is an outgrowth of the official party of the most recent past, military dictatorship of 1963 to 1988.

The different municipalities and states tend to have different policy approaches towards PB which are decided upon at the first annual meeting each year by the people within the municipality, and vary based on the needs-based majority decision of each municipality. Themes vary and include infrastructural themes like education, health and transport as well human rights. There is, however, a flexibility within the themes. It has been seen to be limiting where certain themes are not perceived by the people in the area as being particularly important and thus the level of participation may drop if the purpose is relatively unimportant. Each mayor in Brazil emphasized rules that complemented their political interests and strategies. There have been recorded incidents of rival political party representatives trying to steer the process as much as possible in line with their own party interests.[643] Diverse themes have included women, youth, health, education and infrastructure.

Different initiatives by different Brazilian municipalities have also assisted in the evolution and improvement of the PA model. For

---

640   See generally Abers (1996)
641   Wampler (2007) 7
642   Wampler (2000); Wampler (2007) 7
643   Wampler (2007) 16

example, in Ipatinga, the municipal government sought to create a web-based program in order to improve the communication and the tracking of projects. Citizens enter their projects on computers that the governments place in public schools, public health care facilities, and a public shopping mall. Citizens submit or enter their own policy proposals for debate as well as gain information about what projects have been proposed by others. Once public works projects have been established, the government links a tracking number to each project, which a citizen can then monitor on-line.[644] This has since been adopted by PA as well as many other municipalities.

6.2.   FISCAL DECENTRALISATION IN INDIA: A CASE STUDY OF KERALA

Other countries have also developed forms of citizen participation in the budgetary process, but using different terms such as fiscal decentralisation. India is the prime example of the use of fiscal decentralisation. In 2007 a version of PB was applied based on the PA model, in the city of Pune.[645] The central Government of India and Kerala State however, developed fiscal decentralisation independently of the PA initiative.

The Constitution of the Republic of India[646] defines India in its preamble as a sovereign, socialist, secular, democratic republic.[647] At independence, India had a quasi-federal form of government and a bicameral parliament operating under a Westminster-style parliamentary system.[648] Today, India is perceived as having the classical model of a federation with constitutional delineation of functions and finances between the federal government and the states. There are 25 states and 7 centrally administered territories.[649] It is thus similar to Brazil as each Indian state has a similar three-layered governance structure.[650] While Brazil went one step forward

---

644   Government of Brazil (2008)

645   See generally Vijayalakshmi (2007)

646   Constitution of India (1950)

647   Dutt (1998) 421

648   Wheare (1963) 28

649   Rao (1998) 78

650   See generally Shah (2007)

and recognised municipalities in the 1988 Constitution, India has not done this and as a result there is no recognition in the federal system of the municipal divisions and hence no parallel budgeting provisions. Brazil and India are thus similar as both are large developing countries with formal federations.[651]

India, post-independence and to date, can be considered to be a tax state with elements of a fiscal state.[652] Studies of the tax regime in India between 1985 and 1995 show that states in India raise on average about 35% of their current revenues and disburse about 57% of total public expenditure within the state. Allocations from the central taxes constitute 24% of total revenue while those from state taxes amount to approximately 31%. The amount that can be shared is approximately 24% and the remaining 17% is from non-tax revenue. Central government taxes consist mainly of customs (15% of total central government revenue) and corporation tax (8% of total central government revenue). State sales tax constitutes 16% while other state taxes together amount to less than 6% of total state revenue.[653]

State spending on the other hand constitutes 57% of total expenditure but in reality is broken down to 15% central government sector expenditure and projects. States are however responsible for 85% of social service provision, 60% of administration expenditure and 60% of economic services.[654] The financial autonomy of local governments to initiate new programs and projects is limited. In 1991 fiscal reforms initiated during the decentralisation process led to decrease of central government expenditure, while state transfers were maintained. Thus state expenditure has increased for both capital and current expenditure while income has remained constant.[655] Since 1990-91, state revenue-raising has remained stable, while expenditure has increased by 5%.[656]

---

651   Vaillancourt and Bird (1998) 18

652   See Ormrod-Bonney Model

653   Rao (1998) 83

654   *Ibid.* 84

655   *Ibid.* 85

656   Paul (2007) 32

Local governments are therefore largely dependent on transfers from national government. State revenue sources are limited to property and professional taxes and a limited set of licence fees. The Constitution recognises the inadequacy of state tax powers[657] to meet expenditure needs and thus allows for the sharing of revenues from income tax[658] and the Union excise duty.[659] Grants-in-aid are also provided on a needs basis[660] and with devolution tax, are determined by the Finance Commission.[661] Transfers are thus allocated in accordance with per capita income levels in the different states.[662]

In line with British colonial policy, the Indian social welfare system was set up during British colonisation but only for the European population,[663] significant reforms took place after independence. The British did not establish many social policies other than those aiming at the removal of anti-welfare provisions, such as long-standing malpractices in the realm of marriage, inheritance, and women's social and political participation. Again, this was only made possible due to the political rivalries mainly between different religious communities on the one hand, and the increase in general social discontent that produced new generations of social reformers on the other, which began as early as the first decades of the 19th century.[664] The Constitution of India in article 38(1) stipulates that there shall be the advancement of a social order with social, economic, and political justice as the basis of all institutions of the national life. In Article 38(2), the Indian Constitution lays down that the state shall, in particular, strive to minimize the inequalities in status, facilities, and opportunities, not only amongst individuals but also amongst groups of people who reside in different areas, or engage in different vocations.[665]

---

657   Vaillancourt and Bird (1998) 82

658   Constitution of India (1950) article 270

659   *Ibid.* article 272

660   *Ibid.* article 275

661   *Ibid.* article 280

662   Rao (1998) 82

663   Midgley (1986) 127

664   See generally Aspalter (2003)

665   Constitution of India (1950)

Under Article 42 of the Indian Constitution, the state shall make effective provisions for securing the right to work; education; and public assistance in case of unemployment, old age, sickness, disablement, and in other cases of underserved want. Over the years the government has established, sickness insurance, a pension plan, maternity benefits, special disability benefits, hospital leave, a productivity-linked bonus scheme, various reductions of housing, electricity, and water rates, a deposit-linked life insurance scheme, and death-cum-retirement gratuity for central government employees. Whereas employees and workers in the public and semi-public sector are able to rely on a rather comprehensive system of social security, workers in the private sector—urban or rural—are left out of any such provisions. There are comparatively limited attempts with regard to employment security in some federal states, but there is no social insurance system for old-age pensions. The only schemes that exist are old-age assistance schemes which, are referred to as pension schemes by Central and State Governments.

The massive efforts of the Indian leadership, above all the Congress Party, of the late 1940s and early 1950s to build an Indian welfare state system, although it was residual in nature, was greatly limited to the clientele of government employees and workers in semi-governmental industries. It, however, was seen as successful, it continuously extended in the decades thereafter, especially in the field of population/family planning, but also with regard to health care, employment, nutrition, and social assistance.[666] Hence the Department of Social Welfare of the Central Government only provides initiative and leadership to the respective government authorities in charge of social welfare, and serves mainly as a clearinghouse of information and forum for exchange of ideas and very general policy guidelines. Furthermore, it administers certain central and centrally sponsored schemes, and it deals with matters related to interstate welfare problems.[667] The Constitution also contains a very comprehensive declaration of fundamental rights.[668]

---

666   See generally Aspalter (2003)

667   Dandekar and Rath (1978) 227

668   Bendix (1977) 297

India acceded to both the ICCPR and ICESCR on the 10 April 1979.[669]

6.2.1.   FISCAL BUDGETARY PARTICIPATION IN INDIA

In 1993, a Constitutional Amendment constitutionally recognised and authorised the participation of citizens in governance, although it had not been previously prohibited. This amendment was introduced by the Government of India after several decades of deliberation through two Constitutional Amendments – the 73rd (rural decentralization) and 74th Amendment (urban decentralization) – to give effect to its objectives of decentralization. These amendments stated that elections to local bodies are to take place at least every 5 years and that a three-tier structure was to exist in all parts of the country except in those Indian states where the population is less than 2000. These tiers are Village Panchayats at the smallest level, Block Panchayats at the intermediary level and District Panchayats having a larger jurisdiction. It is up to each state to determine whether the relations among these three tiers should be organised hierarchically or on the basis of the principle of co-responsibility. Other features include provision of an all voter assembly at the village level known as the Gram Sabha with the State Finance Commission for preparing criteria for providing grants to the local bodies, District Planning Committees and State Election Commission. However, apart from Kerala, few states have decisively implemented this constitutional amendment.[670]

Fiscal decentralization in India remains a continually evolving and progressive process. The 74th Amendment provides guidance as to the services that should be local responsibilities, but the list is discretionary. In practice, states have made very few modifications in functional assignments. Key urban functions either remain at the state level, or are allocated in an overlapping and unclear manner among state bodies, parastatal institutions, and urban local bodies.

---

669   Office of the United Nations High Commissioner for Human Rights. Ratifications to the International Covenant on Economic, Social and Cultural Rights (2007), Office of the United Nations High Commissioner for Human Rights. Ratifications to the International Covenant on Civil and Political Rights (2007)

670   Isaac and Heller (2003) 78

On the income side of the budget, the 74th Amendment provides few guidelines as to how urban local bodies should be financed. This aspect of intergovernmental finance is left to states to decide, though programmes and schemes of the central government may offer incentives for particular reforms in tax design or revenue collection. The initial and most determined efforts at democratic decentralization in India have been in the states of Kerala and Bangalore.[671]

6.2.2. KERALA

The trend of decentralisation in Kerala has not been a linear one. The evolution of rural local government in Kerala was not uniform throughout the state since parts of it were under princely rule and the rest under the British province of Madras. The areas under princely rule did not institute Panchayats (rural local government) akin to modern Panchayats before India became independent. In contrast, in the areas under British rule, some rudimentary forms of local government were established. Even after independence, Kerala has been impervious to developments that took place in other parts of the country in the field of Panchayat Raj.[672]

Until 1995, Kerala had only a single tier, the Village Panchayat, and was behind most states in India in the implementation of Panchayat Raj. The only attempt before the 73rd amendment was the District Council experiment in 1991 which did not survive the federal regime change after nation elections in 1995. In the 1990s, changes were already being made, even before the constitutional amendment. Kerala made provisions for an ombudsman for local government, with appellate tribunals at regional and district levels as well as a citizen's charter.[673]

---

671   *Ibid.*

672   The Panchayat Raj is an age-old administrative local self governance system practiced in India, where a group of 5 elders were given the decision making power for an area by the people living in that area. It was adopted on independence into the Constitution of India under article 40 and its weaknesses were corrected through constitutional amendment numbers 73 and 74. See Shivaramu (1997) 1-4, Bendix (1977) 256-357

673   Kerala. Kerala Panchayat Raj Act (1999)

Apart from a suggestion in 1958 by the then head of the Communist Party of India, political parties belonging to both the right and the left never took decentralisation seriously. In 1996, a coalition of left parties led by the Communist Party of India returned to power in Kerala and immediately fulfilled one of its most important campaign pledges by launching the "People's Campaign for Decentralized Planning." The participatory planning experiment was aimed at making the Ninth Five-Year Plan of the state of Kerala a 'people's plan'. The managers of the 'campaign' hoped that as the plan process moved forward, the institutional, legal and procedural bottlenecks to decentralisation of power would be removed as and when they arose.

The Kerala State Government started off the 'campaign' with an announcement in August 1996 that 35–40% of the total planned development funds of the state would be devolved to the local bodies to be spent by these bodies on the basis of the priorities fixed by citizens. The Campaign was structured to nurture and facilitate direct citizen participation based on two principles. Firstly, local government institutions should be transformed into simple delivery service units using the principle of subsidiarity.[674] Secondly, representatives were made continuously accountable and processes transparent.[675]

All 1,214 local governments in Kerala, the municipalities and the three rural tiers of district, block, and gram Panchayats, were given new functions and powers of decision making, and were granted discretionary budgeting authority over 35–40% of the state's developmental expenditures. In addition to devolving resources, state officials sought to directly promote participatory democracy by mandating structures and processes designed to maximize the direct involvement of citizens in planning and budgeting.[676]

The 'People's Campaign for Decentralized Planning' translated into a campaign to mobilise the people through several stages. The first foray was to create a role for the citizens and this was undertaken

---

674   What can best be done and decided at local level should be done there.

675   Isaac and Heller (2003) 80

676   *Ibid.* 78-79

through the Kerala State Planning Board to allow local citizens to shape local development policy and budgeting decisions. The second stage was to charge the local governments within Kerala at this juncture with designing and implementing their own development plans. Additional support was given by the state apparatus through the provision of procedural templates, technical assistance, and key oversight functions and administrative capacity as well as a massive training programme of over 100,000 key resource persons at local and district levels.[677]

Kerala thus chose a participatory institutional structure consisting of four stages. At the first level, Gram Sabhas are held at ward[678] level. The Gram Sabhas are open meetings, presided over by local elected officials, and facilitated by the Key Resource Persons (KRPs). They are always held on holidays, and in public buildings (usually schools). Preparations for the assemblies include extensive publicity, and the distribution of various planning documents. Minutes are kept, and each sub-sector group presents a report of its deliberations and produces a list of "felt needs." This is an open forum where residents identify local development problems, generate priorities, and form sub-sector Development Seminars (DS) where specific proposals first take shape. Subsequent Gram Sabhas select beneficiaries for targeted schemes.

At the second stage development seminars develop integrated solutions for various problems identified at the Gram Sabhas. The DS are constituted of representatives selected by the Gram Sabhas, members of Panchayat samithi, local political leaders, key officials of the area, and experts from the locality and outside. The seminars are required to produce a comprehensive planning document for the Panchayat.

At the third stage Task Forces are selected by the DS and are charged with converting the broad solutions of the seminars into project or scheme proposals to be integrated into the final Panchayat plan. In general, a task force is constituted for each of 10 development sectors, including women's development, and it includes a member

---

677   Heller, Harilal and Chaudhuri (2007) 629.

678   There are 10-12 wards in a Panchayat

of the Panchayat samithi, the relevant local official and representatives selected by the Gram Sabhas.

The fourth phase of the annual planning exercise is the actual formulation of the Panchayat or municipal budget. Drawing from the sectoral projects designed by the task forces, the Panchayat drafts a local plan based on available budgetary resources, which include grant-in-aid,[679] own resources[680] and state or central government project funds.

In both its scope and design, the campaign represents the most ambitious and concerted state-led effort to build local institutions of participatory democratic governance ever undertaken in the subcontinent. Isaac and Heller state that the political and institutional design reflects a social transformation principle similar to PA. Thus every year since 1997, local governments in Kerala have formulated and implemented their own development plans. In the decentralization experiment in India, an important finding of Heller was that the campaign has created structures of participatory governance where none existed before.[681] Not only have resources been devolved, but new institutions have been built, new processes of local decision making have been created and new channels of participation have been opened up. In sum, new loci of governance and new spaces of citizenship now mark Kerala's political and development landscape. One of the most respected and a sceptical commentator on the campaign, Kannan, has offered perhaps one of the most succinct assessments: the campaign has not only created a "public platform for a vigilant civil society," but has also ensured an "enabling environment for development".[682]

6.3.   PARTICIPATION IN THE BUDGET AROUND THE WORLD

At the same time as the WP application of PB in Brazil, there were three other political parties in Central America, the Radical Cause

---

679   The largest component

680   Local taxes and local resource mobilization

681   Isaac and Heller (2003) 78-79

682   See generally Kannan and Pillai (2004)

in Venezuela and the Broad Front in (Montevideo) Uruguay, that were also elected in 1989 and implemented similar participatory programmes in 1990.[683] In 1994, Bolivia passed a Popular Participation Law although the term PB was not adopted. There are other examples, for instance, in the United States, as early as 1986, in Sparks, Nevada, the then city administration involved citizens to participate in the municipal budget by mailing 18,000 households a budget ballot on which citizens were asked to indicate their preferences for spending allocations of the municipality.[684]

However, most accounts agree that a fully-fledged participatory budget was initiated definitively in 1989 in PA.[685] This consensus may be related to the success of the particular model developed in PA. The widespread adoption of PB regimes in Latin America has gone hand-in-hand with the spread of democracy.[686] Thus many local and sub-national governments adopted this system in order to directly involve citizens in state sanctioned policy in order to promote social justice, increase transparency and engage citizens' voices in policy issues.[687]

The real spread of PB worldwide took place after 1996 when the United Nations Habitat II Conference in Istanbul recognised PA's PB process as one of 42 best practices in urban governance.[688] At this point in time India (1993) and the Philippines (1995) were already practicing PB. Since Istanbul, PB has been introduced in one form or another in Guatemala (1996);[689] in the late 1990s in Nicaragua[690] and Thailand;[691] 1998 in Poland[692] and Lebanon;[693]

---

683   See generally Goldfrank (2001); Goldfrank (2002); Chavez (2004); Goldfrank (2005); Goldfrank (2007) 93

684   See generally Simonsen and Robbins (2000) 24

685   See generally Abers (2000); Avritzer (2002); Goldfrank (2003) Wampler (2007) 6, 9

686   See generally De Sousa Santos; Weffort (1989); Roberts (1999); Heller (2001); Avritzer (2002); Barber (2004); Santos (2007)

687   See generally Santos (1998); Avritzer (2002)

688   Goldfrank (2007) 93

689   *Ibid.*

690   *Ibid.*

691   Folscher (*Ibid.*) 174

692   Folscher (2007) 138

693   Folscher (2007) 236

Iraq (1999);[694] in 2000: in Bangladesh,[695] Romania,[696] Bulgaria[697] and Kenya; Peru (2003),[698] and Albania (2004)[699] among others. In addition, while there were less than five European Participatory Budgets in 2000, by 2005 more than 50 European local governments had started to experiment with it. Processes have commenced in Germany, Spain, Italy, and France, and there are also some cases in the UK, Portugal, and Poland, as well as some developments in this direction in Belgium, Norway, and Sweden.[700]

However, there is no single formula or type of participatory budgeting (PB) process; it has always been introduced according to the local contextual social background, history, legal and political context. This has led to the development of a variety of participatory budgeting styles. More recently, institutional funding institutions such as the WB, World Bank Institute, United Nations Development Program (UNDP), and United Nations Habitat Program (Habitat) have begun to promote participation in budgeting as an innovative way to promote transparency, enhance accountability, and encourage more socially equitable forms of spending.

The Indian form of decentralisation in Kerala, as discussed above, although not using the term PB, nevertheless seems not only to fall within the broad definition of PB but also to share many characteristics of the PA model. Indeed, the type and degree of citizen involvement varies from place to place, and PB is expressed through municipal policy in various ways, whether in Brazil, village-based reforms particularly in Kerala, Karnataka and West Bengal; District Councils in Uganda; and Bolivia under its Law of Popular Participation. Thus the discussion that follows will use the term 'participation in budgeting' in order to avoid any confusion about specific models but instead to allow a general analysis and critique

---

694   *Ibid.*

695   Folscher (2007) 175

696   Folscher (2007) 139

697   *Ibid.*

698   Goldfrank (*Ibid.*) 94

699   Folscher (*Ibid.*)

700   See generally Gret and Sintomer (2005)

that will include not only Brazil and India, but diverse examples from all over the world.

6.4.   Resource Allocation through Participation in Budgeting and the Role of Human Rights

The form, type, extent and method all create variables that affect the effectiveness and efficiency of budgetary allocations and thus their impact on development, poverty alleviation and overall human rights. In order to assist and improve participation the one missing link seems to be the quantification of citizen expectations. Participation itself would remain ineffective and incomplete unless benchmarks are set out in a crystallised format and placed at the disposal of the citizenry.

To date, human rights principles are still considered as utopian and no state in the world can claim to have fully achieved them. However, within the participatory context, as seen in the case of India and Brazil, thus far, whether the people are aware of it or not, they make decisions based on need. It is these needs that are arguably the core of human rights and natural rights. If these human rights are thus linked back to the needs expressed they become no longer completely utopian but rather possibly achievable and partially, progressively realistic.

This sub-section will critically analyse participation in budgeting and through the analysis of its outcomes attempt to make suggestions for a possible governance framework that would be best suited or be most conducive for the attempted fulfilment and realisation of human rights through resource allocation.

6.4.1.   The Outcomes of Participation in Budgeting

All accounts agree[701] that throughout the 16-year existence of PB in PA, Brazil, the process has evolved and has been regularly adapted to best suit stakeholder needs. Its success has resulted in, firstly, increased citizen mobilisation as people realised that

---

701   See generally Santos (1998); Abers (2000); Goldfrank (2001); Baiocchi (2002); Baiocchi (2003); Goldfrank (2003); Guidry (2003); World Bank (2003e); Cabannes (2004); Gret and Sintomer (2005); Wampler (2007); Menser and Robinson (January 29, 2008)

participation mattered leading to real changes in everyday life. Most notably, the poorest segments of the city's population have seen an improvement in their living conditions and have largely been involved in the PB process. Secondly, the participation is open to all and the recognition of each voice (one person = one voice) has been important.[702] Community associations have played a key role but have not had any legal privilege and therefore were obliged to clearly show their mobilisation capacity. Thirdly, the creation of participative councils has been decisive in increasing the quality of the public deliberation process, for organising participation all year round and for scrutinising the process. Fourthly, the formal rules and real dynamics of the participation process were the outcome of co-decisions by citizens and local government. Fifthly, the formal criterion of re-distribution is based on the principle of affirmative action. Finally, the process has been based on a clear methodology, which has increased the transparency of public action. It has given the population better access to information and increased the accountability of local government and participatory delegates.[703]

The projects undertaken in PA have achieved almost full water and sewer coverage, a threefold increase in the number of children in municipal schools, and significant increases in the number of new housing units provided to needy families. PA's expenditures in certain areas, such as health and housing, are much higher than the national average, yet the municipalities' administrative costs and overheads have declined over the years. PA has also managed a redistributive regime that is fiscally responsible and transparent. Preliminary results of a national analysis conducted in the late 1990s show that PB tends to lower poverty rates and improve education.[704]

If PB is considered from the vantage point of horizontal accountability, it is apparent that the mayor's office remains firmly in control of the policy-making process. The municipal administration provides information, allocates the political and bureaucratic staff to conduct meetings, and implements projects. PB is a success in PA also because it has the firm support of the municipal administration.

---

702   Wampler (2007) 2

703   See generally Wampler (2004);Baiocchi (2005);Wampler (2007)

704   See generally Baiocchi (2005)

It is not clear whether citizens can legally force the mayor's hand to provide information or implement projects. This means that PB participants must depend partly on the good will and benevolence of the municipal government, which indicates that PB has only partly promoted restrictions on mayoral authority in PA. PB in PA is noteworthy for how it has modified and expanded decision making processes, but the outcomes continue to be limited because the PB's positive results depend on intense support from the municipal government. It is hoped that citizen involvement may decrease the power of the mayor's office over the long term, but for the present the mayor's office remains the most important political actor in PA.

Wampler confirmed the widespread view that PA's PB model has produced good results including an average of 50,000 participants annually, vibrant debates, fairly transparent government processes and the implementation of over USD 400 million of PB projects.[705]

The result of the PA initiative led to the belief that PB is applied based on several presumptions. Firstly, that the distribution of public funds is of utmost importance to the lives of citizens. Secondly, that those citizens are qualified to be directly involved in taking decisions because they are experts in everyday life and have precious local knowledge. Thirdly, that participation is a voluntary political action for everyone. Finally, that PB is costly – but will save a lot of money in the long run.[706]

Many scholars argue that any citizen involvement in local government (including the budget process) is positive and should be cultivated and encouraged by both elected and appointed officials.[707] Others, however, note that citizen participation in the budget process does not always have the desired positive outcomes.[708] Negative outcomes include: loss of decision-making control; the possibility of bad decisions that are politically impossible to ignore; less budget for implementation of actual projects; a time consuming costly process;

---

705   Wampler (2007) 6

706   See generally Baiocchi (2005)

707   See generally University of Southern California Neighborhood Participation Project. (2003); Berner (2001); Franklin and Carberry-George (1999)

708   See generally Ebdon and Franklin (2004)

possible failure creating more hostility toward government; pointless if a public decision is ignored; and poor policy decisions if heavily influenced by opposing interest groups.[709] These differences aside, most public administration scholars agree that citizen participation in government is desirable and should be encouraged, but they concede that such involvement is episodic and sporadic at best, and can, at times, prove detrimental to the functioning and administration of government.[710]

Most scholars and practitioners agree that citizen involvement in governmental process is limited, except when tax increases are proposed. It appears that the financial intricacies of the budget often confuse, bore, or simply do not interest many citizens. Nonetheless, these studies also agree that citizens should be more involved in the budget process.[711]

A)   THE INTENDED CONSEQUENCES: IMPROVED GOVERNANCE

The WB is supporting regional PB efforts in Africa and Latin America focussing on assisting governments in initiating and administering PB. However, the level of active participation by citizens and CSO is directly related to the success of PB especially where governments delegate some decisions to citizens. The criterion for success here involves how the delegation of authority affects the extent of accountability and citizenship rights, PB does not necessarily establish these but it may assist in transformation of the system.[712]

It is argued by Keefer[713] that there are systematic performance differences between younger and older democracies. He adds that this is a result of the inability of political competitors to make credible pre-electoral promises to voters. This takes place in a

---

709   See generally Irvin and Stansbury (2004)

710   See generally Cole (1975); Robert Goodin and John Dryzek (1980); Hirlinger (1992); Verba, Scholzman and Brady (1993); Timney (1998); Vigoda (2002); Kirlin and Kirlin (2002); Irvin and Stansbury (2004); Adams (2004); Blomgren-Bingham, Nabatchi and O'Leary (2005); Yang (2005).

711   Ebdon and Franklin (2004); University of Southern California Neighborhood Participation Project. (2003); Berner (2001); Franklin and Carberry-George (1999).

712   Wampler (2007) 9

713   See generally Keefer (2005)

context of younger states that are more corrupt; exhibit less rule of law, lower levels of bureaucratic quality and secondary school enrolment, and more restrictions on the media; and spends more on public investment and government workers. Keefer and Vlaicu[714], argue that the inability of political competitors to make credible promises to citizens leads them to prefer clientelist policies: to under-provide non-targeted goods, over-provide targeted transfers to narrow groups of voters, and to engage in excessive rent-seeking. They add that other differences that young democracies exhibit, include: different political and electoral institutions; greater exposure to political violence; greater social fragmentation; and failure to explain, either theoretically or empirically, these policy choices.

It is debatable whether or not clientelism has reduced or in fact the source of the money that was dispensed and favours that were granted to citizens and groups has changed. If the legal and policy framework is not clearly drawn and the citizens not well educated on the source of the money, many will continue to see PB simply as an extension of the patronage context and the role of the 'big man' in local politics will remain undisputed.

Manor and Crook in their case study of Kerala illustrate how control over participatory procedures affects the opportunity of citizens to participate. According to legislation, Gram Sabha should hold twice yearly meetings in each village. The purpose of such meetings was to ensure the council's accountability to citizens and to identify priority target populations for assistance. However, councillors in most places abandoned Gram Sabha meetings after the first year or two. Some resorted to subterfuge holding unannounced meetings at times when most villagers were away at work or at the market, or staging Gram Sabha meetings in the Mandal office.[715]

Both Abers and Santos argue that the replacement of clientelism with open and transparent discussions is one of the main reasons for the high legitimacy of PB.[716] The conflict between the municipal government, responsible for the PB and the parliament, where

---

714   See generally Keefer and Vlaicu (2005)

715   Crook and Manor (1998) 29-30

716   Santos (2002) Abers (2000) ch. 8

the governing party never had a majority, has nevertheless been important. As the legislature is responsible for taxation, it blocked all further attempts at tax reform by the executive. PB was an attempt to elaborate an alternative model of governance. From the very beginning, this strategy founded its legitimacy in strengthening civil society. Effective representation thus ensures and supports legitimacy. At many levels it is argued that public administration fails to cater for the needs of today's society and thus PB if effectively and efficiently put into use, may fill in this gap.

Many scholars argue that any citizen involvement in local government (including the budget process) is positive and should be cultivated and encouraged by both elected and appointed officials.[717] Others, however, note that citizen participation in the budget process does not always have the desired positive outcomes.[718] These differences aside, most public administration scholars agree that citizen participation in government is desirable and should be encouraged, but they concede that such involvement is episodic and sporadic at best, and can, at times, prove detrimental to the functioning and administration of government through its inconsistency.[719]

B)   THE UNINTENDED CONSEQUENCES: ACHIEVEMENT OF
        HUMAN RIGHTS

At the inception of participation in budgeting as propounded by the WP, despite the involvement of human rights activists and practitioners, they did not seem to consider the realisation of human rights as a reason for the application of participation. In India again there was no reference to the realisation of human rights principles progressively or otherwise in the communist party's policies in Kerala. However, despite that, it is clearly evident that there are human rights themes and threads running through the entire participatory process.

---

717   See generally University of Southern California Neighborhood Participation Project. (2003); Berner (2001); Franklin and Carberry-George (1999)

718   See generally Ebdon and Franklin (2004).

719   See generally Cole (1975); Robert Goodin and John Dryzek (1980); Hirlinger (1992); Verba, Scholzman and Brady (1993); Timney (1998); Vigoda (2002); Kirlin and Kirlin (2002); Irvin and Stansbury (2004); Adams (2004); Blomgren-Bingham, Nabatchi and O'Leary (2005); Yang (2005).

Brazil finally ratified both the ICCPR and ICESCR on the 24 January 1992 and both conventions entered into force on 24 April 1992.[720] In 1993 Brazil was expected to pass social security reforms but to date this has not taken place.[721] The link to human rights by Brazil includes exercise of the right to health. The Brazilian "Citizens' Constitution" of 1988 established among other rights, health as the right of all, defined its provision as the duty of the state and guaranteed the right to participate in the governance of health, setting the ground for the establishment of institutionalised mechanisms for citizen engagement at municipal, state and national levels. The democratisation of political and societal institutions in the post-dictatorship period; successful mobilisation by the Movimento pela Reforma Sanita'ria[722] gathered momentum and influence over the course of the 1980s; innovative institutional experiments that provided the inspiration for mechanisms for popular involvement and accountability within the state architecture; and a political commitment to the provision of publicly-funded services to all Brazilians.[723]

In Brazil, participation as a process is divided into two, and one is the needs-based theme of the open assemblies and councils that allows them to deal with issues such as youth or culture, mirroring the thematic structure of the municipal administration. For example, one such discussion was a debate between building a pedestrian overpass as opposed to a health care clinic. Participants discussed state responsibility and argued that the state should protect the health of its citizens and provide health care for the poor.[724] The participatory budget implies a redistribution of resources oriented towards the most disadvantaged neighbourhoods, through formal distributive criteria according to which resources have to be allocated. According to the UNDP 2001 report, the quality of life in PA has continuously

---

720   Office of the United Nations High Commissioner for Human Rights. Ratifications to the International Covenant on Civil and Political Rights (2007); Office of the United Nations High Commissioner for Human Rights. Ratifications to the International Covenant on Economic, Social and Cultural Rights (2007)

721   Mesa–Lago (1997) 498

722   Movement for Health Reform

723   Cornwall and Shankland (2008) 2174

724   Wampler (2007) 11

improved since democratization and that PA boasts quality of life indicators similar to that in many OECD countries.[725]

The city of Recife has a thematic plenary on Human Rights (there were 45 elected delegates in 2007). In these thematic forums delegates present proposals of budget allocation aimed at minority groups. The city of Fortaleza also has a Human Rights assembly. The city of Uberlandia (at least in 2004) had as one of its thematic assemblies a specific assembly on "human rights and combating violence".

More recently, the right to housing was also affected at both the federal and grassroots levels when in April 2003, President Lula announced a new housing fund of RD 5.3 billion (USD 1,588,776,642) to fund new housing constructions for lower income families, upgrading of *favelas*, and related municipal programs. It also provided credit for housing construction and improvement. Simultaneously, the financing provided is to be reoriented to cover social projects as well as economic development projects.[726]

In addition, interviews conducted elicited responses to the question of whether PB generally could indirectly or directly be linked to human rights. The responses I received all said that although initially PB was based on social needs these needs varied on the ground and has resulted in competing interests. However, there is no doubt that these societal needs can be perceived as human rights being achieved whether it was the right to a clean and healthy environment through control of smell pollution as in Campinas,[727] the right to health and education or event the freedom of movement.[728]

c)   UNRESOLVED ISSUES

While a lot of positive outcomes are arising from the use of the PA model in Brazil, some problems have arisen. Firstly, initially, the urban infrastructure and elementary education were financed and

---

725   Setzler (2002) 4
726   See generally Mona Serageldin *et al.* (2005)
727   Luis Renato Vedovato Interview 11 (2009)
728   Luis Alberto Interview 9 (2009)

carried out by the central government in Brasilia. In Brazil, the central government has found it difficult to withdraw from some purely local functions such as public markets, local schools, and local bridges more than a decade after the adoption of the 1988 Constitution.[729]

Secondly, a formal statistical analysis of the odds of being elected to a political post shows that, while gender, poverty, and low education have negative effects on the likelihood of being elected, years of participation significantly affect the odds positively. Interaction terms between poverty and low education and years of participation have significant positive effects, suggesting that participation over time tends to increase participatory parity. So while the proportion of elected representatives does show a slightly lesser proportion of women, the poor, and the less educated at elected positions, a more complete study of the available evidence suggests that this effect is significantly tempered by years of participation.

Thirdly, there are a number of negative expectations about the impact of participatory forums on civil society. If participatory forums are parallel to – that is, they co-exist with–civil society, it is not unreasonable to expect they may in certain settings empty out forums of civil society, as they may provide more efficient (and state-backed) ways of addressing certain problems. If participatory forums interface directly with civil society, they might co-opt movements and local decision-making forums may 'balkanize' political life.[730] Cohen briefly addresses another possibility altogether, that deliberative democratic institution might help foster new solidarities and help construct civil society.[731]

6.5.   The Creation of an Environment Conducive to Participation

There are many factors that allowed for successful PB in PA and Kerala as well as other municipalities around the world. All of these diverse factors set the background which allowed for the

---

729   Shah, Thompson and World Bank Institute. Poverty Reduction and Economic Management Division. (2004) 12

730   Fung and Wright (2003) 23

731   Cohen (1996) 112-3

development, spread and eventual success of the projects undertaken by the stakeholders in each state. This section will analyse these factors in light of use or otherwise of human rights principles at the diverse stages of the development of India and Brazil that led them to the use of participation in budgeting. These include academic discourse and the practical application of constitutional and legislative changes; undertakings of political responsibility, accountability, transparency and change; the type, form, level and extent of participation allowed with reference to political decentralisation, its effect and application in the context of political participation and the setting it creates; allowing for the improvement in governance as well the application by extension of human rights concerns and principles.

6.5.1.   THE CONSTITUTIONAL AND LEGISLATIVE FRAMEWORK

Brazil and India approached the application of participation in budgeting from two different angles. The introduction of PB in PA came first through the municipal level. Participation itself has to date never been provided for in legislation, although the framework that allowed its existence was based on constitutional and legislative provisions that were subsequently amended and revised to fit into its evolution. India on the other hand codified fiscal decentralisation and participation through constitutional provisions and this was then filtered down through the system to the state level. However, both countries share the fact that participation was developed as a policy of the political party that came into power, based on its platform in the election campaigns. Thus the first issue to consider in establishing the link between human rights and participation in the budgetary process is the constitutional, legislative and political policy that allows for the exercise of the right to participate in the budgetary process as well as creating the framework in which to situate governance.

During the past 50 years, by subscribing to different variants of central planning paradigms of development, developing and transition economies have by and large followed a path of centralisation, and as a result they are more centralised than industrialised countries were in their early stages of development. The result of the crisis of the fiscal state has translated into responsibilities being devolved from central to local government as well as contact being established between the governors and the governed.[732] For example, as discussed earlier, Brazil was ruled by a military regime from 1964 to 1985, a main characteristic of this period was thus both political and fiscal centralization. In developed states there is a long legacy of citizen involvement with the government. Despite this, even in developed states like the US today, there is attention being accorded to reengaging citizens with government priority setting. As a result, processes like PB began to emerge in order to counter these and related problems.

The reasons for rethinking legislative fiscal arrangements are manifold, and the importance of each factor is country specific. The demise of the collective ownership model prompted a major change in government organisation and geographical boundaries of some countries, especially in Eastern Europe and the former Soviet Union. These countries sought guidance from the principles and practices pursued in industrial countries where market preserving systems of public decision making have evolved over a long period of time. In Africa, both former French and English colonies inherited highly centralised systems of governance geared towards command and control, with little concern for citizens' preferences. Resolution of ethnic conflicts required greater protection of minority rights in politically disenfranchised and fragmented African societies.[733] In Latin America, political reforms empowered people who in turn demanded greater accountability from their governments. In most countries, national governments have failed to ensure regional equity, economic union, central bank independence, a stable macroeconomic environment or local autonomy. In Brazil, the pre-1988 arrangements empowered the federal government with the ability to levy separate special taxes on communication, fuel, electric power, minerals, and transport. The urban infrastructure and elementary education were financed and carried out by the central government.[734]

---

732   Askim and Hanssen (2008) 387

733   See generally Bird and Stauffer (2001)

734   See generally Bomfim and Shah (1994)

6.5.2.   THE POLICIES AND IDEOLOGY

The origins of participation in budgeting are a combination of democratic and left-wing political ideology as discussed earlier in the chapter setting out the historical development of participation in budgeting, in Brazil, while it was the brainchild of communism in India. However, the approach of the different political parties and states that practice participation in budgeting are a mixture between the radical democrats, orthodox left, liberals and conservatives. These diverse reactions may allow for or limit the use of participation in budgeting. However, the one conclusion that can be drawn is that the issue of participation in budgeting seems to cut across many political ideologies and most if not all see merit in, more rather than less participation. By extension, due to the universal acceptance of human rights principles through the treaties and declarations and affirmations by states in complying with the application of human rights principles, the application of participation in budgeting becomes useful as a tool of applying human rights as well as specifically an element of the RTD principles. Despite the divide that has been mainly political between civil and political rights and economic, social and cultural rights, the fact that this tool seems to transverse states of diverse political philosophies arguably can be translated to mean that the application of human rights principles as a whole should not pose a problem.

6.5.3.   INFORMED PARTICIPATION

Citizens in states transitioning from an authoritarian or colonial period may experience a disjuncture between actual lived democracy and formal democracy.[735] Within the developing state context, including states like India and Brazil that are applying participation in budgeting, there is said to be unstable political systems, a large unresponsive, corrupt governance system, dominated by patronage coupled with an emergent civil society that is actively seeking change. This is combined with political indifference and poor economic management.[736] Changes in human rights based legislation and

---

735   Baiocchi (2005) 10

736   Midgley (1986) 2

Constitutions to recognise and/or enforce human rights have taken place in some countries like Brazil. However, whether these changes are made on paper or not, there is little or no connection being made with their application to resource allocation.

Although participation in budgeting may be new in the field of state governance, it is not a new model of budgeting in accounting and finance.[737] Evidence, however, shows that while participation enhances attitudes towards the budget and various other attitudes of participants, it does not always result in increased performance or motivation to perform.[738] In addition, it is argued that there will be no difference between participative and non-participative budgeting if the participants do not perceive it as different. The presence of the perception of freedom in decision making thus provides the key difference.[739]

States and international institutions have adopted a so-called 'multi-stakeholder approach'[740] to global and regional governance, involving more and more business as well as civil society-actors. The rhetoric that surrounds these alleged inclusionary practices tend to make use of a very fluid signifier: 'participation'. It is now claimed more and more that civil society, as well as business actors, are 'participating' in the global political processes that build future societies. At the domestic level, the main stakeholders are the state, civil society and the citizens.

The state always directs the budgetary process. However, civil society and citizens are limited in the space they have in expressing their concerns based on the space given by the state through policy, legislation and the Constitution. For example, Peru has a law allowing for the right to participate. On the other hand, Brazil and PA allow for citizen interaction based on the policy of the political

---

737   It has been used as a technique to enhance participants' attitudes towards organisational budgets and to achieve budgeted objectives. Tiller (1983) 581

738   Brownell (1981); Brownell (1982)

739   Tiller (1983) 582-83

740   This refers to a multi-centred world system where states are no longer the sole actors or stakeholders, but international organizations, business and civil society also play their role in global or regional governance. For more on this see: Rosenau (1990); Hemmati (2002)

party in power in the area, in yet other cases such as Egypt, the government refuses publication of the budget and hence there is no room whatsoever for expression of stakeholders.

Vigoda, Kirlin and Kirlin, Timney, and Yang argue that citizens should be viewed as partners or valued stakeholders, not adversaries or impediments, in governmental process.[741] Stakeholders in the participatory process range from state officials, civil and public servants, trade union representatives, representatives of civil society, elected representatives as well as the citizens themselves.

Sidney Verba, Kay Scholzman, and Henry Brady contend that it is as important to understand who participates in the governmental process as it is to understand what they say and desire from government as a result of their participation.[742] Renee A. Irvin and John Stansbury argue that citizen participation is almost always desirable, but there are conditions that determine when it is effective and when it is not. They consider two tiers of benefits (process and outcomes) and two beneficiaries (government and citizens) in evaluating the effectiveness of the citizen-participation process. Consequently, they state that it is the responsibility of managers and elected officials to facilitate situations whereby citizen participation can have the most positive impact upon the governmental process.[743]

Kaifeng Yang adds to the discussion by stating that it is vital that citizens believe that their participation in government is worthwhile and will have a substantive effect on policy decisions. Public administrators, in turn, must trust citizens and believe that their input is both genuine and meaningful.[744] However, at a time when scholars are pointing out the crisis of the welfare state as a threat to industrialised democracies, participation may be the municipal government innovation that is empowering local citizenry, fostering new activism in civil society and creating a novel form of co-ordination across the state–society divide.[745]

---

741   See generally Yang (2005); Vigoda (2002); Kirlin and Kirlin (2002); Timney (1998).

742   See generally Verba, Scholzman and Brady (1993).

743   See generally Irvin and Stansbury (2004)

744   See generally Yang (2005)

745   Ferreira (2000) as quoted in Baiocchi (2005) 3

Participation by these diverse stakeholders may vary. It may be restricted/unrestricted participation at one or more levels of the fiscal governance structure. At the federal/national level, stakeholders may be allowed to participate. For example in the Republic of South Africa parliamentary provisions allow the Institute of Democracy in South Africa (IDASA) and other NGOs to make presentations based on their understanding of the budget in the national parliament as commentary on it before the Finance Bill is passed. This is, currently an exception and input in most countries tend to be limited to the government ministry/departmental level where the Bill is drawn up as well as discussions with individual Members of Parliament.

In Brazil, the central government has found it difficult to withdraw from some purely local functions such as public markets, local schools, and local bridges more than a decade after the adoption of the 1988 Constitution. However, the main purposes of PB were best set out in the Brazilian case where the political parties involved stated their reasons for applying PB as increasing citizen participation and oversight, transparency, improvement of services to the poor and the development of citizenship.

Wampler best summarises the position on actual citizen participation when he states in discussing Brazil that participants asserted that the process must allow citizens to decide policy outcomes, monitor government activities and change how governments act. Thus a principle of success is the scope and efficiency of the authority that citizens are allowed to exercise.[746]

6.5.4. Quality of Participation

A critical component of the Indian Kerala plan was an elaborate training programme. In its first year, in seven rounds of training at state, district, and local levels, over 15,000 elected representatives, 25,000 officials and 75,000 volunteers received training. 600 state level trainees received 20 days of training as key resource persons; 12,000 district resource persons received 10 days of training and over 100,000 local volunteers received 5 days of training. All elected representatives were required to receive some form of training.

---

746   Wampler (2007) 8-9

Training was accompanied by handbooks and guides of over 4,000 pages of documentation.[747] It is recorded that Kerala has mobilised thousands of people at the Panchayat level to prepare plans for economic development and social justice.[748]

In the USA several diverse techniques are used for participation. Firstly, citizen surveys and forms are used to obtain citizen attitudes on the budget. For example, during 1991–1992 in Eugene, Oregon, an innovative combination of public forums, budget-balancing exercises and representative surveys to determine public support for budgetary spending and balancing alternatives. There were multiple rounds of citizen input and allowed for time for consideration of the alternatives as well as discussion with other forum participants. This approach has come to be referred to as Eugene decisions, and have since been repeated in Sacramento, California, (1996–1997); Lexington, Kentucky (1993); Springfield, Oregon (1988) as well as over 15 other municipalities around the United States.[749]

Secondly, citizen juries and panels are provided with unbiased high quality information with time to deliberate and consider information, with the decisions taken to be representative of citizens. However, the only budgetary participation process was carried out by a CSO, the Jefferson Centre for New Democratic Processes on the US Federal Budget.[750] In 1991 there was also a poll taken on the federal budget deficit and the result was reported to Congress.[751]

6.6.   CONCLUSION

A distillation of the case studies of the two main countries in the world today that are practicing participation in budgeting as well as discussion of other countries with innovations in participation in budgeting show the direction this discourse has taken in light of human rights principles. There is no evidence in either Indian or Brazilian fiscal policy that shows that any consideration was ever

---

747   Isaac and Heller (2003) 83
748   Bandyopadhyay (1997) 2450
749   Simonsen and Robbins (2000) 22–26
750   *Ibid.* 27–28
751   *Ibid.* 29–30

directly made of human rights in deciding upon the participatory processes.

Brazil and India as well as all the other countries applying participation of citizens in the budgeting process are all applying one form or another of the element expressly set out in the Declaration on the Right to Development: participation. However, these case studies are by no means complete or perfect in looking at human right linkages to tax. They are the closest existing model to apply the theoretical concepts discussed in the previous chapters. The ultimate model case study would be one that not only looks into consideration of the needs and wants of people that is expressed through their participation, but also have well set out benchmarks as to what needs to be achieved in not only the short term but also in the long term in both economic and human rights obligations, and this is at best completely utopian. Currently, participation in budgeting stops short of taking into consideration human rights obligations to which all states in the world are party and applying them at the grassroot level through resource allocation to reflect fulfilment of their international and national obligations and commitments. Thus, benchmarking revenue to particular expenditure using human rights principles as the measure does not take anything away from the current participatory processes but rather completes it. How a state municipality or area will recognise that it has achieved sufficiency in a particular issue such as schools, clinics, roads, security is what needs to be benchmarked. Planning the process is key, and using the available tools like the MDGs and human rights principles could lead to the achievement of this goal through realistic and practical benchmarking.

PART 3

CONTEXTUALISING TAXATION AND HUMAN RIGHTS IN KENYA

CHAPTER 7

THE KENYAN CONSTITUENCY DEVELOPMENT FUND

The focus of the immediately preceding chapter narrowed down into how participation is practiced in budgeting processes in Brazil and India. Although neither country made reference to the right to development and human rights, participation is an element of the right to development as discussed in chapter 4. In the actual choice of well-being and development initiatives, key themes for budget allocation include what are today considered to be part of human rights: health, education, housing, social welfare. Kenya is currently undertaking a form of PB which is the focus of this chapter.

The problems that the Kenyan fiscal state and society are grappling with have been discussed in the past chapters with the intention that perhaps this current practice may provide a solution and with a few amendments to the approach provide further solutions not only to the legitimacy of the fiscal state but also the realisation of human rights. In addition to the need to achieve improved social welfare and legitimatise the fiscal state the preceding chapters have brought out the issue of accountability, corruption, clientelism, patronage and the 'big man' system in Kenyan politics. The ensuing discussion will not only analyse the PB in Kenya: the CDF, but will enquire into whether or not the issues set out above, all which form part of the governance practices under the right to development, are being achieved or can be achieved if the CDF process were to be undertaken or analysed within the context of human rights laws in order to improve fiscal legitimacy.

The CDF is the first attempt ever made in Kenya to deliberately and concretely link tax revenue to tax expenditure. Through the CDF citizens are placed in the position of distributing resources which they are aware are sourced from themselves. This chapter will explain and evaluate the development of the CDF, and explore the question of whether human rights could be integrated into the discourse in the allocation of CDF resources.

7.1.   ESTABLISHMENT OF THE CONSTITUENCY DEVELOPMENT FUND

Under the Constituency Development Fund (CDF) Act of 2004[752], for the first time ever in Kenya, each constituency[753] was allocated the functions and abilities to be considered a development unit with fiscal resources from tax revenue being channelled directly to it as a development area. These resources are distributed by a Constituency Development Committee (CDC) made up of the elected representative (Member of Parliament) and a group of grassroot representatives who are assumed to best understand the developmental needs of the constituency.

The CDF can be seen as a development stemming from the already ongoing national discourse and debate since before independence on whether to have a centralised or decentralised government. The CDF also aims to remedy the imbalance in local regional development brought about by partisan politics and clientelism. Its resources are specifically provided to assist only constituency-level development projects, particularly those aiming at combating poverty at the grassroots. The CDF as expressed in the legislation is devoted to community-based projects, which ensures that the prospective benefits are available to a wide cross-section of the inhabitants of a particular constituency. However, the CDF is not to be used to support political bodies/activities or personal award projects. The resources are allocated to the constituency based on requests for funding by any constituency members or institutions for development purposes. The legislation defines development purposes as: infrastructure, health and education, such as schools and clinics.[754]

The CDF Act provides that the government must set aside a proportion of not less than 2.5% of its ordinary revenue for disbursement under the CDF program. Three quarters of this

---

752   Republic of Kenya. The Constituency Development Fund Act (2004)

753   In Kenya the constituency is the unit of political and electoral representation of which there are 210 in the country. Each constituency is further subdivided into locations for local administrative purposes. A district is a grouping of 4-6 constituencies and before the implementation of CDF in 2003, the district was considered the unit of local development.

754   Republic of Kenya. The Constituency Development Fund Act (2004)

amount is divided equally among Kenya's 210 constituencies whilst the remaining one quarter is divided based on a poverty index to cater for poorer constituencies.

Projects under the Act are required by the Act to be community-based, and it also specifies that all projects shall be "development" projects.[755] Thus the CDF funds projects that benefit the community

---

755 Under the CDF Act 2004, section 21 provided that:

21. (1) Projects under this Act shall be community based in order to ensure that the prospective benefits are available to a widespread cross-section of the inhabitants of a particular area.

(2) Any funding under this Act shall be for a complete project or a defined phase, unit or element of a project and may include the acquisition of land and buildings.

(3) All projects shall be development projects and may include costs related to studies, planning and design or other technical input for the project but shall not include recurrent costs of a facility other than as provided for in subsections (9), (10) and (11).

(4) Funds provided under this Act shall not be used for the purpose of supporting political bodies or political activities or for supporting religious bodies or religious activities.

(5) Notwithstanding the provisions of subsection (4), the National Constituency Development Fund Committee may identify a religious body or organization as an appropriate specialized agency for purposes of section 11 with regard to emergency support.

(6) A constituency office project shall be considered as a development project for purposes of the Act and may include appropriate furniture and equipment for the office.

(7) Notwithstanding the provisions of subsection (3), up to a maximum of three per centum of the total annual allocation for the constituency may be used for administration and such use shall be listed in the Second Schedule as a project.

(8) Development projects may include the acquisition of vehicles, machinery and other equipment.

(9) An appropriate amount not more than three per centum of a constituency's annual allocation may be allocated to recurrent expenses of vehicles, equipment and machinery and be listed as a project provided that such items do not belong to a separate entity.

(10) Sports activities may be considered as development projects for purposes of this Act but shall exclude cash awards provided that the allocation to such activities does not exceed two per centum of the total allocation of the constituency in that financial year.

(11) Monitoring and evaluation of ongoing projects and capacity building of various operatives may be considered as a development project provided that not more than two per centum shall be allocated for this purpose.

(12) Environmental activities may be considered as development projects for purposes of this Act provided that the allocation to such activities does not exceed two per centum of the total allocation of the constituency in that financial year.

(13) Each of the projects shall be listed on the Second Schedule including the emergency item under section 11 and, where applicable, the activities under subsections (6), (7), (8), (9), (10, (11) and (12) of this section.

at large, such as construction of schools and health centre buildings, water projects, roads, chiefs' offices, and police posts.[756] The training of CDF committee members can also be supported by CDF. After the 2007 Amendments, the Constituency Development Fund Committee (CDFC) was given more specific project capacities[757] and its limitations were specified.[758]

7.1.1.   THE HISTORICAL MOTIVATIONS FOR THE DEVELOPMENT OF THE CDF

It is generally accepted by many in the Kenyan government and civil society that the concept of the CDF was a novel approach developed within Kenya and was not the domestication of any foreign ideal. Kenya's diverse population demographic and its reflection in the legislature is the place to locate or situate the source of the initiative.

Broadly, the public's realisation of the weakness of the parliamentary system, corruption and the continual failure of the fiscal and development policies in effecting change led to the consistent grassroot demand for constitutional change. This led to the institution of a Constitutional Review Commission in 1998, which following extensive processes of public consultation developed a draft proposal for constitutional revision popularly referred to as the "Bomas Draft". The Bomas Draft provided the guiding framework for articulating an integrated policy on administrative and fiscal decentralization. The people were categorical not only did they

---

756   At the constituency level, the CDF Act specified that up to a maximum of 3% of the total annual allocation may be used on office running expenses, 5% shall be set aside for emergency while not more than 10% shall be allocated to the education bursary scheme annually.

757   It can now also acquire land and buildings, although all assets remain the property of the CDF Board. In addition, the CDF can now set aside money for administration, including rent, salaries of full time staff, allowances and office expenses. There is also a proviso for the allocation of 3% for Constituency Development Fund Committee vehicles and equipment; up to 2% for sports activities (does not include cash awards but includes recurrent expenses). Up to 2% on Monitoring and Evaluation expenses. Up to 2% on environmental activities and finally 5% for emergencies. Up to 15% may be allocated to bursary (including fees for mocks and continuous assessment exams)

758   CDF does not fund private enterprises, merry-go-rounds, religious and political organisations and activities, and recurrent costs.

desire a devolved[759] and decentralised[760] government, but also that without devolution of governance, any attempt at decentralization would be futile.[761]

At the political level, centralisation in post-independence Kenya had many ill effects, the main concern being clientelism. From the President down, the political system became one of patronage. MPs went to State House and the Office of the President to obtain favours. The MPs obtained promises of fiscal resources to benefit their constituency in exchange for giving promises of their continued support in maintaining the centralised state and single party system. However, state fiscal resources were limited and not all MPs were favoured. Thus those MPs that were unable to gain fiscal resources for their constituencies needed to resort to other diverse methods to obtaining financing for local development projects. Curing the need to maintain partisan politics and reduce patronage and clientelism was thus seen to be the main purpose of the setting up of the CDF.[762]

This tradition of reference to the MP for resources to undertake personal and community development projects had built up through the policies of Harambee and Nyayo to the point where the MP became the MP at the grassroot level. However, MPs had limits on their personal financial resources and thus, a limit to the extent of these powers. Their fiscal power included the use of their personal funds and the funds of supporters as well as calling in favours for goods and services. They also used their influence to develop the constituency by using local contacts to fund and construct projects. Once these were exhausted, the MPs resorted to corruption and nepotism, power plays and clientelism at higher levels, as well as, general misuse of positions in order to obtain funding illegally and illegitimately[763] to ensure continual development in their areas

---

759   The delegation of authority (especially from a central to a regional government)

760   The spread of power away from the centre to local branches or governments

761   Opon (2007) this view of society was confirmed when a different draft Constitution which included decentralisation but not devolution as agreed upon by nationwide consultations was put to a referendum and failed to pass as a new Constitution in November of 2005.

762   Kenya Institute of Policy Research and Analysis (2006a)

763   Forcing of general members of society to give a coerced donation for a 'harambee' later resulted in the criminalisation of this form of fund collection.

which translated into grassroot support and thus re-election in the following political term when the cycle re-commenced. The harambee or self-help system was also used to receive money for favours and some of the money would then be used to develop the constituency also as a favour further reinforcing the 'big man' system as the constituents never questioned the source of the funds. On the one hand, corruption is tied to ethnicity and seen to fuel the politics and practices of patronage,[764] while on the other hand, there was the additional issue of ethnicity that came into play and at a certain level tempered the importance of clientelism. Where ethnic communities dominated certain areas there was the inevitable election of hereditary chiefs into the position of local MP. These MPs tended to be more complacent as their ethnic chiefdoms were translated into electoral power and thus this simply maintained and reinforced their position without the need for commensurate action on behalf of their constituents. This type of MP probably felt there was less need to show that development was taking place in their constituencies.

The CDF Act came into existence in the wake of a new regime in 2004, a new push for decentralisation and the rejection by referendum of the draft Constitution. Thus, this legislation can be seen as a development stemming from the already ongoing national endeavour to decentralise the government's resource distribution and reroute its application directly to the grassroot level. The reason for the introduction of this CDF Bill was that it was seen that grassroot development did not seem to be very far-reaching. Before the CDF was implemented, MPs would go to public meetings, usually during the school holidays (as they were based in the urban centres) and ask the District Commissioner (DC)[765] to undertake work like building dispensaries and roads based on their constituents' requests. However, the DCs were perceived as not being very responsive to the needs highlighted by the MPs and they would not usually carry out MPs' requests since their superiors were those in local government and they owed no duty or responsibility to the MPs. This request cycle would continue until the next public meeting. As

---

764   Ghai (2006) 150

765   Usually handled 7 or more constituencies

a result, MPs would use their personal money and money obtained voluntarily and forcibly from other sources to finance activity at constituency level in order to show or prove their effectiveness to their electorate. Hence, the proposed CDF would mean that the use of personal money to fund development, the patronage system of begging for infrastructure and trips to State House would no longer need to continue.[766]

Decentralisation of funds can be mandated by the Constitution, or it can be provided for by specific laws, or finally, can be based on ministerial decisions. Furthermore, decentralisation of funds can be to one or more sub-national levels of government or extra-government agencies. Kenya's decentralisation of funds has involved a mixture of frameworks and governance levels. This means that the people into whose administration such funds are decentralised will have varied capacities to manage them effectively, responsibility not always going to the most competent persons especially where managerial merit is not the sole criterion for accession to fund management.

Benefits that have arisen from its application and are apparent include a reduction of corruption, increasing grass-root development as well as directly attempting to alleviate the financial burden of MPs during campaigns and their terms in office by placing at their disposal government resources for use in their respective constituencies.[767]

7.1.2. THE LEGISLATIVE DEVELOPMENT OF THE CDF

Unlike the policy-based Brazilian[768] and Indian[769] models, the operation of the CDF in Kenya is governed by central state legislation. The CDF Act, 2004 lays down the structure and this is further codified through regulations and circulars which were

---

766   Muriuki Karue Interview 9 (2007)

767   Ciru Gikonyo Interview 2 (2007); Creck Buyonge Interview 4 (2007); Fred Oundo Interview 5 (2007); G Masinde Interview 3 (2007); Justice Mutungi Interview 10 (2007); K Masime Interview 6 (2007); Mohamed Interview 8 (2007); Muriuki Karue Interview 9 (2007); Nixon Nyaga Interview 1 (2007); Owino Opondo Interview 7 (2007)

768   162

769   176

continuously released first by the Ministry of Finance. The 2007 amendments to the CDF Act resulted in the placement of the responsibility of the CDF under the Ministry of Planning and National Development to streamline operations of the fund.[770] This reinforces, however, the centralised control of an attempt to decentralise the governance system. It uses the top-down approach of legislation to allow a certain amount of flexibility and discretion in distribution of resources. The paradox of centralised control over the process of the CDF is in fact the continued control by central government while attempting to placate citizens by providing the illusion of decentralised government.

The Constituency Development Fund (CDF) Act[771] was initially proposed during the Moi Presidential Regime in 1999, by the Member of Parliament (MP) Mr. Muriuki Karue[772] through a Private Member's Bill. The initial Bill is said to have contained the same substantive textual content as the eventual CDF Act, 2004 that was passed through Parliament.[773] However, this 1999 Bill was not passed by Parliament initially for several apparent reasons. Firstly, because it had been introduced by a member of the parliamentary opposition. Secondly, because it proposed that 5% of tax revenue be distributed through the CDF which was considered too high by the government. Finally, MP Karue added that the government simply refused to implement it due to politics from the caucuses.[774] It is arguable whether these were in fact the reasons for which the Bill initially failed to pass through Kenya's Parliament. However, one reason above all remains valid, in bi-partisan politics; minority

---

770   They include the Republic of Kenya. The Constituency Development Fund Act (2004); Republic of Kenya. Constituency Development Fund (Amendment) Act (2007); CDF Regulations; Circulars; Public Procurement and Disposal Act, 2005; Public Procurement and Disposal Regulations, 2006 and CDF Implementation guidelines prepared by the CDF Board. It is important to note that CDF implementation guidelines are constantly evolving, through new circulars, regulations and revisions to the implementation guidelines.

771   Republic of Kenya. The Constituency Development Fund Act (2004)

772   Muriuki Karue Interview 9 (2007).

773   *Ibid.*

774   *Ibid.*

opposition legislation rarely goes through a Parliament dominated by the majority government supporters.[775]

Using the same text, apart from a reduction of the amount of tax revenue to be distributed through the CDF to 2.5%, MP Karue still a member of the opposition again applied for leave of Parliament in early 2002 to reintroduce the Bill through a private member's motion and in October of 2002 leave was granted.[776] In 2003 under the first term of President Kibaki, with the opposition now the ruling party, came the first reading of the CDF Bill, several seminars with various MPs, and a Sub-committee was formed in Parliament to enquire into the Bill. The Bill was passed in December 2003 and came into force in April 2004.[777] The Act became enforceable in mid-year and the poverty index required to implement the Act[778] had not as yet been prepared. Despite this, the government was keen to make the budgetary allocations as soon as possible.[779] Thus, Parliament agreed that each constituency would be granted a flat rate disbursement of 6 million Kenya shillings in the first fiscal year of application.[780]

Under the mandate of section 27(4) (d) of the CDF Act, the National Assembly immediately created a committee of MPs tasked with researching on the status of constituency offices and powers of MPs in these diverse countries, and making recommendations to Parliament.[781] MPs and their advisors were asked to form a committee in order to compare and contrast a number of other

---

775　Access to the Hansard is not public in Kenya and thus my knowledge of Parliamentary debates is limited to interviews and newspaper reports.

776　However, two days later Parliament was dissolved due to the declaration for general elections. Mr Muriuki Karue won his bid for re-election and drafted and introduced in Parliament the CDF Bill. The actual text of the Bill was developed with possible reliance on Indian legislation: Nixon Nyaga Interview 1 (2007) revealed the link to India. However, MP Muriuki Karue claimed that the idea was developed independently by him. Muriuki Karue Interview 9 (2007).

777　Republic of Kenya. The Constituency Development Fund Act (2004)

778　*Ibid.* section 19

779　Muriuki Karue Interview 9 (2007).

780　Republic of Kenya. The Constituency Development Fund Act (2004); Report of the Constituencies Fund Committee pursuant to section 27(4)(d) of the Constituencies Development Fund Act, 2003 (2005)

781　Report of the Constituencies Fund Committee pursuant to section 27(4)(d) of the Constituencies Development Fund Act, 2003 (2005)

countries, including Zambia, India, Brazil, Panama and Canada with the possible Kenyan approach.[782] The report that was then submitted to Parliament reported on No reference was made to the PA process in Brazil or the decentralisation process in India and Kerala.[783]

The 2004 CDF Act contained only one change from the original Bill presented in Parliament in 1999, lowering the minimum distributable tax revenue from 5% to 2.5%.[784] However, since its enactment this provision of the Act has been used by Parliament to increase the allocation. The initial 2.5% of the ordinary revenue collected by the government that was allocated to CDF was increased by Parliament through the annual budget to 7.5% in 2006[785] and 8.3% in 2007 as seen in the figure below.

Figure 5: CDF Allocations 2003-8

	Average Amount per constituency	Total annual Allocation/ % of ordinary government revenue
2003/4	6,000,000	1.26 billion
2004/5	20,000,000	5.6 billion (2.5%)
2005/6	30,000,000	7.2 billion (2.5%)
2006/7	50,000,000	10.038 billion (3.5%)
2007/8	50,000,000	10.1 billion

In actual figures the amount per constituency grew by a third until 2007 when a reduction in the total revenue resulted in the actual amount received per constituency remaining stable despite an increase in the revenue share of 0.8%.

At the administrative level, the National Management Committee (NMC) authorised the creation of the CDF Secretariat which although not legislatively mandated dealt with the administrative requirements of the distribution and oversight of the CDF on behalf of the NMC.

---

782   *Ibid.*

783   Republic of Kenya. Constituency Development Fund (Amendment) Act (2007)

784   Muriuki Karue Interview 9 (2007)

785   Republic of Kenya. Constituency Development Fund (Amendment) Act (2007) section 4(2).

MP M Karue in 2007 through another private member's Bill presented to Parliament the Constituencies Development Fund (Amendment) Bill that was subsequently passed to become the CDF (Amendment) Act.[786] This introduced many critical amendments that resulted in the substantial revision of the CDF application, process and procedures.

7.2. THE CDF CYCLE AND ITS PLACE IN THE NATIONAL BUDGETARY CYCLE

The CDF Act, its procedures and processes have undergone one major amendment that is fundamentally linked to the country's national election process. The inception of the CDF was after the national elections in 2003 and major amendments were only made to the CDF Act after several years of operation in 2007 just before the following national elections. This was not only due to the discovery of misuse of CDF funds but also the discovery of the absence of transition provisions upon change of MP after elections. In addition, at its inception many of its provisions could not be put into effect due to the absence of certain information such as the poverty index.

At its inception, the first flow of funds through the budgetary cycle to the CDF was the immediate disbursement of extra budgetary resources equally to all the 210 constituencies straight down to the grassroots for the state financial year ending 30 June 2004. The project cycle at this initial stage through parliamentary permission tasked the MP with creation of a CDF constituency committee within 30 days of the creation of the CDF in April 2004. This led to the quick initial appointment of committee members by the MP in order to create and activate the financial accounts and receive the budgeted resources allocated.[787] In this initial period there was also no project cycle; instead the CDF Committee at the constituency level simply picked projects of their choice and allocated money for that financial year at their own behest.

The funds flow cycle in this period involved funds being allocated to the CDF line budget based on the poverty index.

---

786   *Ibid.*

787   How this process worked is at best hazy and there is not documentation of it

This poverty index was created in 2004, as a joint project of the WB and the Kenya Bureau of Statistics (KBS),[788] and from the financial year 2004-2005 onwards, the funds were allocated using the proportionalities as set out in the CDF Act and discussed above. Since the CDF budget was given its own line in the national budget, it was initially placed in the budgetary estimates directly under the Ministry of Finance and Treasury. The amount of money allocated to the CDF upon approval by the National Assembly in the budget in June of each year would then be granted as a single amount for the CDF for the year and then transferred to the National Management Committee (NMC) by the Treasury. The sole purpose of the NMC in this situation would be to divide and transfer the money directly into the accounts of the respective constituencies upon approval of the national budget. It was then left to the MP and the CDF Committee at the constituency level to put their projects into action by allocating the funds in accordance with the project proposals that had been submitted and now approved. However, if all the money in the CDF account was not utilised by June of each year, the funds were not returnable to the Treasury at year end like other budgetary allocations.

7.2.1.   THE CURRENT AND POST JULY 2007 AMENDED CDF CYCLE

The project cycle of the CDF as enacted in the CDF (Amendment) Act of 2007 substantially changed not only the form projects could take but also the process of identification of projects and the flow of funds. One critical amendment increased from 30 to 60 days the period to appoint the new members of the CDFC. At the constituency level the MP was required initially to constitute and convene the Constituency Development Fund Committee (CDFC) after a new Parliament is inaugurated. Thus, in Kenya's last elections which took place on the 27 December 2007, the inauguration of

---

788   Nixon Nyaga Interview 1 (2007)

Parliament was on the 15 January 2008[789] and every MP was given up to the 15 March 2008[790] to constitute their respective CDFCs.[791]

The responsibility of the CDF was placed under the Ministry of Planning and National Development.[792] In addition, there is an administrative system set up under the auspices of the Board of the National Management Committee[793] that is required to submit, on a monthly basis to the national Constituency Fund Committee, a summary of project proposals received in the previous month, indicating approval status, a summary of status of disbursements to constituencies, and summary of status of disbursements from Treasury to the National Account.[794] This is done with the assistance of fund managers at every constituency who are ex-officio members of the CDFC and who hold all the records and equipment during

---

789   See generally Norris-Trent (2008)

790   Kenya's financial year commences on the 1 of July each year and ends the following year on the 30 of June. Allocations for the financial years 2006-07 and 2007-08 have been distributed to all the Constituencies and thus one can assume that this duty of the MP has been discharged. See generally allocations on CDF State website, CDF Secretariat (2009)

791   Press Release to Members of Parliament-Elect on the Composition of the CDF Committees (2008) and Republic of Kenya. The Constituency Development Fund Act (2004) section 23(1) of the revised Act

792   Republic of Kenya. Constituency Development Fund (Amendment) Act (2007) Section 2

793   The Board is a body corporate capable of being sued, with perpetual succession and common seal. All CDF property belongs to the Board. It is allowed to borrow and make investments. The Board shall meet 6-18 times per year, and may hold special meetings of up to five persons. All fixed and moveable assets are the property of the Board and are insured under its name. The Board comprises 17 persons in total, one third of whom must be women. It comprises four government officials: the Permanent Secretaries of the ministries of Planning and National Development, and Ministry of Finance, the Clerk of the National Assembly, and the Attorney General. It also comprises 8 qualified persons nominated from institutions listed in the First Schedule as The Kenya Farmers Union, Institute of Engineers of Kenya, Kenya National Chamber of Commerce, Catholic Church, Kenya National Union of Teachers, National Council of Churches of Kenya (NCCK), Supreme Council of the Kenya Muslims (SUPKEM), and Institute of Certified Public Accountants of Kenya. The Minister may appoint another four other persons to achieve regional representation. All appointments must be approved by parliament and have relevant expertise. The Board also comprises the Chief Executive Officer (CEO), who is ex-officio and secretary to the Board. The CEO is appointed on a competitive basis and must be approved by parliament. The CEO must have a relevant university degree and 10 years relevant work experience.

794   Republic of Kenya. Constituency Development Fund (Amendment) Act (2007) section 3

electoral political transition in addition to compiling and maintaining the financial records of the constituency on a monthly basis.[795] In addition the Board is charged with receiving and addressing complaints and disputes and taking appropriate action, appointing the needed officers and other staff for management of the fund, determining the sitting allowances for DPC and CDFC, which are then approved by the National Constituency Fund Committee.

At the administrative level, during the transition period upon dissolution of Parliament on the 22 October 2007[796] in response to constituency level confusion where there was the assumption that the CDFCs dissolved with Parliament, the CDF Secretariat stated that after the 30 October 2007 all financial allocations at constituency level could only take place through the CDF Account Managers[797] and ongoing projects were to continue to completion. In addition, for the remainder of the financial year which then ended on 30 June 2008 no new allocations could be made by the current CDFCs after 30 December 2007. However, the CDFCs were to continue in operation until a new CDFC had been constituted by the MPs elected in the following year.[798]

---

795   The Fund Manager is the custodian of all records and equipment during the term of office and during transition. This person will compile and maintain a record showing all receipts and disbursements on a monthly basis for every project and sub-project in the constituency.

796   Kenyan Government (2007)

797   Press Statement on Management of CDCs following Dissolution of Parliament (30 October 2007)

798   *Ibid.*

Figure 6: CDF Cycle 2007 to Date

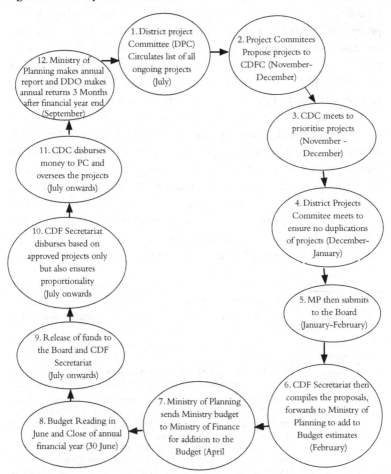

The cycle of identification of projects thus commences in July with the DPC[799] at the beginning of every financial year circulating a list of

---

799   The District Projects Committee comprises all MPs in the district, all chairpersons and mayors of local authorities, the District Commissioner, the District Development Officer who is secretary of the District Projects Committee, all the chairpersons of the Constituency Development Fund Committee, the District Accountant. The relevant district departmental heads may also attend District Projects Committee meetings in an ex-officio capacity. The chairperson is elected from either the MPs or Councillors. The District Project Committee must meet annually and up to a maximum of 6 times a year. The District Project Committee is dissolved upon the dissolution of parliament. The new District Project Committee shall be constituted

ongoing government and council projects to all CDFCs.[800] Between October and December a Project Committee (PC)[801] will propose a project to a CDFC[802] who will ensure that appropriate consultations are made with relevant government departments to ensure realistic project cost estimates. The CDFC[803] ranks projects in order of priority.[804] The MP chairs the CDFC (unless the MP opts out[805]) and tables the list of projects to the DPC, which shall ensure there is no duplication of projects. The MP then submits the DPC approved list to the national Board of Management of the CDF. The CDF Secretariat then compiles the proposals from various constituencies. Upon approval of a project, the PC will implement its project with the assistance of the relevant government department.[806] However, the DPC is held responsible for procurement where contracts exceed Kenya shillings 10 million. It is also responsible for implementation of projects that span two or more constituencies. The Fund Manager submits an annual report 60 days after the financial year end.

---

60 days after a new parliament is inaugurated.

800   However, this does not mean that existence of a similar project can be used to deny funding for a proposed project.

801   A nominated or elected group of persons that may be pre-existing, such as school boards.

802   Under the Revised CDF Act of 2007, the Constituency Development Committee (CDC) was renamed the Constituency Development Fund Committee (CDFC).

803   Under section 23(1) of the Republic of Kenya. Constituency Development Fund (Amendment) Act (2007), the CDFC will have a maximum of 16 persons. The Member of Parliament, Councillors, 1 District Officer, 2 religious representatives, 2 men representatives, 2 women representatives, 1 youth representative, 1 NGO representative, 3 other persons appointed by the MP, and a Fund Manager. Members shall be appointed on three-year renewable terms for a maximum of two consecutive terms. The CDFC must meet at least 12 times but no more than 24 times (including subcommittee meetings). Quorum is one half of the total membership. The CDFC remains in office until elections/by-elections whereby the new MP appoints a new CDFC.

804   This function of the CDFC has remained the same as before the 2007 Amendments although its makeup has been amended and clarified.

805   This option has to date (January 2009) never been exercised.

806   Their other functions include coordinating with the relevant government departments to ensure cost estimates are as accurate as possible. Preparing a work plan for the project. Carrying out procurements for the project. In places where the Project Committee does not have the capacity to undertake procurement, it should be undertaken by the relevant government department. Keeping records of all documents, including receipts, LPOs, invoices, records of delivered materials, etc. Preparation of the financial expenditure report. Finally, monitoring progress of work.

The funds flow commences from the approval by the national budget of the percentage of the ordinary tax revenue of the state for the fiscal year. The funds are then passed to the Minister of Planning who then allocates the budgeted amount to the Board.[807] The CDF Secretariat retains the money in the Board account. The CDF Secretariat then uses the compiled list of approved project proposals from various constituencies to disburse money to the CDF accounts at constituency level. However, unless a project is set out by a CDFC and approved by the Board and the CDF Secretariat, no money will be sent to the accounts of that constituency. The CDFC is responsible for the allocation of funds to various projects and does so as it sees fit.[808] Within its discretion, it determines the instalments with which to release funds to projects. At the end of the financial year, the Board, with approval from the National Constituency Fund Committee, will determine how any excess funds or shortfalls will be handled. The Minister of Planning and National Development[809] tables an annual report on the activities, operations and expenditure of the fund at the end of the financial year.

7.3. LEGITIMATING TAXATION THROUGH THE CDF

Through the structure and provisions of the CDF, there is the possibility of connecting directly and thus bringing to the forefront the connection between the payment of taxation and its use for the good of the taxpayer. The current absence of the legitimation of taxation is an issue addressed by the CDF at a microcosmic level through its direct distribution of a percentage of tax revenue for a fixed set of purposes which are intended to directly improve the lives of citizens at grassroot level. However, it also brings to light the difficulties and issues of concern at national level as the same problems that concern state distribution of the national budget are reflected at this level. These concerns impede and stunt the legitimation process

---

807   It is responsible for administering the fund, approving each and every payment from the fund, ensuring timely and efficient disbursement of funds to each constituency as well as ensuring the efficient management of the fund.

808   The power of the CDFC was also enlarged to allow individual hire and conduct of audits. See Constituency Development Fund Website (2007).

809   The Minister may make regulations and amendments necessary for smooth running of the fund, although parliament must approve them before implementation.

and must therefore be analysed in order to realise the problems that will follow the legitimation of taxation as well as the achievement of human rights principles as it would affect any other process of the application of taxation policy at all levels of the state apparatus.

This analysis in no way means that there have not been actions to remedy the abuse of the CDF process. There are several instances that cut across the themes below that show how the challenges posed by those abusing the process are being answered. However, in support of the checks and balances that can take place and are taking place through the legislative system in Kenya, 17 former officials of the Saboti CDF including the then MP of the area were summoned before the police in April of 2008 and asked to explain how the 100 million was spent from the CDF kitty.[810]

In a different situation, handing over of a CDF failed to take place when the outgoing MP Jackson Rono and his CDF Committee was asked to account for all projects and set out those that were complete and those that were ongoing in Eldama Ravine constituency by the incoming MP Joseph Ayabei.[811]

In Laikipia, the government ordered that investigations be carried out and that the relevant officials vacate their offices while the investigation was ongoing to establish why money allocated to a water project was not used for the required project. The officials were also required to hand over the books of accounts.[812] This stemmed from the report of a Saboti CDF manager having gone missing and presumed murdered after he went to make a location check of 50 ongoing projects and found that none of them existed after which he compiled a report and sent it to the National CDF Management Committee.[813]

Chweya[814] argues that, the CDF does not fit perfectly in any of the models of decentralization. The CDF has been established through an Act of Parliament, but it is not managed through an

---

810   Omonso (2008)

811   Nation Reporter (*Ibid.*)

812   Ndirangu (2007)

813   Omonso and Ng'etich (2008)

814   See generally Chweya (2006)

elected council as is the case of local authorities. The managers, who constitute the CDC, are largely appointees of the MPs. Prior to the establishment of the fund, most MPs struggled to please their constituents using their own funds. This contributed to widespread corruption and abuse of public resources. The availability of the fund therefore, has relieved the MPs from the pressure of resource generation to sustain patron-client relationships. However, it has created new challenges for engaging people in development, and being open to accountability and criticism.

In early 2009 in response to growing concerns about the low utilisation of completed facilities, weak capacity in identifying projects, low and little use of available technical capacity in implementing projects, poor management, few large-scale projects, lack of adequate financial control, allegations of interference, corruption and embezzlement, a CDF Review Taskforce was created and is currently holding public hearings nationwide.[815] The analysis of this thesis may provide ideas for consideration by this taskforce. Resultant themes that included the purposes for which the CDF was created and formed have emerged during its existence. They are in order of importance: development and poverty alleviation; corruption and clientelism; participation; accountability, responsibility and transparency; the mismanagement of state resources and finally decentralisation and the constitutionality of the process of the CDF. All these themes apart from the first one will be discussed in this section. The theme of development and poverty alleviation will be discussed in the next sub-section on its own and in more detail for the purpose of linking it to human rights and for a more detailed analysis.

7.3.1. CORRUPTION AND CLIENTELISM

Corruption and clientelism were very evident at the commencement of the CDF process in 2004 but have since been reduced and controlled through legislative amendments that have improved oversight. However, there remains a continual problem with both corruption and clientelism that is evidenced through different facets

---

815   CDF Secretariat (2009)

of the CDF process both in the project implementation and in the funds flow.

In the process of the implementation of projects, there has been noted collusion between key members of the tender committees and contractors. In some cases government officials may also be part of the collusion. Not only are genuine suppliers locked out of tender process, but the same 2 or 3 corruptible contractors may be repeatedly given work. This includes not only ghost contractors but also contractors with a history of shoddy work. Quotations and specifications for projects may be exaggerated, faulty or substandard buildings are approved by corrupt government officials. In addition there is also the possibility of collusion with fake PC's where CDCs may collude with family members, political allies and acquaintances to set up Project Committees for dubious projects. These PCs then manage the projects but divert most of the funds for personal gain.

Many MPs have been accused of directing the majority of funds to a few locations/divisions based on voter patterns in the constituency. This is a very common occurrence and especially where a constituency does not have a long term plan for development and where information about projects funded is not shared with communities.

A few committees actually illegally amend the books of accounts so that the records reflect development while on the ground no projects or project committees exist. Others keep two sets of books. This is fraud and is a criminal offence. Other CDCs attempt to avoid lengthy procurement regulations by funding projects for small amounts such as 100,000 over 3 years or more. This means the PC cannot meaningfully make good use of the money and that increases the chances of fraud and misallocation.

Some CDF officials have taken advantage of projects funded by other funding bodies such as other devolved funds like LATF, as well as other international and local donors and instead abscond with the money designated for that project. This has actually resulted in the creation of the position of fund managers and requirements in the CDF Amendment Act, 2007 that all CDF projects should have a sign/billboard displaying project information including the total amount allocated, the identity of the contractor/engineers and CDF project reference number.

There remains as a result a critical issue with oversight of the MP and the CDFC. There is thus the need to consider whether to redefine the role of MP and limit the powers of the MP over the fund. One possibility is to ensure that the MP remains as an ex-officio patron of an independent, locally elected CDFC. Thus instead of reducing the element of the 'big man' in Kenyan politics, the problem of clientelism/patronage has instead been reinforced. Making the CDCs independent of the MP would not only remedy this but also overcome the constitutional objection based on the separation of powers principle. His/her role should be to facilitate strategic, long term development planning, arbitrate when there are wrangles and conflicts, and to oversee and ensure the prudent use of funds. No MP and family members or business associates should be allowed to directly benefit from the fund.

Organisations such as the Kenya Anticorruption Commission, the NMC, Public Procurement Appeals and Review Board and other agencies of redress should be compelled to act swiftly and decisively in cases of corruption, failure to do so should be actionable. The CDF Act, individual CDF's record keeping and reporting should be strengthened, standardised and enforced. This will help to seal any loopholes.

7.3.2. PARTICIPATION

The CDCs under the first Kibaki regime, and their selection resulted in controversy with MPs being accused of appointing their relatives, cronies and yes-heads for reasons of patronage and the desire for pliant management.[816] There is a resulting need for the CDFCs to be locally elected/nominated; a mechanism needs to be devised whereby CDCs can be elected or nominated through local means to ensure they represent the public and their interests. Measures also need to be put in place to protect committee members from political interference, have limited terms as committee members and be actively removed for abuse of office.

---

816   Nyaga (2008)

Public participation should be protected by making it mandatory that all CDF processes especially procurement are open to meaningful public involvement. The CDF Act should recognise the right of all members of the public to participate in CDF. This can be achieved by ensuring the CDC is elected or nominated by the public, the CDC and PCs should be compelled to report back to the public and to respond swiftly to their complaints and concerns, all CDF documents should be available to the public and officers who withhold information should be penalised, greater awareness should be carried out so the public understands CDF systems and processes including the record keeping structures. All projects should be originated at grassroots level, if not they should receive grassroots endorsement. Representatives of the PCs should attend in important CDC meetings such as the project selection, and tendering meetings, and all meetings where financial decisions are made. All meetings should be public.

In addition, participation seems to be only skin deep without any actual open and public participation as has been undertaken in both Brazil and India. The aim still seems predominantly for the organised institutions/committees to benefit with one project at a time. Ordinary citizens who may for instance require low cost housing to be built have not managed to access these funds as is taking place in Brazil.

7.3.3.   Accountability, Responsibility and Transparency

The speed with which the CDF Act, 2004 was put into place as well as the speed of the passing of the amendments in 2007 of the CDF Act has meant that there have been many issues of clarification required of roles as well as a strengthening of the accountability structures. From its inception there have been numerous issues of the lack of accountability, transparency and responsibility.

The roles and responsibilities of CDF officers should be clarified to ensure that at each stage liability is specific and clear. At present the CDF committees take decisions under collective responsibility allowing unscrupulous individuals to manipulate this ambiguity.

Attiya Waris

The Kenyan Constituency Development Fund 229

Some MPs tend to dominate all aspects of CDF operations such that no decision can be made or payment made without the MP's approval. In these situations the CDC have no say in the running of the fund and the MP usually works closely with 2-3 officials keeping the rest in the dark. Officials who raise questions or criticisms are likely not to be notified of meetings, and are likely to be dropped from the CDC. In such cases the CDC is not transparent, record keeping is likely to be poor, and information to the public not forthcoming. Such CDCs tend to operate with a lot of secrecy with minimum involvement of the public. Certain contractors are likely to be favoured, and genuine proposals are likely to be ignored in favour of those that favour the MP in one way or other. CDC members are likely to comprise of illiterate and non-technical people who cannot understand the tricks of the MP and his 'kitchen cabinet' who are likely to be the coordinator, treasurer, chairman and secretary. These very people are likely to also be on the tender committee.

The CDF Act charges government with the implementation of CDF, it does not clarify the aspects of implementation. In practice the district development officers (DDOs) and other district officers (DOs) have responsibilities without authority and are easily coerced into approving expenditures of powerful politicians. Conversely government technical departments give technical expertise to CDF through invisible and non-formalised means; BQ's, certificates of completion and so forth are seldom officially signed, allowing technical officers to escape liability. The DDO as the AIE holder should be empowered to demand compliance and conversely liable when complicit in abuse of funds.

The independence of the NMC was called to question and it was replaced by an independent Board, a definitely positive move geared towards improved participation and oversight. However, there still remains the need to strengthen the Board's powers in order to punish errant CDF officials who flout CDF regulations and guidelines. The independence of the Board needs to be safeguarded by securing its budgets, functions and powers through statutory means and de-linking it sufficiently from central government. Legal provisions have been made to improve accountability from the Board through regular, relevant and comprehensive reports including expenditure reports, setting of high performance standards which the Board is accountable to the CDFC through regular, institutionalised, reporting, establishment of rapid response times to public requests and complaints, and reconstitution of its structure. However, this can be further strengthened by extending the accountability to concerned citizens and the public in general who should have the right to demand their accountability.

Some CDCs receive project funds and fail to release funds to the PC. This was especially common with earlier CDF disbursements, but as the press, CSOs[817] and the public[818] have become more vigilant it is hoped that fewer CDCs will be susceptible to misuse. Some CDCs set up parallel accounts where in collusion with officials at the district office they siphon off the money into a separate account to avoid close scrutiny. This is fraud and is a criminal offence.

The CDF Act and guidelines do not protect the role of the labourer. CDF should emphasise the need to pay all labour contracted under CDF at the government rate. There is need to review the law to ensure that CDF projects favour labour intensive means as a way of guaranteeing local labour attractive wages. The present guidelines also do not emphasise on the keeping of labour rolls. Strict standards should be set for all committees and contractors undertaking CDF projects to maintain up-to-date labour rolls. Labour payments should be witnessed by members of the PC/CDC to ensure money intended for labour is not siphoned off.

7.3.4.   MISMANAGEMENT OF STATE FISCAL RESOURCES

Mapesa and Kibua[819] have also argued that the management of the fund has a potential of introducing the politics of rewards and punishment at the local level. Areas which do not support the MP and members of the committee may be excluded from benefiting from the fund. Additionally the funding of projects can be used for manipulation of communities, especially during campaigns for national and civic elections. Further, the fund provides MPs with

---

817   Machuhi (2009)

818   Kwamboka (2009); Kwamboka (2009)

819   See generally Mapesa and Kibua (2006)

the opportunity for stifling free, fair and competitive elections, since they have the exclusive control over the key local resource for development. In the case of the latter, not all civic leaders are members of the CDC, and indeed, those that belong to the committee have potential of exploiting their membership for their own selfish interests.

The role and mandate of the DPC and the Board needed to be strengthened to ensure harmonisation of projects without duplication. Despite the amendments the provision in the Act as amended specifically maintains that duplication does not bar the undertaking of a project, thus this will continue to be a problem. The reason for the inclusion of this provision is inexplicable. The structure of the DPC should be reassessed with the possibility of including the MP in an ex-officio capacity and the accommodation of community representatives. In addition, DPC meetings should be mandatory and all project schedules should be tabled at the DPC for harmonisation and approval as envisaged in the Act, a provision that is currently not being enforced.

7.3.5. DECENTRALISATION AND THE CONSTITUTIONALITY OF THE CDF

Questions have repeatedly been raised about the constitutionality of the CDF Act. To the extent that the Act empowers MPs to conceive and implement "development" projects using taxpayers' funds, it enables parliamentarians to encroach into the duties of the executive contrary to the doctrine of separation of powers. The principle, implied in section 3 of the Kenyan Constitution, demands that each of the three arms of government be assigned specific functions. The functions of the Kenyan Parliament as stated in, *inter alia*, sections 30 and 17(3) of the Kenyan Constitution are limited to legislation and oversight. If the principle of separation of powers were to be applied to the CDF Act, then amendments must be made to leave MPs out of the use of the CDF funds and the implementation and conception of projects. The proper role of MPs under the new set up should be that of independent watchdogs.

The CDF Act may have been inspired by the failure of the Government to devote significant funds to development expenditure. However, allowing Members of Parliament to apportion and expend Government revenues constitutes an encroachment into executive functions and cannot cure the problem. The CDF Act may one day suffer the same fate that befell the Kenya Roads Board Act in the High Court of Kenya where Justice Kasanga Mulwa stated:

> I have no doubt that the enactment of this Act was prompted by good intentions .... (but)...separation of powers is an enduring value of our society, which I feel ought to be protected and maintained. That is so. The doctrine of separation of powers is implicit in the Constitution. ...In my view, any outfit that is composed of members of Parliament and is charged with expenditure of public Funds is commingling of roles of the different organs of state in a manner that is unacceptable. ... I find that it would be against the constitutional principle of separation of powers for members of Parliament to take part in actual spending, then submit their annual estimates to themselves in Parliament through the Public Accounts Committee or the Public Investments Committee. I therefore hold that section 17(1) of the Kenya Roads Board Act is inconsistent with the Constitution to the extent that Members of Parliament participate in the activities of the District Roads Committees in Executive capacities.[820]

It has been argued that under the Kenyan constitutional set-up, the constituency is only envisioned as a political unit and hence it was erroneous (and arguably unlawful) for Parliament to use the CDF Act to convert it into a "development" unit. This argument raises a debatable issue. The CDF Act subtly entrenches the 'Big Man' as the MP and reduces the separation of powers contrary to the provisions of the Kenyan Constitution. In spite of the foregoing parts of this discourse, it is legitimate to argue that the CDF Act does not actually embody any genuine attempt to achieve either equity or equality in the distribution of national resources. First, the underlying principle of *one-man-one-vote* in constituency demarcations has, in Kenyan experience, been ignored and preference given to political expediency to garner votes for political purposes. Accordingly, the current constituencies are unreflective of the true demographic patterns and economic needs within the nation. Section 19(1) (a) of

---

820   *Republic v Kenya Roads Board ex parte John Harun Mwau* (2000)

the CDF Act imposes unqualified equality between constituencies with known disparate demographic patterns. This, coupled with the absence of an objective constituency poverty index, one can legitimately conclude that the provisions of section 19 which take into account the question of relative poverty of the various constituencies cannot achieve equitable distribution of the CDF funds.

In reference to the separation of powers, the proposed amendments seek to do away with the requirement that a third party audit the CDF accounts through the offices of the Auditor-General. This means that Parliament has given itself the power to allocate to itself public resources and retained the power to audit the resources it has allocated itself. The proposed amendments seek to further weaken or remove completely the existing systems that are in place for the public to look in on the activities that the legislators have committed to undertake on the project submission forms tabled before the House and submitted to the Minister of Finance.

The Act gives very wide discretion and an exclusivist role to MPs. Given the extra-constitutional nature of the role of MPs in the operation of the CDF, one can only conclude that the predominant role assigned to MPs was inspired by political considerations rather than legal or other necessity. By giving too many powers to the MPs over the operation of the CDF, and by insisting on implementation of the projects through the departments of Government in the District, the Act negates the principles of devolution, which it seeks to establish through section 3. Among other reasons, MPs, who are the key players in the operation of the CDF, are part of the national government and therefore it cannot be said the Act transfers decision making and implementation to the local levels.

The CDCs are not expected to answer to the Controller and Auditor General, questions on expenditure. The CDF Act thus infringes the principle of accountability, which is the hallmark of a truly democratic system of government provided for under our Constitution. The scenario presented by the Act whereby the legislator makes a law (in this case the CDF Act), participates in implementing the law through the CDC and the DPC, and then accounts for the expenditure to Parliament (in this case to himself) throws democratic accountability overboard. It undermines the concepts of constitutionalism and good governance.

7.4.   LINKING TAXATION USING HUMAN RIGHTS WITHIN THE CDF

Good governance, development and poverty alleviation in the improvement of the general well-being of citizens of a state are all critical elements in the achievement of human rights principles and policies, and have been extensively discussed in the preceding chapters. The development of Kenya to the point of the creation and development of devolved funding has additionally culminated in the need to address the concern of the people, the achievement of a progressively higher standard of living, welfare, dignity and well-being that can possibly be seen through the CDF as a microcosm of the question posed by this thesis, the use of human rights policy and principles as a possible link to join the collection of tax revenue to the distribution of tax expenditure.

7.4.1.   DEFINING DEVELOPMENT AND THE RIGHT TO DEVELOPMENT

The intention of the CDF Act remains a laudable principle. Section 3 states that:

> The provisions of this Act shall apply, as more specifically provided for in the Act, and shall ensure that a specific portion of the national annual budget is devoted to the constituencies for purposes of development and in particular in the fight against poverty at the constituency level.

Section 21 of the CDF Act adds that projects under the Act shall be community based. What, therefore, is a development project? Whether it was a fundamental omission or not on the part of the draftsmen to fail to define the word "development" under the Act, defining a development project would have been an arduous task. However, the draftsmen could have provided criteria for identifying a project as a development project. It is not sufficient for the Act to outlaw the use of CDF funds for political and religious bodies and activities. It can be argued that by failing to define and enlighten constituents on the concept of development that the government had in mind, the CDF Act has paved the way for an eclectic and unstructured expenditure of taxpayers' money in the name of development.

In addition, the CDF Act does not appreciate human development, particularly human resource development, as a prioritised development project. This is demonstrable from the fact that the funding of education of constituents by way of bursaries is severely restricted by section 25(2), where an education bursary scheme is not to exceed 15 percent of the total funds allocated to the constituency in any financial year. This is a narrow and myopic approach to the concept of development, since human resource development, i.e. progressive acquisition of skills and knowledge, is indispensable to the attainment of other aspects of development, whatever the meaning of the term. In Brazil and PA specifically, currently, one theme is decided upon annually and the theme for 2009 is housing. The fixing of the proportion of allocation adds rigidity to the distribution pattern and leaves out the addressing of the real needs of constituents.

Although the amendment to the Act does provide more guidance it still maintains the allocations as set out above, with no definition of the term development. There is no provision in the Act that would exclude the reading of the right to development into the Act and it is on this basis that this thesis analyses the use of tax revenue for the purposes of development and shall thus read into the text of the Act and its application the human right to development, which is a human right.

7.4.2. A KEY ELEMENT OF THE RIGHT TO DEVELOPMENT: PARTICIPATION

Participation, as discussed in Chapters 4 and 5, is one of the core elements of the right to development. The CDF Act uses the terms grassroot and participation extensively. However, the CDF cycle set out above shows clearly that despite this, the system is very much top-down and centre-out in its process of implementation. The various committees of the CDF both at the national level and at the constituency level are faced by 2 major challenges; its legitimacy and whether it has the technical capacity required to administer the fund. Both these challenges tie into the issue of participation.

The composition of the CDFC raises certain issues. First, the Act does not set out any minimum professional qualifications for persons appointed to the committees. The only criteria the MPs are called upon to consider are honesty and integrity; literacy of the person to be appointed to the committee; the knowledge and experience of the persons to be nominated; and the importance of representing the political, gender and ethnic diversity. The guidelines already referred to do not reflect a true representation of constituencies. For example, the Act only provides for one slot for the youth in the membership of the CDFC. Since the youth are the majority of the Kenyan population, it is undemocratic to limit the youth to one slot which also limits their areas of interest, possibly education. This in itself would probably qualify as a constitutional challenge to the CDF Act, because it negates the requirements and principles of a democratic government.

More interestingly, there is no requirement that the MPs be persons with the qualities provided in the guidelines, neither do the regulations bind the MPs to follow the guidelines. MPs are merely called upon to have regard to the qualities when appointing the CDFC. The assumption in the Act is that MPs have the requisite qualities to enable them to efficiently conceive the projects, mobilize the people and oversee the use of the funds. It is debatable, on one hand, whether MPs are persons of unimpeachable honesty and integrity. On the other hand, could a possibly corrupt MP, for instance, constitute, convene and lead a CDFC whose membership must comprise persons of unquestionable honesty and integrity? The most recent corruption in the continuing war on corruption, it is on record that 6 ministers, 1 assistant minister and 7 MPs are either being investigated or are facing corruption charges.[821]

Furthermore, there exists no institutionalised mechanism for the community to nominate individuals who are representative of their interests to the CDFC. Instead, under both the current Act and the

---

821   Shiundu, Barasa and Ngirachu (2009)

amendments, the constitution of the CDC is left entirely to the will of the MP. The community is therefore vulnerable to the prejudices the MP may hold on a partisan, ethnic or class basis.

Incumbent MPs may take advantage of the low level of civic knowledge and use the projects to entrench themselves in the local constituency politics. This will make it increasingly difficult for new political aspirants to make it to political office especially if the local people are misled to associate the CDF funds with the incumbent MP. The ultimate casualty in this scenario will be democracy.

Assuming that this trend is going to be endemic to every CDC, it is time to put in place systems that would ensure that persons nominated to the CDC are representative of the constituency in order to capitalise on the benefits of participatory democracy, which would raise the capacity of the committees to function efficiently. Consequently, decisions arrived at by the said committees would be both technically sound and more acceptable to the community, perhaps by full and open participation at all levels of the process.

The challenges facing the management of the fund, which are not related to the Act, can be backstopped by an enlightened and participative citizenry. The publication of the CDF issues through the media, and sensitisation of communities by civil society organizations have begun bearing fruit. In a number of constituencies, citizens have begun questioning the management of CDC and blowing the whistle. Mombasa County provides a good example where sensitisation of communities is becoming real. Community-based action groups supported by civil society organizations, are checking on the management of the fund. Besides empowering the community through civic education, project committee members also need to be trained and their selection should be based on pre-determined qualifications, to be spelt out in the amended CDF Act.

In sum, the following can help improve the management of CDF. Firstly, promote awareness and participation through civic education. Secondly, institutionalise capacity building. Thirdly, uphold professionalism in constitution of committees. Fourthly, enhance coordination and consolidate effort among stakeholders.

Fifthly, formulate and implement a national monitoring and evaluation framework. Finally, the amendment of the CDF Act.

7.4.3. ACHIEVEMENT OF HUMAN RIGHTS AND THE RIGHT TO DEVELOPMENT

There is no concrete reference made anywhere in the CDF legislation or structure to imply that the state considered human rights principles in the creation of the CDF. My interviews yielded comments criticising the process of linkage to certain issues such as firstly, the failure effectively to link the CDF process and procedure to the people as taxpayers and thus by extension the failure by citizens to perceive that it was their tax money being used for their development.[822] Secondly, that the list of demands being made of the CDF currently make no connection to the human rights or tax contribution of the citizenry.[823]

Although the representative of the Centre for Governance and Development agreed that the CDF definitely linked taxation to economic, social and cultural rights, he tempered his comment with what he perceived as a low understanding of the people generally that the CDF actually involved development and thus no understanding at all that it included issues of human rights. However, he felt that the CDF is doing an extremely good job as regards economic rights. He criticised the CDF from a human rights perspective by stating that it failed to provide for sustainable development as the Act allows only for capital but not recurrent expenditure for development projects as there was no provision for the funding of personnel for staffing the structures built through the CDF projects.[824]

Nevertheless, one aspect is of note. The issue of using human rights as a budgetary policy remains a novel one at the level of both application and theory. However, what is more important in this case is whether one can perceive the possible achievement of human rights principles and policies through the process and procedure of the CDF. This can be set out as follows: the right to education is

---

822   G Masinde Interview 3 (2007)

823   Fred Oundo Interview 5 (2007)

824   K Masime Interview 6 (2007)

being consistently and continually fulfilled by the increase in the number of education bursaries granted and schools being built. The right to health is being improved upon by the construction of more hospitals and clinics. The right to water is being fulfilled by the building of boreholes and wells and the provision of water pipes even if communal to areas where the people had no access to water. The right to work is being fulfilled by requiring that the work undertaken in developing a constituency be locally sourced.

Thus the progressive realisation of socio-economic rights is taking place, and as the Clerk to the National Assembly pointed out quite rightly, as concerns human rights and development, the perception of the people was moving forward quite swiftly as '40-50 years ago people did not know that they had the right to choose what they wanted'.[825]

7.5. CONCLUSION

Those who describe rights as absolutes make it impossible to ask important factual questions. Who decides at what level to fund which cluster of basic rights and for whom? How fair, as well as how prudent, is our current system of allocating scarce resources among competing rights, including constitutional rights? Who exactly is empowered to make such allocative decisions? Attention to the costs of rights leads us not only into problems of budgetary calculations, as a consequence, but also into basic philosophical issues of distributive justice and democratic accountability. Indeed it leads to the philosophical dilemma - what is the relationship between democracy and justice, between principles of collective decision-making, applicable to all important choices, and norms of fairness that we consider valid regardless of deliberative decisions or majority will?[826] The CDF's objectives include firstly, to fund projects with immediate social and economic impact in order to uplift the lives of the people; secondly, to alleviate poverty; and finally for purposes of development and in particular in the fight against poverty at the constituency level.

---

825   Mohamed Interview 8 (2007)

826   Holmes and Sunstein (1999) 131

The CDF is thus a hybrid of de-concentration and devolution, and reflects the contradictions that exist in the power relations between the centre and the periphery. Kenya has a history of centralization of power and resources around the centre, and especially the President. The CDF has particularly moved the power base from the centre to the local level. However, the power it grants is centred on MPs as 'Big Men' and it can be argued is reinforcing a coveted power base at the local level. While it is still too early to make conclusions, there are signs of MPs beginning to build fiefdoms within their constituencies using the fund. Prior to the establishment of the fund, many MPs had very little to do with their constituencies after elections. They had no funds for development and no offices for operations. The norm for constituents was hanging around MPs homes and following them into public places, including bars, hotels and *harambee* functions. This norm was not informed by development issues but rather by client-patron relationships, which was detrimental to constituency development but beneficial to the patrons and their clients.[827]

Most of the above justifications for the fund assume that once the fund is established at the local level, the above mentioned challenges are solved. This is not the case, and so far, experience with the fund shows that there can be unfairness and lack of transparency at the local level. It is common knowledge that, at the local level, there are several divisions based on sub-ethnic, region, class and patron-client relationships. These factors have to be managed at the local level. Secondly, cases of misappropriation and inability to spend the budgeted amount have been experienced in many constituencies and indeed were the cause of the public outcry. Thirdly, cases of either ghost or poorly implemented projects have been noted. Fourthly, the issue of equal distribution of budget allocation, without taking into consideration issues like level of development, area size, and resource endowment of constituencies may not realize the equal allocation, as expected.

CDF is a noble initiative and has brought many benefits to communities around the country. However, CDF has some major

---

827   See generally Oxhorn, Tulchin and Selee (2004)

flaws which if not rectified will undermine the impact of the fund. It would be an error to dispose of the entire CDF initiative on the basis of these emerging issues. It is possible to redress these shortcomings through a widely consultative process where the input from stakeholders is taken into account and integrated into an amended Act. It is prudent to ensure that the legislation governing the CDF is watertight enough to withstand a thorough critique and the rigours of implementation.

CHAPTER 8

CONCLUSION

8.1. CHAPTER SUMMARY

The research question and methodology were identified in the introduction. It drew particular attention to socio-legal theory and to Schumpeter's fiscal sociology and its expanded use since inception. The methodology considered a further expansion as proposed by this thesis: inclusion of human rights law and its possible connection through fiscal sociology to tax law. It outlined and supported the choice of fiscal sociology as a form of inquiry that allows the linkage of tax law to human rights law on several levels, but most importantly that of the state and society.

Chapter 1 discussed the typology of the fiscal state and the OB model as a framework for charting the development of the post-colonial fiscal state. It considered the characteristics critical to the level of the typology and the centrality of the human well-being as expressed through the development of social welfare in the fiscal state. Chapter 2 analysed the process of the introduction of taxation in Kenya through colonisation and its development up to independence in 1963. It considered when the levy of taxation commenced and whether the law and society recognised the need for certain benefits as a result of the payment of tax. Chapter 3 then continued the analysis from independence in 1963 to date.[828] It looked into the continuing challenges not only to the legitimacy of the post-colonial fiscal state but to its progression and achievement of the level of the fiscal state with improved well-being and social welfare provisions.

Chapter 4 then turned to the possible solution to the challenges posed by the preceding chapter: the fiscal realisation of human rights. It discussed the obstacles and impediments not only to the realisation in the post-colonial fiscal state generally, but also to Kenya specifically. The critical development within well-being,

---

828   30 September 2009

development and human rights: participation was then drawn upon in chapter 5 and 6. The process of PB and its utilisation of participation of society in the distribution of tax resources at the discretion of the state was analysed in the context of Brazil and India where it has developed through diverse approaches. Finally Chapter 7 brings Kenya back into the centre of the discussion and analyses the CDF as a method of PB that can be used in the long run to not only legitimise the post-colonial fiscal state but also to realise human rights progressively.

8.2.   The Research Question

The research question that has guided the entire discourse of this thesis is: Can the fiscal state be legitimised through the realisation of human rights? It arose out of the impression of a distinct division between tax law and human rights law. There seemed to be no connection between the funds that society provides to the state and the state's responsibility to improve the well-being of the society. Human rights are thus not only ideals that encompass human dignity, but are laws that are enforceable. Each chapter sought to analyse the role of the state as it attempts to develop society using its limited fiscal resources.

The challenges to tax law include the limited resources available at the disposal of the state; the lack of political will to improve society; the mismanagement of the state apparatus; the lack of trust between the state and society to improve their well-being. The challenges of human rights law are their high resource requirements; the lack of political will to implement them; the lessening of power of the state over the people that they represent and the lack of societal ownership.

8.3.   General Conclusion

The typology of the fiscal state in planning the development of the post-colonial fiscal state is the only currently existing typology. Its systematic development is strongly centred on the development of the developed states more particularly Europe. Only limited and very basic analysis has taken place on its application to developing states and the impact of colonialism. However, the typology of the OB model is an extremely well-developed one, and place can and has been found for particular parts of the development of the post-colonial fiscal state. within its characteristics The most important discussion is about the fiscal system and the elements within the fiscal state of welfare, participation, governance and accountability and their improvement.

The post-colonial fiscal state has a challenge to attempt to achieve the level of the fiscal state while dealing with both limited resources and a fiscal state that has limited fiscal legitimacy. These obstacles together lead to various limitations. Developing countries in their endeavour to improve the lifestyles of their people and the amenities available to them continue to face difficulties because of this on several fronts. Past failed attempts include the usage of ideas from international lending institutions. The argument in many circles today is that the time has come to find state-specific solutions that are home-grown as much as possible.

This thesis attempts to reanalyse the developmental point at which developing nations seem to be at and attempt through the lens of one country, Kenya, to attempt to posit a new tax policy initiative: to re-link tax revenue and tax expenditure through the view of society in order to relegitimise its collection and distribution. This thesis then takes a step forward and posits a second argument that a tool for re-legitimation is international human rights principles and policies. The thesis then joins two seemingly disjointed fields – that of tax and human rights.

Through the lens of human rights, one sees that the right to development if perceived as an umbrella right including all rights together can be used to mandate the reallocation of tax resources in a just manner that also allows for the people and citizens to perceive the utility of the state. Participation, which is a key element of the right to development, is currently being practiced in the field of state budgeting in many states, although without actually referring to human rights. In Kenya, the participatory element is exercised albeit in a limited manner in the CDF.

The theory being posited is itself novel as there is no literature that sets out to create within taxation the responsibility of realising human rights and vice versa. The existing case studies especially Brazil, India and Kenya all proved that there was no reference made to human rights obligations when tax revenue was being discussed and distributed. However, the second limb as to whether this is indeed a possibility remains strong. Interactions in Kenya and Brazil with experts in the field proved that although there was no intent there was indeed a change in the standards of human rights and a re-legitimation of taxation in these states as people realised that there was indeed a limit to the state's resources and that they had a voice in its use and distribution.

Has this research fulfilled Schumpeter's criteria in its utilisation of fiscal sociology? In other terms, has the study premised knowledge on the basis of historical, political, legal, economic and cultural factors for the analysis of a fiscal state? The answer is both yes and no. Although there has been a sustained attempt to contrast these elements, laws, choices and perceptions, this has resulted in different perspectives: the state-societal relationship has been kept at the forefront in the discussion of its functioning and reflection in the developing and evolving contexts in the law. Legal form of thought, however, is only beginning to involve the issue of participation and this deficit compounded by too little empirical information on the individual participants. This is an echo of other studies that use analytical techniques rather than centralising empirical research. Epistemologically, analysis of key data and texts reveal key characteristics which may not be statistically representative but offer crucial insights.

In addition, despite the absence of initial references to human rights, subsequent attempts are being made to draw human rights into the societal discourse at the grassroot level. The re-conceptualisation of human rights especially in social welfare and development as being a societal rather than a state-driven process will go a long way in practically realising the state's responsibility in improving the well-being of its people and realising human rights. An open declaration of the limit to resources, a specific allocation of these resources for societal distribution, allowing freedom of choice in what the resources are used for will not only legitimise the post-colonial fiscal state in the eyes of society but also realise human rights.

8.4. CONCLUSION

There are a number of ways in which the state fulfils its human rights obligations and legitimises its power to collect resources, while in other ways it has failed to do so. This book has tried to show this as fully as possible: however, further empirical research by others in the future would be desirable. In conclusion, human rights should be taken into consideration as a way for states to allow space for their citizens to perceive the right to tax and to be willing taxpayers while at the same time increasing the awareness of the state responsibility in collection and distribution of taxation. To summarise this conclusion and perhaps the form and content of this research as a whole, this thesis ends with the words of Goldscheid that it commenced with:

> There is hardly any other aspect of history ... so decisive for the fate of the masses as that of public finances. Here one hears the pulse beat of nations at its clearest here one stands at the source of all social misery[829]

---

829   Goldscheid (1962) 2

APPENDICES

Appendix 1: Scholars, Fiscal Sociology and its Application to the Concept of the Fiscal State

Approaches to Taxation	Schumpeter	Ormrod	Bonney	Daunton	Tilly	Musgrave
Fiscal Sociology	Yes	Yes	Yes	Yes	Yes	No
Fairness	Yes	No	No	Yes	Yes	No
War causes transition of states	Yes	Yes	Yes	Yes	Yes	Yes
Transition is linear	Yes	Yes	Yes	Yes	No (cyclical)	No

Source: Author

Appendix 2: Annual Collections by Tax Type

ANNUAL TAX REVENUE

(IN MILLION Ksh)

	2000/ 2001	2001/ 2002	2002/ 2003	2003/ 2004	2004/ 2005	2005/ 2006	2006/ 2007	2007/ 2008
IMPORTS	86°992	83°474	89°297	97°174	110°201	94°788	117°909	132°654
Import Duty	28°664	21°286	18°332	21°958	23°149	21°388	27°910	32°539
Excise Duty	28°285	32°110	35°932	40°109	44°855	29°187	32°742	34°050
VAT On Imports	24°131	24°452	28°780	27°362	32°473	34°034	44°744	53°634
IDF	5°912	5°626	6°253	7°745	9°724	10°179	12°513	12°431
DOMESTIC	82°541	87°274	99°478	115°690	143°767	179°533	209°825	252°022
Pay As You Earn (PAYE)	28°887	32°894	36°350	43°906	53°325	61°503	72°470	86°140
Personal Tax	2°050	2°018	2°008	2°217	3°051	2°801	2°977	3°228
Corporation Tax	17°620	18°087	23°297	26°354	31°947	38°799	43°146	57°434
Withholding Tax	7°511	7°573	9°350	9°445	11°792	12°300	14°180	18°826
Other Taxes	178	255	209	287	487	402	256	525
Capital Gains Tax (*Suspended*)	–	–	–	–	–	–	–	–
VAT Domestic	26°295	26°447	27°586	31°411	40°183	42°151	51°829	57°374

Excise Duty - Domestic						17°615	19°609	22°070
Excise on airtime			678	2°070	2°982	3°962	5°358	6°397
Turnover Tax								28
TOTAL REVENUE	169°533	170°748	188°775	212°864	253°968	274°321	327°734	384°676

Source – KRA various publications

Appendix 3: Annual Collections as Percentage of Total Revenue

PERCENTAGE CONTRIBUTION TO TOTAL TAX REVENUE								
	2000/ 2001	2001/ 2002	2002/ 2003	2003/ 2004	2004/ 2005	2005/ 2006	2006/ 2007	2007/ 2008
IMPORTS	51,31	48,89	47,30	45,65	43,39	34,55	35,98	34,48
Import Duty	16,91	12,47	9,71	10,32	9,11	7,80	8,52	8,46
Excise Duty	16,68	18,81	19,03	18,84	17,66	10,64	9,99	8,85
VAT On Imports	14,23	14,32	15,25	12,85	12,79	12,41	13,65	13,94
IDF	3,49	3,29	3,31	3,64	3,83	3,71	3,82	3,23
DOMESTIC	48,69	51,11	52,70	54,35	56,61	65,45	64,02	65,52
Pay As You Earn (PAYE)	17,04	19,26	19,26	20,63	21,00	22,42	22,11	22,39
Personal Tax	1,21	1,18	1,06	1,04	1,20	1,02	0,91	0,84
Corporation Tax	10,39	10,59	12,34	12,38	12,58	14,14	13,16	14,93
Withholding Tax	4,43	4,44	4,95	4,44	4,64	4,48	4,33	4,89
Other Taxes	0,10	0,15	0,11	0,13	0,19	0,15	0,08	0,14
Capital Gains Tax (*Suspended*)	0,00	0,00	0,00	0,00	0,00	0,00	0,00	0,00
VAT Domestic	15,51	15,49	14,61	14,76	15,82	15,37	15,81	14,91
Excise Duty - Domestic	0,00	0,00	0,00	0,00	0,00	6,42	5,98	5,74

Excise on airtime	0,00	0,00	0,36	0,97	1,17	1,44	1,63	1,66
Turnover Tax	0,00	0,00	0,00	0,00	0,00	0,00	0,00	0,01
TOTAL REVENUE	100,00	100,00	100,00	100,00	100,00	100,00	100,00	100,00

Source – KRA various publications

Appendix 4: Annual Collections as Percentage of GDP

PERCENTAGE CONTRIBUTION TO TOTAL TAX REVENUE								
	2000/ 2001	2001/ 2002	2002/ 2003	2003/ 2004	2004/ 2005	2005/ 2006	2006/ 2007	2007/ 2008
IMPORTS	9,18	8,12	8,57	8,50	8,67	6,05	7,63	7,63
Import Duty	3,03	2,07	1,76	1,92	1,82	1,37	1,81	1,87
Excise Duty	2,99	3,12	3,45	3,51	3,53	1,86	2,12	1,96
VAT On Imports	2,55	2,38	2,76	2,39	2,55	2,17	2,90	3,08
IDF	0,62	0,55	0,60	0,68	0,76	0,65	0,81	0,71
DOMESTIC	8,71	8,49	9,55	10,11	11,31	11,47	13,58	14,49
Pay As You Earn (PAYE)	3,05	3,20	3,49	3,84	4,19	3,93	4,69	4,95
Personal Tax	0,22	0,20	0,19	0,19	0,24	0,18	0,19	0,19
Corporation Tax	1,86	1,76	2,24	2,30	2,51	2,48	2,79	3,30
Withholding Tax	0,79	0,74	0,90	0,83	0,93	0,79	0,92	1,08
Other Taxes	0,02	0,02	0,02	0,03	0,04	0,03	0,02	0,03
Capital Gains Tax (*Suspended*)	0,00	0,00	0,00	0,00	0,00	0,00	0,00	0,00
VAT Domestic	2,78	2,57	2,65	2,75	3,16	2,69	3,35	3,30
Excise Duty – Domestic	0,00	0,00	0,00	0,00	0,00	1,12	1,27	1,27

Excise on airtime	0,00	0,00	0,07	0,18	0,23	0,25	0,35	0,37
Turnover Tax	0,00	0,00	0,00	0,00	0,00	0,00	0,00	0,00
TOTAL REVENUE	17,89	16,62	18,13	18,61	19,98	17,52	21,21	22,12

Source – KRA various publications

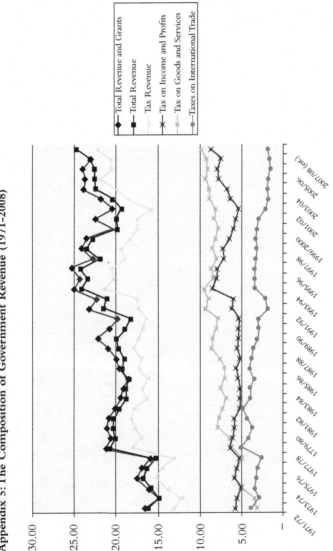

Appendix 5: The Composition of Government Revenue (1971-2008)

Appendix 6

Economic growth by decade

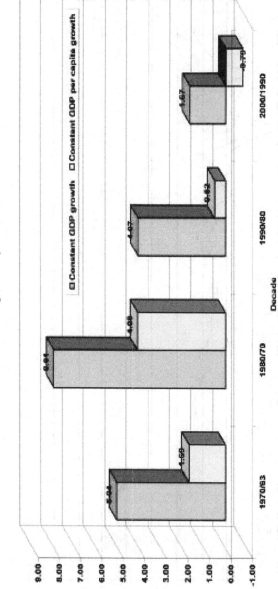

Appendix 7

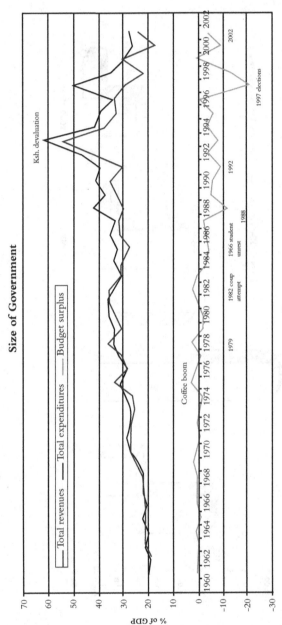

Size of Government

— Total revenues — Total expenditures —— Budget surplus

Ksh. devaluation

Coffee boom

1979

1982 coup attempt

1966 student unrest

1992

1997 elections

2002

% of GDP

Year

Appendix 8

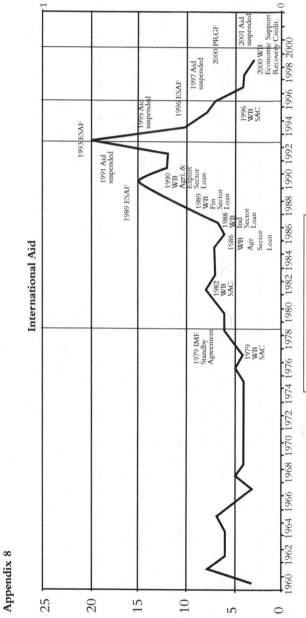

International Aid

- Aid (% of GNI) — IMF agreements

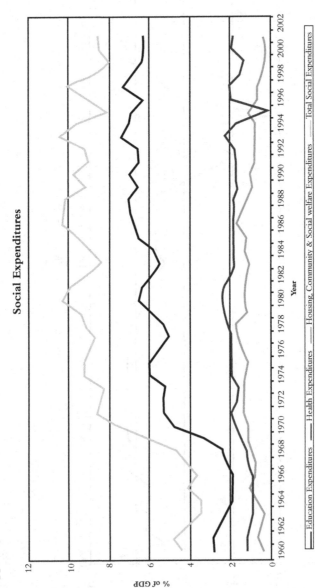

Appendix 9

Social Expenditures

Education Expenditures — Health Expenditures — Housing, Community & Social welfare Expenditures — Total Social Expenditures

Kenya's MTEF Budget Framework

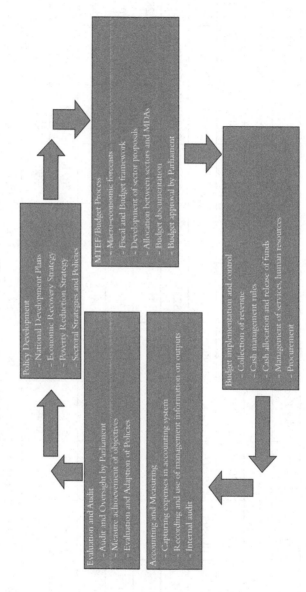

Policy Development
- National Development Plans
- Economic Recovery Strategy
- Poverty Reduction Strategy
- Sectoral Strategies and Policies

MTEF/Budget Process
- Macro-economic forecasts
- Fiscal and Budget framework
- Development of sector proposals
- Allocation between sectors and MDAs
- Budget documentation
- Budget approval by Parliament

Budget implementation and control
- Collection of revenue
- Cash management rules
- Cash allocation and release of funds
- Management of services, human resources
- Procurement

Accounting and Measuring
- Capturing expenses in accounting system
- Recording and use of management information on outputs

Evaluation and Audit
- Audit and Oversight by Parliament
- Measure achievement of objectives
- Evaluation and Adaption of Policies
- Internal audit

Appendix 11: Real and Nominal Tax Yields (Ksh million)

	Total Tax		Sales Tax		Income Tax		Excise Duties		Import Duties	
	Nominal	Real	Nominal	Real	Nominal	Real	Nominal	Real	Nominal	Real
1996	127030	127030	29850	29850	48375	48375	23687	23687	22594	22594
1997	147893	132997	34468	30996	55578	48980	28382	25523	27167	24431
1998	155524	131244	39205	33084	55235	46612	28733	24247	28444	24003
1999	156966	125272	40944	32677	53317	42551	28493	22740	28605	22829
2000	164112	119094	50221	36445	53429	38773	28318	20550	28804	20903
2001	162464	111430	50872	34891	55862	38314	32077	22001	21584	14804
2002	190297	125443	57185	37696	67529	44515	42671	28129	19895	13115
2003	203169	122023	58983	35425	70862	42560	47590	28583	21907	13157
2004	211957	113955	62967	33853	78777	42353	45304	24357	21392	11501
2005	298901	145806	78603	38343	115601	56390	55557	27101	25732	12552

Nominal (current prices); Real (constant prices)

Appendix 12: Real and Nominal Tax Bases (Ksh Million) Domestic Factor

	Incomes		Private Consumption		Imports		GDP	
	Nominal	Real	Nominal	Real	Nominal	Real	Nominal	Real
1996	449,621	449,621	359,442	359,442	168,486	168,486	528,739	528,739
1997	536,264	482,252	453,176	407,532	190,674	171,469	623,235	560,463
1998	596,539	503,409	513,249	433,121	197,789	166,911	694,028	585,677
1999	639,056	510,021	540,400	431,285	206,401	164,725	743,478	593,358
2000	685,436	497,414	609,862	442,570	247,804	179,829	967,838	702,350
2001	770,028	528,140	685,607	470,238	290,108	198,976	1,020,022	699,604
2002	850,910	560,916	693,171	456,935	257,710	169,881	1,022,208	673,835
2003	850,910	581,636	805,162	483,581	281,844	169,276	1,136,288	682,455
2004	850,910	608,477	954,649	513,252	364,205	195,809	1,282,504	689,518
2005	-	-	-	-	430,740	210,117	1,415,155	690,319

BIBLIOGRAPHY

Constitution of the Republic of France (1793).

(1940). *Hay v Commissioner of Income Tax*. East African Court of Appeal, East African Court of Appeal. 7: 7.

Constitutional (Amendment) Act (1986).

The Constitution of Kenya Review Act (2000).

(2000). *Republic v Kenya Roads Board exparte John Harun Mwau* High Court of Kenya. CA 1372 of 2000.

Abers, R. N. (1996). "From Ideas to Practice: *The Partidos dos Trabalhadores and Participatory Governance in Brazil.*" Latin American Perspectives 23(4): 35-53.

Abers, R. N. (2000). Inventing Local Democracy: *Grassroots Politics in Brazil.* Boulder, CO, Lynne Rienner.

Acemoglu, D., S. Johnson, et al. (2001). "The colonial origins of comparative development: an empirical investigation." *American Economic Review* 91(5): 1369-1401.

Adams, B. (2004). "Public Meetings and the Democratic Process." *Public Administration Review* 64: 43-54.

Adar, K. G. and I. M. Munyae (2001). "Human Rights Abuse in Kenya Under Daniel Arap Moi, 1978-2001." *African Studies Quarterly.*

Adongo, A. and R. Rop (2004). KENYA: Women Praise Kibaki's Directive to Drop Tax on Sanitary Towels. IRIN. Nairobi.

Ahmad, I. A. (2001). An Islamic Perspective on the Wealth of Nations. *The Economics of Property Rights Cultural, Legal and Philosophical Issues.* S. Pejovich: 7-8.

Akech, J. M. M. (2000). "Judicial Review of Spending Powers: Should Kenyan Courts Entertain Taxpayers Actions?" *Journal of African Law* 44: 195-217.

Alexander, R., B. Paterline, et al. (2007). "Citizen Involvement in the County Budget Process in Georgia." *International Social Science Review* 82(3/4): 163.

Alfredsson, G. and A. Eide (1999). *The Universal Declaration of Human Rights : a common standard of achievement,* The Hague ; London ; Kluwer.

Alston, P. (1987). "Out of the Abyss: The Challenges Confronting the New

U. N. Committee on Economic, Social and Cultural Rights." *Human Rights Quarterly* 9(3): 332-381.

Alston, P., M. Robinson, et al. (2005). *Human rights and development : towards mutual reinforcement*. Oxford, Oxford University Press.

Alvarez, S. E. and E. Dagnino (1998). *Cultures of politics/politics of cultures : revisioning Latin American social movements*. Boulder, Colorado; Oxford, Westview Press.

Alwy, A. and S. Schech (2004). "Ethnic Inequalities in Education in Kenya." *International Education Journal* 5(2): 266-274.

Anon (2008). Part XVII of the Local Government Act requires local authorities to keep proper Accounts. The East African. Nairobi.

Ansiliero, G. and L. H. Paiva (2008). "The recent evolution of social security coverage in Brazil." *International Social Security Review* 61(3): 1-28.

Arcelus, F. J., B. Sharma, et al. (2005) "The Human Development Index Adjusted for Efficient Resource Utilization." *WIDER Research Paper* No 2005/08, 12.

Armitage, D. (2000). The Ideological Origins of the British Empire. Cambridge, Cambridge University Press

Askim, J. and G. S. Hanssen (2008). "Councillors' receipt and use of citizen input: Experience from Norwegian local government." *Public Administration* 86(2): 387-409.

Aspalter, C. (2003). The State and the Making of the Welfare System in India. Hong Kong, University of Hong Kong.

Assembly of Heads of State and Governments of the African Union (1994). African Union Declaration on Social Development. African Union. AHG/Decl. 5(XXX).

Assembly of Heads of State and Governments of the African Union (1995). Relaunching Africa's Economic and Social Development: The Cairo Agenda, African Union. AHG/Res 236 (XXXI) Annex.

Astorga, P., A. R. Berges, et al. (2005). "The standard of living in Latin America during the twentieth century." *Economic History Review* 58(4): 765-+.

Austin, G. (2008). "The 'Reversal of Fortune' book and the Compression of History: Perspectives from African and Comparative Economic History." *Journal of International Development* 20: 996-1027.

Avritzer, L. (1993). Modernity and democracy in Brazil : an interpretation of the Brazilian path of modernization: iii, 259 leaves.

Avritzer, L. (2002a). "Democracy and the public space in Latin America." from http://www.netLibrary.com/urlapi.asp?action=summary&v=1 &bookid=81008

Avritzer, L. (2002b). New Public Spheres in Brazil: Local Democracy and Deliberative Politics. Belo Horizonte Universidade Federal de Minas Gerais.

Ayany, S. G. (1983). A History of Zanzibar: A Study in Constitutional Development 1934-1946. Nairobi, Kenya Literature Bureau.

Backhaus, J. (2002). "Fiscal sociology - What for?" *American Journal of Economics and Sociology* 61(1): 55-77 at 73.

Backhaus, J. (2002). "Fiscal sociology - What for?" *American Journal of Economics and Sociology* 61(1): 55-77.

Backhaus, J. (2002). "Fiscal Sociology What For?" *American Journal of Economics and Sociology* 61(1): 55-76 at 73.

Baierle, S. (1998). The Explosion of Experience: The Emergence of a new Political Ethical Principle in Popular Movements in Porto Alegre, Brazil. *Cultures of politics/politics of cultures : revisioning Latin American social movements.* S. E. Alvarez, E. Dagnino and A. Escobar. Boulder, Colo. ; Oxford, Westview Press.

Baiocchi, G. (2001). "Participation, activism, and politics: The Porto Alegre experiment and deliberative democratic theory." *Politics & Society* 29(1): 43-72.

Baiocchi, G. (2002). "Synergizing Civil Society: State-Civil Society Regimes in Porto Alegre, Brazil." *Political Power and Social Theory* 15: 3-86.

Baiocchi, G. (2003a). Participation, Activism and Politics: The Porto Alegre Experiment. *Deepening democracy : institutional innovations in empowered participatory governance.* A. Fung and E. O. Wright. London, Verso: 45-76.

Baiocchi, G. (2003b). *Radicals in power : the Workers' Party (PT) and experiments in urban democracy in Brazil.* London ; New York

New York, Zed Books ;

Distributed in the USA exclusively by Palgrave.

Baiocchi, G. (2005). *Militants and citizens : the politics of participatory democracy in Porto Alegre.* Stanford, Calif., Stanford University Press ; London :

Eurospan [distributor].

Baiocchi, G. (2006). The Citizens of Porto Alegre: In which Marco borrows bus fare and enters politics *The Boston Review*. Boston.

Baldwin, P. (1990). The Politics of Solidarity: Class Bases of the European Welfare State 1875–1975 Cambridge.

Bandyopadhyay, D. (1997). People's Participation in Planning. *Economic and Political Weekly*. September: 2450-2454.

Barber, B. R. (2004). Strong democracy : participatory politics for a new age. Berkeley, Calif. ; London, University of California Press.

Barsh, R. L. (1991). "The Right to Development as a Human Right - Results of the Global Consultation." *Human Rights Quarterly* 13(3): 322-338.

Basok, T. and S. Ilcan (2006). "In the Name of Human Rights: Global Organizations and Participating Citizens." *Citizenship Studies* 10(3): 309-327.

Bendix, R. (1977). *Nation-building and citizenship : studies of our changing social order*. Berkeley, University of California Press.

Bennett, N. R. (1978). *A History of the Arab State of Zanzibar*. London, Methuen and Co Ltd.

Berner, M. (2001). "Citizen Participation in Local Government Budgeting." *Popular Government* 66: 23-30.

Bevan, D. P., P. Collier, et al. (1990). *External Shocks and the Kenyan Economy* Oxford, Oxford University.

Bird, R. M. and T. Stauffer, Eds. (2001). *Intergovernmental Fiscal Relations in Fragmented Societies*. Helbig and Lichtenhahn, Bale.

Bitrán, R. and U. Giedion (2003). Waivers and exemptions for health services in developing countries. *World Bank: Social Protection Discussion Paper Series*.

Blomgren-Bingham, L., T. Nabatchi, et al. (2005). "The New Governance: Practices and Processes for Stakeholder and Citizen Participation in the Work of Government." *Public Administration Review* 65: 547-58.

Boahen, A. A. (1987). *African Perspectives on Colonialism*. Baltimore and London, John Hopkins University Press.

Bomfim, A. and A. Shah (1994). "Macroeconomic Management and the Division of Powers in Brazil - Perspectives for the 1990S." *World*

Development 22(4): 535-542.

Bonney, R. (1995). *The Origins of the Modern State in Europe, Thirteenth to Eighteenth Centuries: Economic Systems and State Finance,* Oxford.

Bonney, R. (1999). *The Rise of the Fiscal State in Europe, c 1200-1815.* Oxford, Oxford University Press.

Bradshaw, Y. and M. Wallace (1996). *Global Inequalities.* Thousand Oaks, Calif., Pine Forge Press.

Bratton, M., R. B. Mattes, et al. (2005). *Public opinion, democracy, and market reform in Africa,* Cambridge University Press.

Brennan, G. and J. M. Buchanan (1980). *The power to tax : analytical foundations of a fiscal constitution.* Cambridge, Cambridge University Press.

Brett, E. A. (1973). Colonialism and Underdevelopment in East Africa: *The Politics of Economic Change* 1919-1939. Nairobi, Heinemann.

Briggs, A. (1961). "The Welfare-State in Historical-Perspective." *Archives Europeennes De Sociologie* 2(2): 221-258.

British Cabinet (1931). Closer Union in East Africa, Her majesty's Stationery Office.

British Colonial Government (1948). Report to United Nations on Administration of Tanganyika for 1947. London.

British Colonial Government (1952). Report to United Nations on Administration of Tanganyika for 1951. London.

British Colonial Government (1953). Report to United Nations on Administration of Tanganyika for 1952. London.

British Colonial Government (1955). Report to United Nations on Administration of Tanganyika for 1954. London.

British Empire (1922). *British Empire Report.* C. Secret. London, Crown Printers. 63: 8.

British Empire (1932). Conclusions of Meeting. B. Cabinet. London, British Crown. 35.

British Empire (1933). Conclusions of Meeting. B. Cabinet. London, British Crown. 38.

Brown, I., Ed. (1989). *The economies of Africa and Asia during the inter-war depression.* London, Routledge.

Brown, N. J., P. Quiblier, et al. (1994). *Ethics & agenda 21 : moral implications of a global consensus.* New York, United Nations Environmental

Programme.

Brownell, P. (1981). "Participation in Budgeting, Locus of Control and Organizational-Effectiveness." *Accounting Review* 56(4): 844-860.

Brownell, P. (1982). "The Role of Accounting Data in Performance Evaluation, Budgetary Participation, and Organizational-Effectiveness." *Journal of Accounting Research* 20(1): 12-27.

Bruton, H. J., C. Hill, et al., Eds. (1996). *The evaluation of public expenditure in Africa* Washington DC, World Bank.

Buckley, R. B. (1903). "Colonization and Irrigation in the East African Protectorate." *The Geographical Journal* 4(21): 349-371.

Burgess, R. and N. Stern (1993). "Taxation and Development." *Journal of Economic Literature* 31(June): 762-830.

Cabannes, Y. (2004). "Participatory budgeting: a significant contribution to participatory democracy." *Environment and Urbanization* 16(1): 27-46.

Camargo, J. M. and F. H. G. Ferreira (2000). The Poverty Reduction Strategy of The Government of Brazil: A Rapid Appraisal. *Second Global Poverty Report*, United Nationa Development Programme.

Campbell, J. L. (1993). "The State and Fiscal Sociology." *Annual Review of Sociology* 19: 163-185.

Carpenter, M. (2009). "The capabilities approach and critical social policy: Lessons from the majority world?" *Critical Social Policy* 29: 351.

Carrier, J. and I. Kendall (1986). "Categories, Categorizations and the Political-Economy of Welfare." *Journal of Social Policy* 15: 315-335.

CDF Secretariat (30 October 2007). Press Statement on Management of CDCs following Dissolution of Parliament. M. o. Planning. Nairobi, Government Printers.

CDF Secretariat (2008). Press Release to Members of Parliament-Elect on the Composition of the CDF Committees. M. o. Planning. Nairobi, Government Printer.

CDF Secretariat. (2009). "CDF Review Taskforce." Retrieved 25/9/09, 2009, from http://www.cdfreview.org/index.php?option=com_cont ent&task=view&id=20&Itemid=1.

CDF Secretariat. (2009). "Constituencies Allocations." 2009, from <http://www.cdf.go.ke/index.php?option=com_content&task=category&se ctionid=30&id=104&Itemid=70>.

Center for Governance and Democracy(CGD) (2001). A Survey of Seven Years of Waste. *Policy Brief* Nairobi, Center for Governance and Democracy.

Chapman, A. (1996). "A Violations Approach for Monitoring the International Covenant on Economic, Social and Cultural Rights." *Human Rights Quarterly* 18(1): 23-66.

Chapra, M. U. (1976). The Islamic Welfare State and Its Role in the Economy. *Studies in Islamic Economics.* K. Ahmad. Jeddah, The Islamic Foundation: 143-169 at 161.

Chavez, D. (2004). *Polis & demos : the left in municipal governance in Montevideo and Porto Alegre.* Maastricht, Netherlands, Shaker Publ.

Choudry, M. A. and A. Rahman (1986). "Macroeconomic Relations in the Islamic Economic Order." *International Journal of Social Economics* 13(6): 60 at 63.

Christiano Carvalho Interview 8 (2009). A. Waris. Sao Paulo.

Chweya, L. (2006) "Constituency Development Fund: A Critique." *The African Executive.*

Ciru Gikonyo Interview 2 (2007). A. Waris. Nairobi.

Cobham, A. (2006). Recommendation to the Dept for International Development of the United Kingdom: Funding a welfare state in Africa. *The Guardian London.*

Cohen, J. (1996). Procedure and Substance in Deliberative Democracy. *Democracy and difference : contesting the boundaries of the political.* S. Benhabib. Princeton, N.J., Princeton University Press: 95-119.

Cole, R. C. (1975). "Citizen Participation in Municipal Politics." American *Journal of Political Science* 19: 761-81.

Collignon, S. (2007). "The Three Sources of Legitimacy for European Fiscal Policy." *International Political Science Review/ Revue internationale de science pol* 28(2): 155-184.

Collins, D., J. Quick, et al. (1996). "The fall and rise of cost sharing in Kenya: the impact of phased implementation." *Health Policy and Planning* 11(1): 52-63.

Commission for Africa (2005). Our Common Interest: Report for the Commission for Africa. London.

Commission on Human Rights. The Right to Development (1977).

Committee Against Torture. Consideration of Reports Submitted by States Parties Under Article 19 of the Convention: Conclusions and Recommendations of the Committee Against Torture: Hungary (2006).

Committee on Economic Social and Cultural Rights. Concluding observations of the Committee on Economic, Social and Cultural Rights: Kenya (1993).

Committee on Economic Social and Cultural Rights. General comment No. 9 The domestic application of the Covenant: Substantive Issues Arising In the Implementation of the International Covenant on Economic, Social and Cultural Rights (1998).

Committee on the Convention on the Rights of the Child. General Comment No 5: General Measures of Implementation for the Convention on the Rights of the Child (2003).

Committee on the Rights of the Child. Consideration of Reports Submitted by States Parties Under Article 44 of The Convention : Concluding observations: Bolivia (2005).

Connolly, W., Ed. (1984). *Legitimacy and the State,* Blackwell.

Constituency Development Fund Website (2007) "Minister Appoints CDF Chairman."

Cooper, F. (1997). Modernizing bureaucrats, backward Africans, and the development concept. *International Development and the Social Sciences: Essays on the History and Politics of Knowledge.* F. Cooper and R. Packard. Berkeley: 64–92.

Cooper, F. (2002). *Africa since 1940. The Past of the Present, New Approaches to African History.* Cambridge MA, New York, Cambridge University Press.

Cornwall, A. and A. Shankland (2008). "Engaging citizens: Lessons from building Brazil's national health system." *Social Science & Medicine* 66: 2173-2184.

Costa, L. A. M. C. d. (2006). The old (literally) of gold of the Brazilian currency. *Terra Magazine.* Brazil, Terra magazine.

Creck Buyonge Interview 4 (2007). A. Waris. Nairobi.

Crook, R. C. and J. Manor (1998). *Democracy and decentralisation in South Asia and West Africa.* Cambridge, Cambridge University Press.

Dahlgren, G. (1991). "Strategies for health financing in Kenya - the difficult birth of a new policy." *Scandinavian Journal of Social Medicine* 46: 67-81.

Dandekar, V. M. and N. Rath (1978). *Poverty in India*. Pune, Indian School of Political Economy.

Daunton, M. (1994). "The entrepreneurial state 1700-1914." *History Today* 44(5): 11-17 at 17.

Daunton, M. (2001). *Trusting Leviathan: The politics of taxation in Britain 1799-1914*. Cambridge, Cambridge University Press.

Davis, H. E., J. J. Finan, et al. (1977). *Latin American diplomatic history : an introduction*. Baton Rouge, Louisiana State University Press.

Davis, L. E. and R. A. Huttenback (1988). *Mammon and the Pursuit of Empire. The Economics of British Imperialism*. Cambridge MA, New York, Cambridge University Press

De Sousa Santos, B. "Participatory budgeting in Porto Alegre: Toward a redistributive democracy." *Politics & Society* 26(4): 461-510.

Dickinson, A. (1970). *The Stamp Act 1765-66*. New York, Franklin Watts.

Diffie, B. W., B. C. Shafer, et al. (1977). *Foundations of the Portuguese empire, 1415-1580*. Ontario, Burns and MacEachern.

Dilley, M. R. (1966). *British policy in Kenya Colony*. London, Cass.

Director General (1976). *Employment, Growth and Basic Needs: A One World Problem*. World Employment Conference, International Labour Organisation.

Dixon, J. and R. P. Scheurell (2002). *The state of social welfare : the twentieth century in cross-national review*. Westport, Conn., Praeger.

Donnelly, J. (1982). "Human Rights as Natural Rights." *Human Rights Quarterly* 4(3): 391-405.

Donnelly, J. (2003). *Universal human rights in theory and practice*. Ithaca, Cornell University Press.

Dutt, S. (1998). "Identities and the Indian state: An overview." *Third World Quarterly* 19(3): 411-434.

Ebdon, C. and A. Franklin (2004). "Searching for a Role for Citizens in the Budget Process." *Public Budgeting and Finance* 24: 32-49.

Esping-Andersen, G. (1990). *The three worlds of welfare capitalism*. Cambridge, Polity.

European Union. *European Convention on Human Rights* (1953).

Everest-Phillips, M. and R. Sandall (2008) "Linking Business Tax Reform with Governance: How to Measure Success." *In Practice*, 1-4.

Fahnbulleh, M. (2006). "In search of economic development in Kenya: Colonial legacies & postindependence realities." *Review of African Political Economy* 33(107): 33-47.

Ferreira, M. C. (2000). "Participation and Political Behavior in the State of São Paulo." Public Opinion.

Ferrero (1983). Study of the New Economic Order and the Promotion of Human Rights (UN Doc E/CN.4/Sub.2/1983/24.

Fieldhouse, D. K. (1973). *Economics and Empire, 1830-1914* London.

Financial Commissioner (1932). Report of the Financial Commissioner Lord Moyne: Certain Questions in Kenya. C. Affairs. London, Her Majesty's Stationery Office.

Flora, P. and A. J. Heidenheimer (1981). *The Development of welfare states in Europe and America*. New Brunswick ; London, Transaction.

Folscher, A. (2007). Participatory Budgeting in Asia. *Participatory budgeting.* A. Shah. Washington, D.C., World Bank: 157-189.

Folscher, A. (2007). Participatory Budgeting in Central and Eastern Europe. *Participatory budgeting.* A. Shah. Washington, D.C., World Bank: 127-156.

Folscher, A. (2007). Participatory Budgeting in the Middle East and Africa. *Participatory budgeting.* A. Shah. Washington, D.C., World Bank: 225-241.

Fox, M. (6 July 2009) "Budgets by the People: Participatory democracy, Brazil-style, is running into problems." *IN THESE TIMES.*

France, R. o. (1789). Declaration of the Rights of Man, Government of France.

Franklin, A. and B. Carberry-George (1999). "Analyzing How Local Governments Establish Service Priorities." *Public Budgeting and Finance* 19: 31-46.

Fred Oundo Interview 5 (2007). A. Waris. Nairobi.

Freire, P. (1970a). *Pedagogy of the oppressed.* [New York], Herder and Herder.

Freire, P. (1970b). *Cultural action for freedom.* [Cambridge], Harvard educational review.

Freire, P. and P. Freire (1973). *Education for critical consciousness.* New York,, Seabury Press.

Fuchs, M. (1985). *Soziale Sicherheit in der Dritten Welt: Zugleich eine Fallstudie Kenia.* Baden Baden.

Fukuda-Parr, S., T. Lawson-Remer, et al. (2008) "Measuring the Progressive Realization of Human Rights Obligations: An Index of Economic and Social Rights Fulfillment." *University of Connecticut: Department of Economics Working Paper Series.*

Fung, A. and E. O. Wright (2003). *Deepening democracy : institutional innovations in empowered participatory governance.* London, Verso.

G Masinde Interview 3 (2007). A. Waris. Nairobi.

Ganji (1969). The Realization of Economic, Social and Cultural Rights: Problems, Policies, Progress (UN Doc E/CN.4/1108/Rev.1), United Nations.

General, U. N. S. (1985). *Study by the Secretary General on Popular Participation* (UN Doc E/CN.4/1985/10).

Ghai, Y. (1999). The Kenyan Bill of Rights: Theory and Practice. *Promoting human rights through bills of rights.* P. Alston, Oxford University Press: 187-282.

Ghai, Y. (2006). Redesigning the State for "Right to Development". *Development as a Human Right: Legal Political and Economic Dimensions.* B. Andreassen and S. Marks. London, Harvard School of Public Health: 141-166.

Ghai, Y. P. and J. P. W. B. McAuslan (1970). *Public Law and Political Change in Kenya.* London, Oxford University Press.

Gikonyo, W. (2008). The CDF Social Audit Guide. OSEIA. Nairobi, Open Society.

Goldfrank, B. (2001). *Deepening Democracy through Citizen Participation? A Comparative Analysis of Three Cities.* Annual Meeting of the American Political Science Association, San Francisco.

Goldfrank, B. (2002). Urban experiments in citizen participation: deepening democracy in Latin America.

Goldfrank, B. (2003). Making Participation Work in Porto Alegre. *Radicals in power : the Workers' Party (PT) and experiments in urban democracy in Brazil.* G. Baiocchi. London ; New York, Zed Books. Palgrave.

Goldfrank, B. (2005). "The Politics of Deepening Local Democracy: Decentralization, Party Institutionalization, and Participation." *Conference Papers -- Midwestern Political Science Association.*

Goldfrank, B. (2007). Lessons from Latin America's Experience with Participatory Budgeting. *Participatory budgeting.* A. Shah. Washington, D.C., World Bank: 92.

Goldfrank, B. and A. Schneider (2006). "Competitive institution building: The PT and participatory budgeting in Rio Grande do Sul." *Latin American Politics and Society* 48(3): 1-31.

Goldscheid, R. (1962). *A Sociological Approach to Problems of Finance. Classics in the Theory of Public Finance.* R. A. Musgrave and A. T. Peacock. London, Macmillan and Company.

Goulet, D. (1989). "Participation in Development: New Avenues." *World Development* 17(2): 165-178 at 165.

Government of Brazil. (2008). "City of Ipatinga Participatory Budgeting." Retrieved 21 April 2009, from http://www.ipatinga.mg.gov.br.

Government of Kenya (1969). *Economic Survey.* Nairobi, Government Printers.

Government of Kenya (1980). Sessional Paper no 4 "Economic Prospects and Policies". Nairobi, Government Printers.

Government of Kenya (1983). Kenya National Development Plan 1984-88. Nairobi, Government Printers.

Government of Kenya (1986). Sessional Paper No. 1/86 on Economic Management for Renewed Growth. Nairobi, Government Printers.

Government of Kenya (1989). Working Paper on Government Expenditures in Kenya Nairobi, Government Printers.

Government of Kenya (2003). Kenya Economic Recovery Strategy for Wealth and Employment Creation 2003-2007. M. o. P. a. N. Development. Nairobi, Government Printers.

Government of the United States of America (1970). *Goldberg v Kelly.* US, US. 397: 254.

Government of the United States of America (1975). *Goss v Lopez.* US, US. 419: 565.

Government of the United States of America (1976). *Mathews v Eldridge.* US, US. 424: 319.

Gower (1959). Gower to Secretary of State for the Colonies.

Gray, J. M. S. (1957). *The British in Mombasa, 1824-1826. Being the history of Captain Owen's protectorate, etc. [With illustrations.],* pp. viii. 216.

Macmillan & Co.: London.

Gret, M. and Y. Sintomer (2005). *The Porto Alegre experiment : learning lessons for better democracy.* London ; New York

New York, Zed Books ;

Distributed exclusively in the U.S. by Palgrave.

Grindle, M. S. (1996). *Challenging the state: crisis and innovation in Latin America and Africa.* Cambridge, Cambridge University Press.

Grosh, B. (1991). *Public Enterprise in Kenya: What Works, What Doesn't, and Why.* Boulder, Lynne Reiner.

Group of Experts on the UN Programme on Public Administration and Finance (1997). Political, Social and Economic Realities in Developing Countries and in Countries with Economies in Transition, United Nations.

Grugel, J. and N. Piper (2009). "Do Rights Promote Development?" *Global Social Policy* 9: 79-98.

Guidry, J. A. (2003). "Not Just Another Labor Party: The Workers' Party and Democracy in Brazil." *Labor Studies Journal* 28: 83-108.

Hammersley, M. and P. Atkinson (1983). *Ethnography, Principles in Practice.* London, Tavistock Publications.

Hanson, S. (6 August 2009) "Corruption in Sub-Saharan Africa." *International Reporting Project.*

Harnecker, M. (1999). Delegating Power to the People: Participatory budget in Porto Alegre, World Bank.

Heller, P. (2001). "Moving the State: The Politics of Democratic Decentralization in Kerala, South Africa, and Porto Alegre." *Politics & Society* 29(1): 131.

Heller, P., K. N. Harilal, et al. (2007). "Building Local Democracy: Evaluating the Impact of Decentralization in Kerala, India." *World Development* 35(4): 626.

Heller, P. S. (1974). "Public Investment in LDC's With Recurrent Cost Constraint: The Kenyan Case." *Quarterly Journal of Economics* 88(2): 251-277.

Hemmati, M. (2002). *Multi-Stakeholder Processes for Governance and Sustainability. Beyond Deadlock and Conflict.* London, Earthscan.

Henkin, L. (1984). International Human Rights and Rights in the United

States. *Human rights in international law : legal and policy issues.* T. Meron. Oxford, Clarendon Press. 1: 43.

Henkin, L. (1987). *International Law,* Martinus Nijjhof.

Her Majesty's Stationery Office (1940). Statement of Policy on Colonial Development and Welfare.

Himbara, D. (1994). "The Failed Africanization of Commerce and Industry in Kenya." *World Development* 22(3): 469-482.

Hirlinger, M.W. (1992). "Citizen-Initiated Contacting of Local Government Officials: A Multivariate Analysis." *Journal of Politics* 54: 553-63.

Holmes, S. and C. R. Sunstein (1999). *The cost of rights : why liberty depends on taxes.* New York ; London, W.W. Norton.

Holtham, G. and A. Hazlewood (1976). *Aid and inequality in Kenya : British development assistance to Kenya.* London, Croom Helm in association with the Overseas Development Institute.

Hopkins, A. G. (1999). "Back to the future: From national history to imperial history." *Past & Present*(164): 198-243.

Horvath, R. J. (1972). "A Definition of Colonisation." *Current Anthropology* 13(1): 45-57 at 47.

Howard, C. (1993). "The hidden side of the American welfare state." *Political Science Quarterly* 108(3): 403.

Human Rights Committee. General Comment No. 14: Nuclear weapons and the right to life (Article. 6) (1984).

Human Rights Committee (1990). General comment No. 3: The nature of States parties' obligations (article 2, paragraph. 1, of the Covenant) in Compilation of General Comments and General Recommendations Adopted by Human Rights Treaty Bodies, United Nations: 15.

Human Rights Committee (2003). Report on Mexico Produced by the Committee under Article 20 of the Convention, and Reply from the Government of Mexico, United Nations.

Huxley, E. (1939). "The Book of the Quarter: The Invaders of East Africa " *Journal of the Royal African Society* 38(152): 347-356.

Huxley, E. J. G. (1935). *White man's country : Lord Delamere and the making of Kenya.* London, Macmillan and Co. Ltd.

Ignatieff, M., A. Gutmann, et al. (2003). *Human Rights as Politics and Idolatry,* Princeton University.

Illich, I. (1978). *Toward a history of needs.* New York, Pantheon Books.

Illich, I. (1983). *Deschooling society,* Harper & Row.

Illich, I. D. (1975). *Medical nemesis: the expropriation of health,* London: Calder and Boyars.

Ingelhart, R. (1997). Postmaterialistic Values and the Erosion of Institutional Authority. *Why People Don't Trust Government.* J. S. Nye, P. D. Zelikow and D. C. King. Cambridge,MA, Harvard University Press.

Ingham, K. (1965). *A history of East Africa.* London, Longmans.

International Alliance of Inhabitants (2009) "*W Nairobi W Appeal for the right to live in Nairobi with dignity and justice.*"

International Bank for Reconstruction and Development (1963). The economic development of Kenya : report of a mission organized by the IBRD at the request of the Government of Kenya and the United Kingdom. Baltimore, John Hopkins Press.

International Labour Office (1952 (1982)). Convention of the International Labour Office (ILO) on 'Minimum Standards of Social Security' *Convention No. 102 of 1952.* C. a. R. ILO. Geneva, International Labour Office

Intute (2008). Brazil, Intute.

Irish, M. R. (1974). "International Double Taxation Agreements and Income Tax at Source." *International and Comparative law Quarterly* 23: 292-316.

Irvin, R. A. and J. Stansbury (2004). "Citizen Participation in Decision-Making: Is it Worth the Effort." *Public Administration Review* 64: 55-65.

Isaac, T. M. T. and P. Heller (2003). Democracy and Development: Decentralized Planning in Kerala. *Deepening democracy : institutional innovations in empowered participatory governance.* A. Fung and E. O. Wright. London, Verso.

Javed Burki, S. and M. Ul Haq (1981). "Meeting basic needs: An overview." *World Development* 9(2): 167-182.

Justice Mutungi Interview 10 (2007). A. Waris. Nairobi.

K Masime Interview 6 (2007). A. Waris. Nairobi.

KACC (2009). Press Release: Achievements in Investigations. KACC. Nairobi, Government of Kenya.

Kagari, M. (2004) "Kenya: Not Yet Uhuru." *East Africa Police Programme,*

11, 14.

Kannan, K. P. and V. N. Pillai (2004). Development as Freedom: A Interpretation of the Kerala Model, Centre for Developing Studies: 39.

Karingi, S. N. and B. Wanjala (2005) *"The Tax Reform Experience of Kenya."* UNU Wider Publication.

Kay, J. A. and M. A. King (1990). *The British tax system.* Oxford ; New York, Oxford University Press.

Keefer, P. (2005) "Clientelism, credibility and the policy choices of young democracies."

Keefer, P. and R. Vlaicu (2005). Democracy, credibility and clientelism. *Meetings of the American Political Science Association, September 2005,* World Bank Policy Research Working Paper 3472.

Kelley, D. (2000). A Life of One's Own: Individual Rights and the Welfare State. *International Human Rights in Context: Law, Politics,* Morals. H. J. Steiner and P. Alston. Oxford, Oxford University Press: 257.

Kenya Constituencies Fund Committee (2005). Report of the Constituencies Fund Committee pursuant to section 27(4)(d) of the Constituencies Development Fund Act, 2003. K. N. Assembly. Nairobi, Clerk's Chambers, National Assembly.

Kenya Institute of Policy Research and Analysis. (2006a). "Constituency Development Fund." *The Democratic Governance Support Programme (DGSP)* Retrieved 1/3/09, 2009, from http://www.kippra.org/Constituency.asp.

Kenya Institute of Policy Research and Analysis (2006b). Draft Baseline Survey Report on Decentralised Funds in Kenya: A Review of Bondo, Bungoma, Nakuru, Machakos, Kirinyaga, Wajir, & Mombasa Districts and Nairobi Province. Nairobi, Kenya Institute of Policy Research and Analysis.

Kenya Institute of Public Policy Research and Analysis (2004). Tax Compliance Study. Nairobi, Tax Policy Unit, Macroeconomics Division, Kenya Institute of Public Policy Research and Analysis.

Kenya National Audit Office (2006-7). The Report of the Controller and Auditor General Together with the Appropriation Accounts Other Public Accounts and the Accounts of the Funds of 2006-2007. C. a. A. General. Nairobi, Government of Kenya. 2009.

Kenya National Audit Office. (2009). "Kenya National Audit Office."

Retrieved 6th April 2009, 2009, from http://www.kenao.go.ke/
index.html.

Kenyan Government (2007). Kenya: Kibaki: Speech on the dissolution of
the Ninth Parliament (22/10/2007).

Kerala, G. o. Kerala Panchayat Raj Act (1999).

Kimenyi, M. S. and J. M. Mbaku (2004). Ethnicity, Institutions and
Governance in Africa. *Devolution and development: governance prospects
in decentralizing states*. M. S. Kimenyi and P. Meagher. Hants, Ashgate
Publishing: 105-136.

Kiringai, J. and G. West (2002). Budget Reforms and the Medium-Term
expenditure Framework in Kenya. *Working Paper*. K. I. o. P. R. a.
Analysis. Nairobi, Kenya Institute of Policy Research and Analysis.

Kirlin, J. J. and M. K. Kirlin (2002). "Strengthening Effective Government
— Citizen Connections through Greater Civic Engagement,." *Public
Administration Review* 65: 80-85.

Knorr, K. E. (1963). British colonial theories, 1570-1850. London, F. Cass.

Kuran, T. (1995). "Economics and the Islamic Sub-Economy." *Journal of
Economic Perspectives* 9(4): 155-186 at 159.

Kwamboka, E. (2009). Constituents sue MP over fund misappropriation.
The Standard Online Edition. Nairobi, Standard Newspapers.

Kwamboka, E. (2009). Court allows Otuoma to access CDF kitty. *The
Standard Online Edition*. Nairobi, Standard Newspapers.

Lauren, P. G. (2003). *The evolution of international human rights : visions seen*.
Philadelphia ; [Great Britain], University of Pennsylvania Press.

Legovini,A. (2002).Kenya:Macro Economic Evolution since Independence,
UNDP.

Lesbaupin, I. (2000). "Brazil: Civil society since democratization (1985-
2000)." *Caravelle-Cahiers Du Monde Hispanique Et Luso-Bresilien*(75):
61-75.

Levi, M. (1988). *Of Rule and Revenue*. Berkeley, University of California
Press.

Levy, B. and S. J. Kpundeh, Eds. (2004). *Building state capacity in Africa: new
approaches, emerging lessons*. Washington DC, World Bank Development
Institute.

Lewis, J. (2000). *Empire State-Building: War and Welfare in Kenya 1925-52*.

Oxford, James Curry.

Lewis, J. E. (2000). ""Tropical East Ends" and the Second World War: some contradictions in Colonial Office welfare initiatives." *Journal of Imperial and Commonwealth History* 28(60): 1.

Leys, C. (1975). *Underdevelopment in Kenya : the political economy of neo-colonialism, 1964-1971.* Nairobi, Kenya, East African Educational Publishers.

Linden, M. v. d., M. Dreyfus, et al., Eds. (1996). *Social Security Mutualism: The Comparative History of Mutual Benefit Societies,* Peter Lang.

Lockhart, J. and S. B. Schwartz (1983). *Early Latin America : a history of colonial Spanish America and Brazil.* Cambridge Cambridgeshire ; New York, Cambridge University Press.

Lord Hailey (1938). An African Survey: *A Study of Problems Arising in Africa South of the Sahara* Oxford.

Low, D. A. and J. Lonsdale (1976). Introduction: towards the new order, 1945–1963. *History of East Africa, III.* D. A. Low and A. Smith. Oxford,.

Lugard, F. J. D. (1965). *The dual mandate in British tropical Africa.* London, F. Cass.

Lugard, F. J. D. B. (1913-18). Memorandum Number 5: Taxation. *Political Memoranda: Revision of Instructions to Political Officers on Subjects Chiefly Political and Administrative.* F. J. D. B. Lugard. London, F Cass: 163-215.

Luis Alberto Interview 9 (2009). A. Waris. Sao Paulo.

Luis Renato Vedovato Interview 11 (2009). A. Waris. Sao Paulo.

Macgregor, J. and S. P. C. Schuftan (1998). "Downsizing the civil service in developing countries: the golden handshake option revisited." *Public Administration and Development* 18(1): 61-76.

Machuhi, E. (2009). Kenya: Rights Activists Denied CDF Records Nation on the Web. Nairobi, *Nation Newspapers.*

MacLean, R. (2005). *Encyclopedia of African History Volume 1.* K. Shillingdon. 1: 693-699.

Maina, W. (1996). Constitutional Crisis in Kenya: An Inquiry into the Origins, Nature and Prospects of Reform. *IPAR Project on Constitution-Making in Kenya.* Kenya.

Mapesa, B. M. and T. N. Kibua (2006). An Assessment of the Management and Utilisation of the Constituency Development Fund in Kenya.

Discussion Paper Series. Nairobi, Kenya Institute of Policy Analysis and Research.

Marmor,T. R.,J. L. Mashaw, et al. (1990). America's misunderstood welfare state : persistent myths, enduring realities. New York, Basic Books.

Marques, R. (2004). Fiscal Sociology: Setting a Research Agenda Annual meeting of the American Sociological Association, San Francisco, CA, www.allacademic.com.

Marquetti, A. (2005). Characteristics of Brazilian cities experiencing the Participatory Budgeting, Pontifícia Universidade Católica do Rio Grande do Sul.

Marshall,T. H. (1950). Citizenship and social class and other essays, Cambridge U.P.

Marston, D. (2002). The French-Indian War, 1754-1760, Osprey Publishing.

Martin, B. G. (1974). "Arab Migrations to East Africa in Medieval Times " International Journal of African Historical Studies 7(3): 367-390.

Mbithi, P. M. and R. Rasmusson (1977). Self Reliance in Kenya: the case of Harambee. Uppsala, Scandinavian Institute of African Studies.

Mbugua, J. K., G. H. Bloom, et al. (1995). "Impact of user charges on vulnerable groups: the case of Kibwezi in rural Kenya." Social Science & Medicine 41(6): 829-835.

McAuslan, P. and J. McEldowney, Eds. (1985). Law, legitimacy, and the constitution : essays marking the centenary of Dicey's Law of the Constitution. London, Sweet & Maxwell.

McCorquodale, R. and M. A. Baderin (2007). Economic, social and cultural rights in action. Oxford, Oxford University Press.

Mclaughlin, E. and J. Baker (2007). "Equality, Social Justice and Social Welfare: A Road Map to the New Egalitarians." Social Policy & Society 6(1): 53-68.

Meebelo, H. S. (1971). Reaction to Colonialism. Manchester, Manchester University Press.

Menser, M. and J. Robinson (January 29, 2008). Participatory Budgeting: From Porto Alegre, Brazil to the U.S., Liberty Tree Local Democracy

Mesa-Lago, C. (1997). "Social Welfare Reform in the Context of Economic-Political Liberalization: Latin American Cases." World Development 25(4): 497-517.

Midgley, J. (1986). *Community participation, social developments and the state.* London, Methuen.

Midgley, J. (1986). Participation and Social Work Services. *Community participation, social developments and the state.* J. Midgley. London, Methuen: 126-144.

Mill, J. S. (1963). Principles of Political Economy. *Collected works.* J. M. Robson. Toronto,, University of Toronto Press. 3: 962.

Ministry of External Relations Brazil (2008). Brazil and the United Nations. B. Ministry of External Relations, Government of Brazil.

Ministry of Finance Brazil. (2008). "The Brazilian Tax System." Retrieved 5/7/08, from http://www.receita.fazenda.gov.br/principal/Ingles/ SistemaTributarioBR/BrazilianTaxSystem/default.htm.

Mohamed Interview 8 (2007). A. Waris. Nairobi.

Molohan, M. J. B. (1959). *Detribalization.* Dar es Salaam.

Mona Serageldin et al. (2005). Assessment of Participatory Budgeting in Brazil. Washington DC, Inter American Development Bank.

Moore, M. (2001). "Political Underdevelopment: What Causes 'Bad Governance'." *Public Management Review* 3(3): 1-34.

Moore, M. (2004). "Revenues, State Formation and the Quality of Governance in Developing Countries." *International Political Science Review* 25(3): 297-319.

Moore, M. (2004). "Revenues, state formation, and the quality of governance in developing countries." *International Political Science Review* 25(3): 297-319.

Moore, M. and L. Rackner (2004). "The New Politics of Taxation and Accountability in Developing Countries." *Institute of Development Studies Bulletin* 33(3).

Moses, S., F. Manji, et al. (1992). "Impact of user fees on attendance at a referral centre for sexually transmitted diseases in Kenya." *Lancet* 340: 463-466.

Moyi, E. and E. Ronge (2006). Taxation and Tax Modernization in Kenya: A Diagnosis of Performance and Options for Further Reform. Nairobi, Institute of Economic Affairs.

Moynihan, D. P. (2007). Citizen Participation in Budgeting: Prospects for Developing Countries. *Participatory Budgeting.* A. Shah. Washington, World Bank: 55-87 at 56.

Mueller, D. C. (1997). *Perspectives on public choice.* Cambridge, Cambridge University Press.

Mumford, A. (2001). *Taxing culture : towards a theory of tax collection law.* Burlington, VT, Ashgate.

Mumford, A. (2008). "Towards a Fiscal Sociology of Tax Credits and the Fathers' Rights Movement." *Social and Legal Studies* 17(2): 217-235.

Mungeam, G. H. (1966). British rule in Kenya 1895-1912. The establishment of administration in the East Africa Protectorate. [With portraits and maps.]. [*Oxford studies in African affairs.*], pp. xii. 329. Clarendon Press: Oxford.

Munro, J. F. (1987). "Shipping Subsidies and Railway Guarantees: William Mackinnon, Eastern Africa and the Indian Ocean, 1860-93." *The Journal of African History* 28(2): 209-230.

Muriuki Karue Interview 9 (2007). A. Waris. Nairobi.

Murunga, G. (2007). The State, Its Reform and the Question of Legitimacy in Kenya. *Beyond state failure and collapse: making the state relevant in Africa.* G. K. Kieh. Plymouth, Lexington Books: 115-150.

Musgrave, R. A. (1992). "Schumpeter's Crisis of the Tax State: *An Essay in Fiscal Sociology.*" *Journal of Evolutional Economics* 2: 89-113.

Mwabu, G., J. Mwanzia, et al. (1995). "User charges in government health facilities in Kenya: effect on attendance and revenue. ." *Health Policy and Planning* 10: 164-170.

Naik, J. P. (1975). *Equality, quality and quantity : the elusive triangle in Indian education.* Bombay, Allied.

Naik, J. P. (1977). *Some perspectives on non-formal education.* Bombay, Allied Publishers.

Naik, J. P., J. P. Naik, et al. (1977). *An Alternative system of health care services in India : some proposals.* Bombay, Allied Publishers.

Nation Reporter (2008). Row Over CDF hinders handing over ceremony. *Daily Nation.* Nairobi, Nation Newspapers.

National Taxpayer's Association (2006). Concept Note. Nairobi, National Taxpayer's Association.

Ndegwa, S. N. (1997). "Citizenship and Ethnicity: An Examination of Two Transition Moments in Kenyan Politics." *The American Political Science Review* 91(3): 599-616.

Ndirangu, M. (2007). Probe Ordered into Laikipia CDF Cash misuse claims. *Daily Nation*. Nairobi, Nation Newspapers: 9.

Ndulu, B. J. and F. W. Mwega (1994). Economic Adjustment Policies. *Beyond Capitalism Vs Socialism in Kenya and Tanzania* J. D. Barkan. Boulder, Colo.; London, Lynne Reinner: 101-128.

New Zealand. Core Document Forming Part of the Reports of States Parties: New Zealand (2006).

Nickel, J. (1987). *Making Sense of Human Rights: Philosophical Reflections on the Universal Declaration of Human Rights*. Berkeley, University of California Press.

Nixon Nyaga Interview 1 (2007). A. Waris. Nairobi.

Nkinyangi, J. A. (1982). "Access to Primary Education in Kenya: The Contradictions of Public Policy." *Comparative Education Review* 26(2): 199-217.

Nonet, P. and P. Seznick (2000). *Law and Society in Transition: Towards Responsive Law*, Transaction Publishers.

Norris-Trent, C. (2008) "Bitter face-off in first parliament session." *France 24*

Nyaga, N. (2008). Why MPs are so Cagey: CDF and the Politics of Transition. *Daily Nation*. Nairobi, Nation Newspapers: 11.

Nyambura-Mwaura, H. (2009). Kenya sees 2009/10 budget deficit at 3.5 pct of GDP Reuters. Nairobi, Reuters.

Nyerere, J. (1969). Stability and Change in Africa. *Africa Contemporary Record. Annual survey and documents, 1968-1969*. C. Legum. London, Rex Collings. 2: C 30-31.

O'Callaghan, F. L. (1900). Uganda railway.

O'Neill, O. (1996). *Towards justice and virtue : a constructive account of practical reasoning*. Cambridge; New York, Cambridge University Press.

O'Rawe, M. (1999). The United Nations: Structure versus Substance (Lessons from the Principal Treaties and Covenants). *Human Rights: An Agenda for the 21st Century*. A. Hegarty and S. Leonard. London, Cavendish: 15-33 at 29.

Ocaya-Lakidi, D. (1977). Manhood, Warriorhood and Sex in East Africa. *The Warrior tradition in modern Africa*. A. A. A. Mazrui. Leiden, E J Brill: 134-165.

Ochieng', W. R. (1985). *A History of Kenya*. London, Macmillan.

Ochieng, W. R. and R. M. Maxon (1992). *An economic history of Kenya*. Nairobi, Kenya, East African Educational Publishers.

Odhiambo, M., W.V. Mitullah, et al. (2006). *Management of Resources by Local Authorities: The Case of Local Authority Transfer Fund in Kenya*. Nairobi, Claripress.

Offe, C. and J. Keane (1984). *Contradictions of the welfare state*. London, Hutchinson.

Office of the United Nations High Commissioner for Human Rights. Ratification Status of the ICCPR (2004).

Office of the United Nations High Commissioner for Human Rights (2004). Ratification Status of the ICESCR.

Office of the United Nations High Commissioner for Human Rights. Ratifications to the International Covenant on Civil and Political Rights (2007).

Office of the United Nations High Commissioner for Human Rights. Ratifications to the International Covenant on Economic, Social and Cultural Rights (2007).

Okoth-Ogendo, H.W. O. (1972). *The politics of constitutional change in Kenya since independence, 1963-69*. London, Royal African Society.

Omonso, G. (2008). Police to Quiz 17 over CDF Cash *Daily Nation*. Nairobi, Nation Newspapers: 31.

Omonso, G. and D. Ng'etich (2008). Fund Manger got Death Threats *Daily Nation*. Nairobi, Nation Newspapers.

Opon, C. (2007). Towards an Integrated Decentralization Policy in Kenya. *ActionAid International Kenya (AAIK) consultative meeting on Decentralization Policy*. Nairobi, Social Sector Division African Research and Resource Forum.

Organisation of the African Union. African Charter of Human and Peoples Rights (1982).

Ormrod, W. M., M. Bonney, et al. (1999). *Crises, Revolutions and Self-Sustained Growth: Essays in European Fiscal History, 1130-1830*. Stamford, Shaun Tyas.

Overseas Development Institute (2008). Achieving economic and social rights: The challenge of assessing compliance.

Owino Opondo Interview 7 (2007). A. Waris. Nairobi.

Oxhorn, P., J. S. Tulchin, et al. (2004). *Decentralisation, Democratic Governance and Civil Society in Comparative Perspective.* Washington DC, Woodrow Wilson centre Press.

Oyugi, L. N. (2005). *Fiscal decentralisation in Kenya : the case of local authority transfer fund.* Nairobi, Institute of Policy Analysis and Research.

Pakenham, T. (1991). *The scramble for Africa, 1876-1912,* Weidenfeld & Nicolson.

Pampel, F. C. and J. B. Williamson (1989). *Age, class, politics, and the welfare state.* Cambridge, Cambridge University Press.

Paul, S. (2007). India: Civic Participation in Sub-National Budgeting. *Participatory budgeting.* A. Shah. Washington, D.C., World Bank.

Payne, C. (2009). "Bringing Home the Bacon or Not? Globalization and Government Respect for Economic and Social Rights." *Human Rights Review* 10(3): 413-429.

Perham, M. (1963). *The Colonial Reckoning: The Reith Lectures:* 1961. London, Collins The Fontana Library 77-78.

Perz, S. G., J. Warren, et al. (2008). "Contributions of racial-ethnic reclassification and demographic processes to indigenous population resurgence - The case of Brazil." *Latin American Research Review* 43(2): 7-33.

Peterson, J. (2003). Policy Networks. *Political Science Series 90.* Vienna, IHS.

Plant, R. (1986). Needs, Agency and Rights. *Law, rights, and the welfare state.* C. J. G. Sampford and D. J. Galligan. London ; Wolfeboro, N.H., Croom Helm: 22-48.

Pogge, T. W. M. (2008). *World poverty and human rights, Polity.*

Prabhakaran, M. P. (1990). *The Historical Origin of India's Underdevelopment: A World System Perspective.* Lanham, University Press of America.

Prado, J. C. (1967). *The Colonial Background to Modern Brazil. Berkeley and Los Angeles,* University of California Press.

Project, M. (2005). A Practical Plan to Achieve the Millennium Development Goals, United Nations.

Przeworski, A., M. Alvarez, et al. (2003). *Democracy and development: political institutions and well-being in the world.* Cambridge, Cambridge University Press.

Rao, M. G. (1998). India: Intergovernmental Fiscal Relations in a Planned Economy. *Fiscal decentralization in developing countries.* F.Vaillancourt and R. M. Bird. Cambridge, Cambridge University Press: 78-114.

Raphael Moya Interview 12 (2009). A. Waris. Sao Paulo.

Republic of Benin. Constitution of the Republic of Benin (1990).

Republic of India (1950). Constitution of India Government of India.

Republic of Kenya (1965). African Socialism and its Application to Planning in Kenya Government Printers.

Republic of Kenya. The Constituency Development Fund Act (2004).

Republic of Kenya. Draft Constitution of Kenya (2004).

Republic of Kenya (2006). Aide Memoire: Kenya's Candidature to the Human Rights Council. M. o. F. A. K. M. t. N. York. New York, United Nations.

Republic of Kenya. Constituency Development Fund (Amendment) Act (2007).

Republic of Kenya. The Constitution of the Republic of Kenya ((1988) 1992).

Republic of South Africa (1997). *Soobramoney v. Minister of Health* (KwaZulu-Natal). BCLR, Constitutional Court of South Africa. 12: 1696.

Republic of South Africa (2000). *South Africa v. Grootboom.* BCLR, Constitutional Court of South Africa. 11: 1169.

Republic of South Africa (2002). *Treatment Action Campaign v. Minister of Health.* BCLR, High Court of South Africa, Transvaal Provincial Div. 4: 356(T).

Robert Goodin and John Dryzek, " 10 (1980):273-92 (1980). "Rational Participation: The Politics of Relative Power." *British Journal of Political Science* 10: 273-92.

Roberts, A. D., Ed. (1986). *The Cambridge History of Africa* Volume 5. Cambridge, Cambridge University Press.

Roberts, K. M. (1999). *Deepening democracy : the modern left and social movements in Chile and Peru.* Stanford, Calif., Stanford University Press.

Roper, S. and L. Barria (2009). "Political Science Perspectives on Human Rights." *Human Rights Review* 10(3): 305-308.

Rosenau, J. (1990). *Turbulence in World Politics.* Hemel Hempstead, Havester Wheatsheaf.

Ross, W. M. (1968). *Kenya from Within*. London, Frank Cass.

Sampford, C. J. G. and D. J. Galligan (1986). *Law, rights, and the welfare state*. London ; Wolfeboro, N.H., Croom Helm.

Santos, B. d. S. (1998). "Participatory budgeting in Porto Alegre: Toward a redistributive democracy." *Politics & Society* 26(4): 461-510.

Santos, B. d. S. (2002). *Towards a New Legal Common Sense*. London, Buttterworths.

Santos, B. d. S. (2007). *Democratizing democracy : beyond the liberal democratic canon*. London ; New York, Verso.

Schmidt-Traub, G. (2009). "The Millennium Development Goals and human rights-based approaches: moving towards a shared approach." *International Journal of Human Rights* 13(1): 72-85.

Schumpeter, J. A. (1950). "The March into Socialism." *The American Economic Review* 40: 446-456.

Schumpeter, J. A. (1954). *History of Economic Analysis*. London, George Allen and Unwin Ltd.

Schumpeter, J. A. (1991). The Crisis of the Tax State. *The Economics and Sociology of Capitalism*. R. Swedberg. New Jersey, Princeton University Press: 99-140.

Secretary of State for the Colonies (1924). Cabinet Memorandum: Position of Indians in Kenya. B. Cabinet. London, British Crown.

Secretary of State for the Colonies (1925). Cabinet Memorandum: East African Development Loan. B. Cabinet. London, British Crown.

Secretary of State for the Colonies (1925). Report of the East African Commission. C. Affairs. London, Her Majesty's Stationery Office.

Secretary of State for the Colonies (1933). Cabinet Memorandum: Report on Kenya. B. Cabinet. London, British Crown.

Secretary of State for the Colonies Lord Ormsby-Gore (1925). Report of the Secretary of State for the Colonies Lord Ormsby-Gore on the East African Commission. C. Affairs. London, Her Majesty's Stationery Office.

Seeley, J. (1987). "Social Welfare in a Kenyan Town: Policy and Practice, 1902-1985." *Afr Aff (Lond)* 86: 541-566.

Sengupta, A. (2000). "Realizing the right to development." *Development and Change* 31(3): 553-578 at 570-571.

Sengupta, A. (2003a). The Right to Development as a Human Right. *Boston: Francois-Xavier Bagnoud Center, Harvard University.*, Francois-Xavier Bagnoud Center, Harvard University. 31: 4.

Setzler, M. (2002). Social Resources and Subnational Democratic Reform: Overcoming the Voter's Dilemma in Urban Brazil, University of Texas.

Shah, A. (2004) "Corruption and Decentralized Public Governance."

Shah, A. (2004). "Fiscal decentralization in developing and transition economies: progress, problems, and the promise."

Shah, A. (2007). *Participatory budgeting.* Washington, D.C., World Bank.

Shah, A., T. Thompson, et al. (2004). *Implementing decentralized local governance : a treacherous road with potholes, detours, and road closures.* Washington, D.C., World Bank World Bank Institute Poverty Reduction and Economic Management Division.

Shimoli, E. and K. Koross (2009). CDF Cash was used to pay census clerks. *Daily Nation.* Nairobi, Nation Newspapers: 1-2.

Shiundu, A., L. Barasa, et al. (2009). Ministers, MPs Under KACC Probe Named. *Nation Newspapers.* Nairobi, Nation Newspapers.

Shivaramu, K. (1997). *Democratic decentralization in Panchayati Raj system.* New Delhi, M.D. Publications.

Shivji, I. G. (1976). *Class Struggles in Tanzania.* London, Monthly Review Press.

Shue, H. (1996). *Basic rights : subsistence, affluence, and U.S. foreign policy.* Princeton, N.J., Princeton University Press.

Simonsen, W. and M. D. Robbins (2000). *Citizen participation in resource allocation.* Boulder, Colorado; Oxford, Westview Press.

Singh, C. (1965). "The Republican Constitution of Kenya: Historical Background and Analysis." *The International and Comparative Law Quarterly* 14(3): 878-949.

Singh, M. (1969). *History of Kenya's Trade Union Movement to 1952.* Nairobi, East African Publishing House.

Smith, A. G. (1997). *Human Rights and Choice in Poverty.* Westport, Greenwood Publishing.

Smith, M. (2004). "The Human Right to Development: Between Rhetoric and Reality." *Harvard Human Rights Law Journal* 17: 137-168.

Smith, R. K. M. (2007). *Textbook on International Human Rights.*

Socio-Legal Studies Association. (2004). "What is the Socio-Legal Studies Association? ." from *http://www.ukc.ac.uk/slsa/index.htm#top* <*http://www.ukc.ac.uk/slsa/index.htm*.

Sorrenson, M. P. K. (1968). *Origins of European Settlement in Kenya*. Nairobi, Oxford University Press.

Souza, C. (2001). "Participatory budgeting in Brazilian cities : limits and possibilities in building democratic institutions." *Environment and Urbanization* 13(1): 159-184.

Souza, C. (2005) "Brazil's Tax System: The Dilemmas of Policy Reform." *FOCAL Policy Paper*, 12.

Standard, E. A. (1913). East African Standard. *East African Standard*. Nairobi.

Steiner, H. J. and P. Alston, Eds. (2000). *International Human Rights in Context: Law, Politics, Morals*. Oxford, Oxford University Press.

Steiner, H. J., P. Alston, et al. (2007). *International human rights in context : law, politics, morals : text and materials* Henry J. Steiner, Philip Alston, Ryan Goodman. Oxford, Oxford University Press.

Stichter, S. (1982). *Migrant Labour in Kenya: Capitalism and African Response, 1895–1975*. London.

Stoljar, S. (1984). *An analysis of rights*. London, Macmillan.

Strandes, J. (1961). *The Portuguese Period in East Africa*. Nairobi, East African Literature Bureau.

Streeten, P. (1980). "Basic Needs and Human-Rights." *World Development* 8(2): 107-111.

Subrahmanyam, G. (2004). Schizophrenic Governance and Fostering Global Inequalities in the British Empire: The UK Domestic State Versus the Indian and African Colonies, 1890-1960. Chicago, American Political Science Association.

Subramanian, V. K. (1979). *The Indian financial system*. New Delhi, Abhbinav.

Swallow, B. (2005). "Potential for Poverty Reduction Strategies to Address Community Priorities: Case Study of Kenya." *World Development* 33(2): 301-321.

Swamy, G. (1994). Kenya: Patchy, intermittent commitment. *Adjustment in Africa: lessons from country case studies*. H. I and F. R. Washington DC, World Bank.

T, H. R. (1904). "The Opening up of British East Africa." *Journal of the*

Royal African Society 4(13): 44-55.

Taliercio, R. R. (2004). *The Design, Performance, and Sustainability of Semi-Autonomous Revenue and Authorities in Africa and Latin America.* London, Routlege.

Taxiete Interview 10 (2009). A. Waris. Sao Paulo.

The Federal State of Brazil (1988). The Federal Constitution of Brazil. Legislature, Brazil.

Tignor, R. L. (1993). "Race, Nationality, and Industrialization in decolonizing Kenya, 1945-1963." *The International Journal of African Historical Studies* 26(1): 31-64.

Tiller, M. G. (1983). "The Dissonance Model of Participative Budgeting - an Empirical Exploration." *Journal of Accounting Research* 21(2): 581-595.

Tilly, C. (1992). *Coercion, Capital, and European States, AD 990-1990.* Oxford, Basil Blackwell.

Timney, M. (1998). Overcoming Administrative Barriers to Citizen Participation: Citizens as Partners, Not Adversaries. *Government is Us: Public Administration in an Anti-Government Era.* C. S. King and C. Stivers. Thousand Oaks, CA, Sage: 88-101.

Titmuss, R. M. (1958). *Essays of 'The Welfare State.',* pp. 232. George Allen & Unwin: London.

Tlakula, P. (2004). *Human Rights and Development. Human Rights, the Rule of Law and Development in Africa.* P. T. Zeleza and P. J. McConnaughay. Philadelphia, University of Pennsylvania Press: 109-119.

Twomey, P. (2007). Human Rights-based Approaches to Development. *Economic, social and cultural rights in action.* R. McCorquodale and M. A. Baderin. Oxford, Oxford University Press: 47.

United Nations Resolution on the Permanency of Sovereignty over Natural Resources. Geneva, United Nations.

United Nations. Charter of the United Nations (1945).

United Nations. The Proclamation of Tehran in Final Act of the International Conference on Human Rights (1968).

United Nations. Declaration of Principles and Programme of Action of the World Employment Conference (1976).

United Nations. Report of the World Conference on Agrarian Reform and Rural Development (UN Doc. A/54/485) (1979).

United Nations. Global Consultation on the Right to Development as a Human Right (1990).

United Nations (1995). *Copenhagen Declaration on Social Development.* World Summit for Social Development Copenhagen 1995 Copenhagen.

United Nations. Core Document Forming Part of the Reports of States Parties: Bosnia and Herzegovina (2004).

United Nations. (2004). "Status of Ratifications of the Principal International Human Rights Treaties." Retrieved 9th June 2004, from http://www.unhchr.ch/pdf/report.pdf.

United Nations. Core Document Forming Part of the Reports of States Parties: Bolivia (2005).

United Nations. (2006). "Inaugural Session of the Human Rights Council." Retrieved 24/7/09, 2009, from http://www.un.org/ga/60/elect/hrc/.

United Nations. (2009). "Growth in United Nations membership, 1945-present." Retrieved 22/7/09, 2009, from http://www.un.org/en/members/growth.shtml.

United Nations Centre for Human Rights (1991). *The realization of the right to development : global consultation on the right to development as a human right.* New York, United Nations.

United Nations General Assembly. Implementation of Recommendations on Economic and Social Matters (1947).

United Nations General Assembly. Reports on World Economic Conditions and Trends (1947).

United Nations General Assembly. Economic Development of Underdeveloped Countries (1948).

United Nations General Assembly. Universal Declaration of Human Rights (1948).

United Nations General Assembly. Financing of Economic Development of Underdeveloped Countries (1950).

United Nations General Assembly. Resolution on the Permanency of Sovereignty over Natural Resources (1962).

United Nations General Assembly. International Covenant on Civil and Political Rights (1966).

United Nations General Assembly. International Covenant on Economic, Social and Cultural Rights (1966).

United Nations General Assembly. Proclamation of Tehran (1968).

United Nations General Assembly. Declaration on Social Progress and Development (1969).

United Nations General Assembly. Declaration on Friendly Relations between States (1970).

United Nations General Assembly. Charter of Economic Rights and Duties of States (1974).

United Nations General Assembly. Alternative Approaches and Ways and Means within the United Nations System for Improving the Effective Enjoyment of Human Rights and Fundamental Freedoms: (1977).

United Nations General Assembly. Declaration on the Right to Development (1986).

United Nations General Assembly. Vienna Declaration and Program of Action: World Conference on Human Rights (1993).

United Nations General Assembly. Nature of the General Legal Obligation Imposed on States Parties to the Covenant (2004).

United Nations International Children's Fund (2007) "Eyes on the Budget as a Human Rights Instrument."

University of Southern California Neighborhood Participation Project. (2003) "Promises of Participation." *University of Southern California Neighborhood Participation Policy Brief* 1, 1-5.

Vaillancourt, F. o. and R. M. Bird, Eds. (1998). *Fiscal decentralization in developing countries*. Cambridge, Cambridge University Press.

Verba, S., K. Scholzman, et al. (1993). "Citizen Activity: Who Participates? What Do They Say?" *American Political Science Review* 87: 303-19.

Vickery, K. P. (1986). *Black and White in southern Zambia : the Tonga Plateau economy and British imperialism, 1890-1939*. New York, Greenwood Press.

Vigoda, E. (2002). "From Responsiveness to Collaboration: Governance, Citizens, and the Next Generation of Public Administration." *Public Administration Review* 65: 527-40.

Vijayalakshmi, V. (2007). Pune citizens to decide how the municipality spends money. *The Earth Times*. Pune.

Wahome, M. (2009). Roads Board And Revenue Collector Emerge Tops. *Nation Newspapers*. Nairobi, Nation Newspapers.

Wampler, B. (2000). *A Guide to Participatory Budgeting*. Conference on the Participatory Budget Porto Alegre, Brazil.

Wampler, B. (2004). "Expanding Accountability Through Participatory Institutions: Mayors, Citizens, and Budgeting in Three Brazilian Municipalities." *Latin American Politics and Society* 46(3): 13-16.

Wampler, B. (2007). *Participatory budgeting in Brazil : contestation, cooperation, and accountability*. University Park, Pa., Pennsylvania State University Press.

Wanjala, S. C. (1993). "Law and the protection of dignity of the individual in the under-developed state: The Kenyan example." *University of Nairobi Law Journal*.

Warutere, P. (2005). The Goldenberg conspiracy: The game of paper gold, money and power *Occasional Paper,* Institute of Security Studies.

Wasike, W. S. K. (2001). Road Infrastructure Policies in Kenya: Historical Trends and Current Challenges. *Infrastructure and Economic Services Division*. Nairobi, KIPPRA.

Webber, C. and A. Wildavsky (1986). *A History of Taxation and Expenditure in the Western World*. New York, Simon and Schuster.

Weber, M. (1972). *Economy and Society* Routledge.

Weffort, F. (1989). Why Democracy? *Democratizing Brazil : problems of transition and consolidation*. A. C. Stepan. New York, Oxford University Press.

Weston, B. (1992). Human Rights. *New Encyclopedia Britannica*. 20: 656.

Wheare, K. C. (1963). *Federal government*. London, New York,, Oxford University Press.

Wilensky, H. L. (1975). *The welfare state and equality : structural and ideological roots of public expenditures*. Berkeley ; London, University of California Press.

Wilkinson, J. C. (1981). "Oman and East Africa: New Light on Early Kilwan History from the Omani Sources." *International Journal of African Historical Studies* 14(2): 272-305.

Willis, J. (2005). Swahili: Mombasa, Fort Jesus, the Portuguese 1589-1698. *Encyclopedia of African History* Volume 1. K. Shillingdon. 1: 1515-1517.

Wolfe, M. and U. N. R. I. f. S. Development (1983). *Participation: The View from Above*. Geneva, United Nations Research Institute for Social Development.

Wolff, R. D. (1974). *The economics of colonialism: Britain and Kenya, 1870-1930*. New Haven, Yale University Press.

Woodman, G. R. (1988). The decline of folk-law social security in common-law Africa. *Between Kinship and the State: Social Security and Law in Developing Countries*. F. v. B.-B. e. al. Dordrecht: 69-88.

World Bank (1981). *World development report, 1981*. New York, Published for the World Bank Oxford University Press.

World Bank (1992). World development report 1992. New York, Published for the World Bank Oxford University Press: 277.

World Bank (2003). Case Study 2 - Porto Alegre, Brazil: Participatory Approaches in Budgeting and Public Expenditure Management. *Social Development Notes*, World Bank.

World Bank. (2009). "Participation and Civic Engagement." Retrieved 24/9/09, 2009, from http://web.worldbank.org/WBSITE/ EXTERNAL/TOPICS/EXTSOCIALDEVELOPMENT/EXTP CENG/0,,menuPK:410312~pagePK:149018~piPK:149093~theSite PK:410306,00.html.

World Conference on Human Rights. Vienna Declaration and Programme of Action (1993).

World Trade Organisation. Marrakesh Agreement Establishing the World Trade Organization (1994).

Wrigley, C. C. (1978). Neo-mercantile policies and the new imperialism. *The Imperial Impact: Studies in the Economic History of Africa and India* C. Dewey and A. G. Hopkins. London.

Xu, K., C. James, et al. (2006). An Empirical Model of Access to Health Care, Health Care Expenditure and Impoverishment in Kenya: Learning from Past Reforms and Lessons for the Future. Health Systems Financing Discussion Paper. Geneva, World Health Organization Department of Health Systems Financing.

Yang, K. (2005). "Public Administrators' Trust in Citizens: A Missing Link in Citizen Involvement Efforts." *Public Administration Review* 65: 273-85.

Ylvisaker, M. (1978). "The Origins and Development of the Witu Sultanate

" *International Journal of African Historical Studies* 11(4): 669-688.

Zeleza, P. T. and P. J. McConnaughay, Eds. (2004). *Human Rights, the Rule of Law and Development in Africa.* Philadelphia, University of Pennsylvania Press.

INDEX

A

Accountability   2, 5, 10, 24, 94-95, 107, 110-12, 118-20, 123-24, 147, 157, 159, 162, 173-74, 186, 188, 190-91, 193, 196-97, 207, 225, 228-29, 230, 233-34, 239, 245

Accountable 20-21, 123, 151, 169, 182, 230

Administration   6, 11, 13, 20, 31, 33-34, 39-42, 45, 47, 53-54, 57, 60, 62-63, 67-71, 73-76, 79n276, 84n298, 85-86, 94-95, 109, 111n394, 117, 128, 132, 142, 168-169, 172-174, 177, 185, 188, 190, 192-193, 209, 210n757, 213

Africa, African   24-25, 40, 42-43, 47, 50, 53, 54n149, 55n155, 57, 61-63, 65-90, 125, 131n450, 159, 190, 197, 201

Arab   51, 53-59, 62, 73, 82, 130, 134

Asian   59, 62, 68,71-72, 75, 77-79, 83, 87n312, 90, 93, 96

Avoidance 1n6, 2, 24n53, 94

B

Backhaus   9, 15, 21, 27, 28, 46, 90

Belief   2, 25, 189

Bonney 11, 21-22, 28-33, 39, 41, 43, 46, 47, 53, 90, 177, 249

Brazil   14, 57, 58, 134n456, 161-174, 176-77, 184, 186-87, 193-199, 201-03, 207, 213, 216, 228, 235, 244, 246

Britain   41, 48, 59, 80, 84

British   5n13, 40, 42-43, 49, 51-52, 54, 57, 59-76, 80, 84-86, 88, 96, 178, 181

Brown   58, 109n387

Printed in the United States
By Bookmasters